Lecture Notes in Computer Science　　13573

More information about this series at https://link.springer.com/bookseries/558

Shadi Albarqouni · Spyridon Bakas ·
Sophia Bano · M. Jorge Cardoso ·
Bishesh Khanal · Bennett Landman ·
Xiaoxiao Li · Chen Qin · Islem Rekik ·
Nicola Rieke · Holger Roth · Debdoot Sheet ·
Daguang Xu (Eds.)

Distributed, Collaborative, and Federated Learning, and Affordable AI and Healthcare for Resource Diverse Global Health

Third MICCAI Workshop, DeCaF 2022
and Second MICCAI Workshop, FAIR 2022
Held in Conjunction with MICCAI 2022
Singapore, September 18 and 22, 2022
Proceedings

 Springer

Editors
Shadi Albarqouni (iD)
University of Bonn
Bonn, Germany

Spyridon Bakas (iD)
University of Pennsylvania
Philadelphia, PA, USA

Sophia Bano
University College London
London, UK

M. Jorge Cardoso (iD)
King's College London
London, UK

Bishesh Khanal (iD)
NepAl Applied Mathematics and Informatics
Kathmandu, Nepal

Bennett Landman
Vanderbilt University
Brentwood, TN, USA

Xiaoxiao Li (iD)
University of British Columbia
Vancouver, BC, Canada

Chen Qin
University of Edinburgh
Edinburgh, UK

Islem Rekik
Istanbul Technical University
Istanbul, Turkey

Nicola Rieke (iD)
NVIDIA GmbH
Munich, Bayern, Germany

Holger Roth (iD)
NVIDIA Corporation
Santa Clara, CA, USA

Debdoot Sheet
Indian Institute of Technology
Kharagpur, India

Daguang Xu (iD)
NVIDIA Corporation
Santa Clara, CA, USA

ISSN 0302-9743   ISSN 1611-3349 (electronic)
Lecture Notes in Computer Science
ISBN 978-3-031-18522-9   ISBN 978-3-031-18523-6 (eBook)
https://doi.org/10.1007/978-3-031-18523-6

This Springer imprint is published by the registered company Springer Nature Switzerland AG
The registered company address is: Gewerbestrasse 11, 6330 Cham, Switzerland

Preface DeCaF 2022

Machine learning approaches have demonstrated the capability of revolutionizing almost every application and every industry through the use of large amounts of data to capture and recognize patterns. A central topic in recent scientific debates has been how data is obtained and how it can be used without compromising user privacy. Industrial exploitation of machine learning and deep learning (DL) approaches has, on the one hand, highlighted the need to capture user data from the field of application in order to yield a continuous improvement of the model, and on the other hand it has exposed a few shortcomings of current methods when it comes to privacy.

Innovation in the way data is captured, used, and managed, as well as how privacy and security of this data can be ensured, is a priority for the whole research community. Most current methods rely on centralized data stores, which contain sensitive information and are often out of the direct control of users. In sensitive contexts, such as healthcare, where privacy takes priority over functionality, approaches that require centralized data lakes containing user data are far from ideal, and may result in severe limitations in what kinds of models can be developed and what applications can be served.

Other issues that result in privacy concerns are more intimately connected with the mathematical framework of machine learning approaches and, in particular, DL methods. It has been shown that DL models tend to memorize parts of the training data and, potentially, sensitive information within their parameters. Recent research is actively seeking ways to reduce issues caused by this phenomenon. Even though these topics extend beyond distributed and collaborative learning methods, they are still intimately connected to them.

The third MICCAI Workshop on Distributed, Collaborative and Federated Learning (DeCaF 2022) aimed at creating a scientific discussion focusing on the comparison, evaluation, and discussion of methodological advancement and practical ideas about machine learning applied to problems where data cannot be stored in centralized databases; where information privacy is a priority; where it is necessary to deliver strong guarantees on the amount and nature of private information that may be revealed by the model as a result of training; and where it's necessary to orchestrate, manage, and direct clusters of nodes participating in the same learning task.

During the third edition of DeCaF, 18 papers were submitted for consideration, and, after peer review, 14 full papers were accepted for presentation. Each paper was rigorously reviewed by at least three reviewers in a double-blind review process. The papers were assigned to reviewers considering (and avoiding) potential conflicts of interest and recent work collaborations between peers. Reviewers were selected from among the most prominent experts in the field from all over the world.

Once the reviews were obtained, the area chairs formulated final decisions over acceptance, conditional acceptance, or rejection of each manuscript. These decisions were always taken according to the reviews and could not be appealed. In the case of conditional acceptance, authors had to make substantial changes and improvements to their paper according to reviewer feedback. The nature of these changes aimed to increase the scientific validity as well as the clarity of the manuscripts.

Additionally, the workshop organizing committee granted the Best Paper Award to the best submission presented at DeCaF 2022. The Best Paper Award was assigned as a result of a secret voting procedure where each member of the committee indicated two papers worthy of consideration for the award. The paper collecting most votes was then chosen by the committee.

The double-blind review process with three independent reviewers selected for each paper, united with the mechanism of conditional acceptance, as well as the selection and decision process through meta-reviewers, ensured the scientific validity and the high quality of the works presented at the third edition of DeCaF, making our contribution very valuable to the MICCAI community, and in particular to researchers working on distributed and collaborative learning. We would therefore like to thank the authors for their contributions and the reviewers for their dedication and fairness when judging the works of their peers.

August 2022

Shadi Albarqouni
Spyridon Bakas
M. Jorge Cardoso
Bennett Landman
Xiaoxiao Li
Chen Qin
Nicola Rieke
Holger Roth
Daguang Xu

Preface FAIR 2022

As we witness a technological revolution that is spinning diverse research fields including healthcare at an unprecedented rate, we face bigger challenges ranging from the high cost of computational resources to the reproducible design of affordable and innovative solutions. While AI applications have been recently deployed in the healthcare systems of high-income countries, their adoption in developing and emerging countries remains limited.

Given the breadth of challenges faced, particularly in the field of healthcare and medical data analysis, we presented the first Workshop on Affordable AI and Healthcare (FAIR) aiming to i) raise awareness about the global challenges in healthcare, ii) strengthen the participation of underrepresented communities at MICCAI, and iii) build a community around affordable AI and healthcare in low resource settings.Our workshop stands out from other MICCAI workshops as it prioritizes and focuses on developed AI solutions and research suited to low infrastructure, point-of-care-testing, and edge devices. Examples include, but are not limited to, AI deployments in conjunction with conventional X-rays, ultrasound, microscopic imaging, retinal scans, fundus imaging, and skin lesions. Moreover, we encouraged works that identify often neglected diseases prevalent in low resource countries and propose affordable AI solutions for such diseases using medical images. In particular, we were looking for contributions on (a) making AI affordable for healthcare, (b) making healthcare affordable with AI, or (c) pushing the frontiers of AI in healthcare that enables (a) or (b).

In the second edition of the FAIR workshop (FAIR 2022), held in conjunction with MICCAI 2022 (Singapore), nine papers, eight regular and one white paper, were submitted for consideration, and after the peer review process, only four regular papers were accepted for publication (an acceptance rate of: 50%) along with the white paper. The topics of the accepted submissions are around deep ultrasound segmentation, portable OCT image quality enhancement, self-attention deep networks, and knowledge distillation in a low-regime setting. Papers were presented both virtually and in-person in Singapore.

We followed the same review process as the main MICCAI conference by employing a double-blind review process with three to four reviewers per submission. Reviewers were selected from a pool of excellent researchers in the field, who have published at top-tier conferences, and manually assigned to the papers avoiding potential conflict of interest. Submissions were ranked based on the overall scores. Final decisions about acceptance/rejection and oral presentations were made by the Program Chairs according to ranking, quality, and the total number of submissions. Springer's Editorial Policy was been shared with the authors to aid the preparation of camera-ready versions.

We would like to thank the authors for their contributions and the reviewers for their commitment, patience, and constructive feedback. Also, we would like to thank the publicity committee and the advisory committee for their support.

August 2022

Shadi Albarqouni
Sophia Bano
Bishesh Khanal
Islem Rekik
Nicola Rieke
Debdoot Sheet

Organization

Organization Committee DeCaF 2022

Shadi Albarqouni	University of Bonn and Helmholtz AI, Germany
Spyridon Bakas	University of Pennsylvania, USA
M. Jorge Cardoso	King's College London, UK
Bennett Landman	Vanderbilt University, USA
Xiaoxiao Li	University of British Columbia, Canada
Chen Qin	University of Edinburgh, UK
Nicola Rieke	NVIDIA, Germany
Holger Roth	NVIDIA, USA
Daguang Xu	NVIDIA, USA

Program Committee DeCaF 2022

Aaron Carass	Johns Hopkins University, USA
Dianwen Ng	Nanyang Technological University, Singapore
Dong Yang	NVIDIA, USA
Jingwei Sun	Duke University, USA
Jonny Hancox	NVIDIA, UK
Klaus Kades	German Cancer Research Center (DKFZ), Germany
Konstantin Pandl	Karlsruhe Institute of Technology, Germany
Kun Han	University of California, Irvine, USA
Maximilian Zenk	German Cancer Research Center (DKFZ), Germany
Meirui Jiang	Chinese University of Hong Kong, Hong Kong, China
Micah J. Sheller	Intel Corporation, USA
Muhammad Habib ur Rehman	King's College London, UK
Pengfei Guo	Johns Hopkins University, USA
Sarthak Pati	University of Pennsylvania, USA
Shenglai Zeng	University of Electronic Science and Technology of China, China
Shunxing Bao	Vanderbilt University, USA
Vishwesh Nath	NVIDIA, USA
Wenqi Li	NVIDIA, USA
Xiangyi Yan	University of California, Irvine, USA

Yangsibo Huang	Princeton University, USA
Yawen Wu	University of Pittsburgh, USA
Yuankai Huo	Vanderbilt University, USA
Zhen Chen	City University of Hong Kong, Hong Kong, China
Ziyue Xu	NVIDIA, USA

Organization Committee FAIR 2022

Shadi Albarqouni	University of Bonn and Helmholtz AI, Germany
Sophia Bano	University College London, UK
Bishesh Khanal	NAAMII, Nepal
Islem Rekik	Istanbul Technical University, Turkey
Nicola Rieke	NVIDIA GmbH, Germany
Debdoot Sheet	Indian Institute of Technology Kharagpur, India

Publicity Committee FAIR 2022

Yenisel Plasencia Calaña	Maastricht University, The Netherlands
Linda Marrakchi-Kacem	National Engineering School of Tunis, Tunisia
Yunusa Mohammed	Algorizmi Health Ltd., Nigeria
Aya Salama	Algorithm tech., Egypt
Farah Shamout	NYU Abu Dhabi, UAE

Steering Committee FAIR 2022

Diana Maetus	Centrale Nantes/LS2N, France
Rakesh Mullick	GE Healthcare, India
Nassir Navab	TU Munich, Germany
Terry Peters	Western University, Canada
Aisha Walcott-Bryant	IBM Research - Africa, Kenya

Program Committee FAIR 2022

Alaa Bessadok	Helmholtz AI, Germany
Alessandro Casella	Italian Institute of Technology, Italy
Amelia Jiménez-Sánchez	IT University of Copenhagen, Denmark
Anees Kazi	TU Munich, Germany
Anirban Mukhopadhyay	TU Darmstadt, Germany
Anita Rau	University College London, UK
Fadi Kacem	University of Carthage, Tunisia
Hassan Mohy-ud-Din	LUMS, Pakistan
Juana Puyal	University College London, UK
Krishna Chaitanya	ETH Zurich, Switzerland

Mahesh Shakya	NAAMII, Nepal
Omar Al-Kadi	University of Jordan, Jordan
Rafat Damseh	United Arab Emirates University, UAE
Tinashe Mutsvangwa	University of Cape Town, South Africa

Contents

Affordable AI and Healthcare

Distributed, Collaborative, and Federated Learning

Incremental Learning Meets Transfer Learning: Application to Multi-site Prostate MRI Segmentation

Chenyu You[1]([✉]), Jinlin Xiang[2], Kun Su[2], Xiaoran Zhang[3], Siyuan Dong[1], John Onofrey[4], Lawrence Staib[1,3,4], and James S. Duncan[1,3,4]

[1] Electrical Engineering, Yale University, New Haven, CT, USA
chenyu.you@yale.edu
[2] Electrical and Computer Engineering, The University of Washington, WA, USA
[3] Biomedical Engineering, Yale University, New Haven, CT, USA
[4] Radiology and Biomedical Imaging, Yale School of Medicine, New Haven, CT, USA

Abstract. Many medical datasets have recently been created for medical image segmentation tasks, and it is natural to question whether we can use them to sequentially train a single model that (1) performs better on all these datasets, and (2) generalizes well and transfers better to the unknown target site domain. Prior works have achieved this goal by jointly training one model on multi-site datasets, which achieve competitive performance on average but such methods rely on the assumption about the availability of all training data, thus limiting its effectiveness in practical deployment. In this paper, we propose a novel multi-site segmentation framework called **incremental-transfer learning (ITL)**, which learns a model from multi-site datasets in an end-to-end sequential fashion. Specifically, "incremental" refers to training sequentially constructed datasets, and "transfer" is achieved by leveraging useful information from the linear combination of embedding features on each dataset. In addition, we introduce our ITL framework, where we train the network including a site-agnostic encoder with pretrained weights and at most two segmentation decoder heads. We also design a novel site-level incremental loss in order to generalize well on the target domain. Second, we show for the first time that leveraging our ITL training scheme is able to alleviate challenging catastrophic forgetting problems in incremental learning. We conduct experiments using five challenging benchmark datasets to validate the effectiveness of our incremental-transfer learning approach. Our approach makes minimal assumptions on computation resources and domain-specific expertise, and hence constitutes a strong starting point in multi-site medical image segmentation.

Keywords: Incremental learning · Transfer learning · Medical image segmentation

---

C. You and J. Xiang—Equal contribution.

S. Albarqouni et al. (Eds.): DeCaF 2022/FAIR 2022, LNCS 13573, pp. 3–16, 2022.
https://doi.org/10.1007/978-3-031-18523-6_1

1   Introduction

Many medical image datasets have been created over the year, and recent break-through achieved by supervised training accelerates the pace in medical image segmentation. Despite great promise, many prior works have limited clinical value, since they are separately trained on small datasets in terms of scale, diversity, and heterogeneity of annotations. As a result, such single-site methods [10,14,21,22,29,31,32,35–41] are vulnerable to unknown target domains, and linearly expand parameters since they assume to train a new model in isolation when adding new datasets. This jeopardizes their trustworthiness and practical deployment in real-world clinical environments.

In this paper, we carry out the **first-of-its-kind** comprehensive exploration of how to build a multi-site model to achieve strong performance on the training domains and can also serve as a strong starting point for better generalization on new domains in the clinical scenarios. Multi-site training [1,3,7,8,11,24,25] has been proposed to consolidate the generalization on multi-site datasets, but it has the following limitations: (1) it still exhibits certain vulnerability to different domains (*i.e.*, different imaging protocols), which yields sub-optimal performance [1,13,34]; (2) due to various constraints (*i.e.*, imaging time, privacy, and copyright status), it could become challenging or even infeasible for the requirement on the availability of all training data in a certain time phase. For example, when a new site's data will be available after training, the model requires retraining, which largely prohibits the practical deployments; and (3) consider the relatively small size of the single medical imaging dataset, simply training a dense network from scratch usually leads to sub-optimal segmentation quality because the model might over-fit to those datasets.

Our **key idea** is to combine the benefits of incremental-learning (IL) and transfer-learning by sequentially training a multi-dataset expert: we continually train a model with corresponding pretrained weights as new site data are incrementally added, which we call **Incremental-Transfer Learning** (ITL). This setting is appealing as: (1) the common IL setting [4,5,15,17,23,27,28,42] is to train the base-learner when different site datasets gradually come; thus the effectiveness of this approach heavily depends on the optimality of the base-learner. Consider each single medical image dataset is usually of relatively small size, it is undesirable to build a strong base-learner from scratch; (2) transfer-learning [26,30,33,43,44] typically leads to better performance and faster convergence in medical image analysis. Inspired by these findings above, we develop a novel training strategy for expanding its high-quality learning abilities to our multi-site incremental setting, considering both *model-level* and *site-level*. Specifically, our system is built upon a site-agnostic encoder with pretrained weights from natural image datasets such as IMAGENET, and at most two segmentation decoder heads wherein only one head is trainable, and the other is fixed associated with specific sites - a parameter-efficient design. Our intuition is that the shared site-agnostic encoder network with pretrained weights encodes regularities across different medical image datasets, while the target and source segmentation decoder heads model the sub-distribution by our proposed site-level incremental loss, resulting

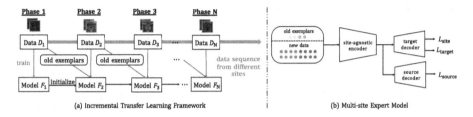

(a) Incremental Transfer Learning Framework   (b) Multi-site Expert Model

Fig. 1. Overview of (a) our proposed Incremental Transfer Learning framework, and (b) the multi-site expert model. Note that in this study, we only use one multi-site expert model and one source decoder network, which will not introduce additional parameter.

in an accurate and robust model that transfers better to new domains without sacrificing performance. We conduct a comprehensive evaluation of ITL on five prostate MRI datasets. Our approach can consistently achieve competitive performance and faster convergence compared to the upper-bound baselines (*i.e.*, isolated-site and mixed-site training), and has a clear advantage on overall segmentation performance compared to the lower-bound baselines (*i.e.*, multi-site training). We also find that our simple approach can effectively address the forgetting issues. Our experiments demonstrate the benefits of modeling both multi-site regularities and site-specific attributes, and thereby serve as a strong starting point on this important practical setting.

2 Method

2.1 Problem Setup

In ITL, a model incrementally learns from a sequential site stream wherein new datasets (namely, medical image segmentation tasks with new sites) are gradually added during the training, as illustrated in Fig. 1. More formally, we denote the sequence of multi-site datasets to be trained as a multi-domain data sequence $\mathcal{D} = \{D_1, D_2, \cdots, D_N\}$ of N sites, and i-th site D_i contains the training images $X = \{x_j\}_{j=1}^{M}$ and segmentation labels $Y = \{y_j\}_{j=1}^{M}$, where $x_j \in \mathbb{R}^{H \times W \times 3}$ is the augmented image input, and $y_j \in \{0, 1\}^{H \times W}$ is the ground-truth label. Here the augmented input setting is appealing: the axial context naturally provided by a 3D volume can uniquely yield more robust semantic representations to the downstream tasks. We assume access to a multi-site expert model $F_i = \{E_i, G_i\}$ for i-th (site) phase, including a pretrained model as a site-agnostic encoder network E_i with the weight θ_i, a target decoder network G_i^t with the weight θ_i^t. During training, we additionally attach a source decoder network G_i^s (*i.e.*, using G_{i-1}^s from previous phrase) with the weight θ_i^s. In the i-th incremental (site) phase, the multi-site expert model has access to two types of domain knowledge: the site-specific knowledge from the current dataset D_i and old exemplars P_i. The latter refers to a set of old exemplars from all previous training datasets $D_{1:i-1}$ in

Table 1. Information about five different sites from three benchmark datasets.

Dataset	Modality	# of cases	Field strength (T)	Resolution (in/through plane) (mm)	Coil	Source
Site0	MRI	30	3	0.6–0.625/3.6–4	Surface	NCI-ISBI13 [2]
Site1	MRI	30	1.5	0.4/3.0	Endorectal	NCI-ISBI13 [2]
Site2	MRI	19	3	0.67–0.79/1.25	-	I2CVB [12]
Site3	MRI	12	1.5	0.625/3.6	Endorectal	PROMISE12 [16]
Site4	MRI	13	1.5 and 3	0.325–0.625/3–3.6	-	PROMISE12 [12]

the memory protocol $\mathcal{M}$. This is highly nontrivial to preventing the challenging "catastrophic forgetting" problem [20] of the current dataset i against previous sites in clinical practice. Note that, in this study, we only use one multi-site expert model and one source decoder network, which will not introduce additional parameters. Based on the setting above, we define the ITL problem below.

Problem of ITL. *In the current site i, our goal is to continuously learn a multi-site expert model based on the knowledge from both (D_i, P_i) and the pretrained weight, making the model (1) generalizes well on the unseen data at site i, and (2) achieves competitive performance on the previous sites.*

2.2 Preliminary

Our goal is to build a strong multi-site model by learning a site-agnostic encoder with pretrained weights as well as a segmentation decoder over multi-site datasets. This naturally raises several interesting questions: *How well will ITL-based methods perform in multi-site medical image datasets? Will transfer learning make the base learner stronger on the unseen site? If yes, can they perform stably well?* To answer the above questions, a prerequisite is to define the upper bound and lower bound. Here we introduce three common paradigms for multi-site medical image segmentation: (1) isolated-site training, (2) mixed-site training, and (3) multi-site training. It is well-known that the isolated-site and mixed-site training approaches can achieve state-of-the-art performance when evaluating the same dataset, while the performance catastrophically drops when evaluating new datasets. On the other hand, the multi-site training approach often yields inconsistent performance across multiple sites. For all training paradigms, we minimize Dice loss between the predicted outputs and the ground truth label.

Upper Bound. We consider two training paradigms (*i.e.*, isolated-site and mixed-site training) as our upper bound baseline. For isolated-site training, given each site D_i, we train isolated-site models separately. The architecture of the isolated-site model consists of a pretrained encoder E_i and a segmentation decoder network, same architecture as G_i. Then, we apply different isolated-site models to predict results based on the site-specific data at inference. However, this approach dramatically increases memory and computational overhead, making it practically challenging at scale. For mixed-site training, we train one full model on the full mixed-site data D, and then use the well-trained model for inference. However, it requires the simultaneous presence of all data in training and inference.

Lower Bound. For multi-site training, we sequentially train only one model coupled with the pretrained weights on all sites. This can get rid of large parameter counts, making it appealing in practice. However, due to the forgetting quandary, it inevitably suffers from severe performance degradation. This naturally questions: *can we improve performance on multi-site medical image segmentation with minimal additional memory footprint?* In the following, we give an affirmative answer.

2.3   Proposed Incremental Transfer Learning Multi-site Method

To address the aforementioned problems, we develop the incremental transfer learning framework to perform well on the training distribution and generalize well on the new site dataset with minimal additional memory. To our best knowledge, we are **the first work** to apply incremental transfer learning to the limited clinical data regimes. To control the parameter efficiency, we decompose the model into a share site-agnostic encoder E_i and two segmentation decoder heads (*i.e.*, source decoder G_i^s and target decoder G_i^t). In this way, we can keep the network parameters the same when adding a new site. Specifically, G_i^s is designed to transfer the knowledge of a previously learned site, and G_i^t is designed to comprehensively train on a new site and previous datasets. During training, we only update G_i^t while G_i^s is frozen. It is worth mentioning that our proposed framework is independent of the encoder architecture, and can be easily plugged in other pretrained vision models.

The full ITL algorithm is summarized in Algorithm 1. We describe our ITL algorithm as follows. We first randomly initialize G_i^t, G_i^s, and then iteratively train our full model (*i.e.*, a pretrained encoder E_i and two decoders G_i^t, G_i^s) with N-site training samples. Bounded by the computational requirements, it is challenging or even infeasible to retain all data for training. Inspired by recent work [23], to maintain the knowledge of previous sites, we "store" all the old site data exemplars in the memory protocol $\mathcal{M}_i$. In the i-th incremental (site) phase, we first load P_i, and then use both P_i and D_i to train F_i initialized by θ_i^s. This setting is appealing as (1) it can substantially alleviate the imbalance between the old and new site knowledge, and (2) it is efficient to train on them. Of note, we do not use the source decoder when training on the first-site dataset. We formulate ITL as *model-level* and *site-level* optimization.

Model-Level Optimization. To perform better on all these training distributions, we propose improving generic representations by distilling knowledge from previous data. In each incremental phase, we jointly optimize two groups of learnable parameters in our ITL learning by minimizing the *model-level* incremental

---

Algorithm 1. Incremental-Transfer Learning(ITL) Algorithm

Require: Dataset: $\mathcal{D}$; Hyper-parameters: α, δ, γ
1: Initialize the $\mathcal{M}$ *(Memory)* : $\mathcal{M}$
2: Initialize the Model F_0: *Pretrained Encoder* $\longrightarrow E_0, G_0$
3: **for** $i = 1,2,3,....\text{N}$ **do**
4: **for** All training Sample in D_i and $\mathcal{M}_{i-1}$ **do**
5:   $\mathcal{L}_{\text{target}} = \sum_{j=0}^{N-1} \alpha_j \mathcal{L}_{\text{Dice}}^{E_i, G_i^t}(\mathcal{M}_j, Y_j)$ or 0 When $N = 1$
6:   $\mathcal{L}_{\text{source}} = \sum_{j=0}^{N-1} \delta_j \mathcal{L}_{\text{Dice}}^{E_i, G_i^s}(\mathcal{M}_j, Y_j)$ or 0 When $N = 1$
7:   $\mathcal{L}_{\text{model}} = \mathcal{L}_{\text{source}} + \mathcal{L}_{\text{target}}$
8:   $\mathcal{L}_{\text{site}} = \mathcal{L}_{\text{Dice}}^{E_i, G_i^t}(\mathcal{D}_i, Y_i)$
9:   $\mathcal{L}_{\text{all}} = \mathcal{L}_{\text{site}} + \mathcal{L}_{\text{model}}$
10:   $F_i = (E_i, G_i^t)$ by minimizing the $\mathcal{L}_{\text{all}}$
11: **end for**
12: Update Memory: $\mathcal{M} + \gamma\% D_N \longrightarrow \mathcal{M}$
13: Save Teacher Model: G_N
14: **end for**

---

loss (*i.e.*, $\mathcal{L}_{\text{model}} = \mathcal{L}_{\text{target}} + \mathcal{L}_{\text{source}}$) on all training samples (*i.e.*, $D_i \bigcup D_{0:i-1}$): (1) a share site-agnostic encoder E_i and a target decoder G_i^t; (2) a share site-agnostic encoder E_i and a source decoder G_i^s. This helps ITL avoid catastrophic forgetting of prior site-specific knowledge.

Site-Level Optimization. The above *model-level* optimization is used to maintain previously learned knowledge. In contrast, this step is design to train the multi-site model to learn site-specific knowledge on the newly added site. Specifically, we minimize the site-level incremental loss $\mathcal{L}_{\text{site}}$ between the probability distribution from F_i and the ground truth. This essentially learns the site-specific knowledge for the downstream medical image segmentation tasks. Of note, $\mathcal{L}_{\text{source}}$, $\mathcal{L}_{\text{target}}$, and $\mathcal{L}_{\text{site}}$ use the Dice loss. The overall loss combines the *model-level* loss and the *site-level* loss as follows:

$$\mathcal{L}_{\text{all}} = \mathcal{L}_{\text{model}} + \mathcal{L}_{\text{site}}. \tag{1}$$

3   Experiments

Datasets and Settings. We evaluate our proposed incremental transfer learning method on three prostate T2-weighted MRI datasets with different sub-distributions: NCI-ISBI13 [2], I2CVB [12], and PROMISE12 [16]. Due to the diverse data source distributions, they can be split into five multi-site datasets, which is similar to [19]. Table 1 provides some dataset statistics. For pre-processing, we follow the setting in [18] to normalize the intensity, and resample all 2D slices and the corresponding segmentation maps to 384×384 in the axial plane. For all five site datasets, we randomly split each original site dataset into training and testing with a ratio of 4:1. For each site training, we divide the data from the previous site into a small subset with a certain portion (*i.e.*, 1%, 3%, 5%), and combine it with the current site data for training.

Table 2. Comparison of segmentation performance (DSC[%]/95HD[mm]) across datasets. Note that a larger DSC (↑) and a smaller 95HD (↓) indicate better performing ITL models. We use four models pretrained on IMAGENET: ResNet-18, ResNet-34, ResNet-50, and ViT under different portions (*i.e.*, 1%, 3%, 5%) of exemplars from previous data for every incremental phase. We consider multi-site training as the lower bound, isolated-site, and mixed-site training as the upper bound.

Backbone	Scheme	HK		UCL		ISBI		ISBI1.5		I2CVB	
		DSC[%]	95HD[mm]	DSC[%]	95HD[mm]	DSC[%]	95HD[mm]	DSC[%]	95HD[mm]	DSC[%]	95HD[mm]
RES-18	Multi	59.38	64.17	66.26	54.19	54.38	73.40	66.89	44.49	84.54	11.70
	1%	67.82	56.08	67.12	58.05	59.47	70.46	77.34	34.77	82.94	6.06
	3%	71.60	18.41	82.18	23.92	72.26	20.91	81.53	19.21	84.08	13.75
	5%	81.81	5.50	84.45	13.95	84.52	15.65	89.32	10.11	86.72	11.70
	Isolated	93.46	2.06	88.29	6.20	93.35	2.04	90.89	7.53	88.74	13.93
	Mixed	92.17	7.60	83.38	12.22	91.70	2.46	90.08	9.20	89.12	13.86
RES-34	Multi	57.75	55.13	64.87	52.50	57.47	65.38	65.61	56.83	91.46	8.83
	1%	67.40	24.18	79.55	30.43	69.61	44.69	84.68	18.71	89.38	15.24
	3%	80.90	28.41	82.57	22.18	75.89	26.26	84.68	10.57	90.35	13.15
	5%	80.46	22.92	87.79	17.32	88.14	14.64	90.29	8.57	91.30	8.52
	Isolated	93.87	1.89	89.03	4.05	92.28	2.19	92.57	7.96	91.57	7.98
	Mixed	93.85	1.71	87.81	16.85	91.49	3.35	93.82	5.30	92.58	6.64
RES-50	Multi	63.24	53.98	64.79	56.59	72.95	26.63	69.41	49.89	90.40	8.21
	1%	69.01	60.70	69.85	44.21	75.30	28.74	80.27	20.10	90.08	8.02
	3%	78.72	16.89	83.74	12.81	84.96	8.51	86.95	6.18	92.34	5.24
	5%	92.46	2.92	88.79	10.97	92.16	2.04	92.18	4.87	91.35	2.12
	Isolated	93.73	2.12	89.03	7.23	93.26	4.39	93.48	5.10	93.20	2.40
	Mixed	94.38	1.34	88.28	9.77	92.71	9.43	92.27	5.29	90.45	5.29
VIT	Multi	66.94	53.57	65.85	54.69	92.66	6.37	72.80	51.35	90.56	7.02
	1%	71.99	48.61	85.29	11.35	75.99	17.87	84.73	12.32	90.11	7.23
	3%	79.33	20.84	88.16	7.08	85.48	7.97	87.64	9.95	90.07	6.94
	5%	93.25	1.37	87.62	9.23	92.22	4.82	91.62	2.82	91.87	6.59
	Isolated	94.44	1.88	88.80	8.21	93.23	4.76	92.47	6.27	93.23	6.43
	Mixed	93.30	1.38	87.20	9.21	92.86	9.29	86.92	12.28	92.01	6.99

Training and Evaluation. In this study, we implement all models using Pytorch. We set H, W as 384, α, δ as 0.5, and the batch size as 5. To mitigate the overfitting, we augment the data by random horizontal flipping, random rotation, and random shift. We adopt ResNet family [9] (*i.e.*, ResNet18, ResNet34, ResNet50) and ViT [6] (*i.e.*, R50+ViT-B/16 hybrid model) as our pretrained encoder. We evaluate the model performance by Dice coefficient (DSC) and 95% Hausdorff Distance (95HD). For a fair comparison, we adopt the same decoder architecture design in [18] are shown in Appendix Table 4, and do not use any post-processing techniques. All of our experiments are conducted on two NVIDIA Titan X GPUs. All the models are trained using Adam optimizer with $\beta_1 = 0.9$, $\beta_2 = 0.999$. For 100 epochs training, a multi-step learning rate schedule is initialized as 0.001 and then decayed with a power of 0.95 at epochs 60 and 80.

Main Results. We conduct extensive experiments on five benchmark datasets. We adopt four models: ResNet-18, ResNet-34, ResNet-50, and ViT. We select three portions (*i.e.*, 1%, 3%, 5%) of exemplars from previous data for every incremental phase. Our results are presented in Table 2 and Appendix Fig. 2. First and foremost, we can see ITL-based methods generalize across all datasets under two exemplar portions (*i.e.*, 3% and 5%), yielding the competitive segmentation quality comparable to the upper bound baselines (*i.e.*, isolated-site and mixed-site training), which are much higher than the lower bound counterparts. The 1% exemplar portion seems slightly more challenging for ITL, but its superiority over the lower bound counterparts is still solid. A possible explanation for this finding is that using two exemplar portions (*i.e.*, 3% and 5%) maintains enough information of ITL, which mitigates the catastrophic forgetting, while ITL trained in the setting of 1% exemplar portion is not powerful enough to inherit prior knowledge and generalize well on newly added sites. Second, we consistently observe that ITL using larger models (*i.e.*, ResNet-50 and ViT) generalize substantially better than those using small models (*i.e.*, ResNet-18 and ResNet-34), which demonstrate competitive performance across all datasets. These results suggest that our ITL using the large model as our pretrained encoder leads to substantial gains in the setting of very limited data.

4   Analysis and Discussion

We address several research questions pertaining to our ITL approach. We use a ResNet-18 model as our encoder in our experiments. For comparisons, all models are trained for the same number of epochs, and all results are the average of three independent runs of experiments. To study the effectiveness of our proposed ITL framework, we performed experiments with 5% exemplars ratio.

Table 3. Comparison of segmentation performance in different phases.

HK		UCL		ISBI		ISBI1.5		I2CVB	
DSC[%]	95HD[mm]	DSC[%]	95HD[mm]	DSC[%]	95HD[mm]	DSC[%]	95HD[mm]	DSC[%]	95HD[mm]
94.06	1.96	-	-	-	-	-	-	-	-
93.68	1.98	88.74	8.72	-	-	-	-	-	-
93.20	1.83	87.38	9.30	92.87	1.82	-	-	-	-
90.37	8.34	86.73	12.75	89.84	13.32	91.57	11.05	-	-
88.88	8.91	85.14	10.97	85.98	14.23	89.74	13.11	88.46	12.15

Does Transfer Learning Lead to Better ITL? We draw two perspectives that may intuitively explain the effectiveness of transfer learning in our proposed ITL framework. As a first test of *whether transfer learning makes the base-learner stronger*, we plot the training loss/validation loss (*i.e.*, $\mathcal{L}_{all}$) to iteration to demonstrate the convergence improvements in Appendix Fig. 3. We can see that training from pretrained weights can converge faster than training from scratch. Another (perhaps not so surprising) observation we can get from Appendix Fig. 3 is that using pretrained weights usually yields slightly smaller loss compared to training from scratch. We then ask *whether transfer learning produces increased performance on multi-site datasets*. Since each single medical image dataset is usually of relatively small size, training the model from scratch tends to overfit a particular dataset. To evaluate the impact of transferring learning, we compare w/pretraining to w/o pretraining. As shown in Appendix Table 7, training from scratch does not bring benefits to the ITL framework. Instead of training from scratch, we find that simply incorporating transfer learning significantly boots the performance of ITL while achieving faster convergence speed, suggesting that transfer learning provides additional regularization against overfitting.

Does ITL Generalizes Well on Multi-site Datasets? We investigate whether the ITL framework generalizes well on multi-site datasets. We report the segmentation results of different phases in Table 3, from which we observe that ITL achieves good performance in different phases. This reveals that our approach is greatly helpful in reducing forgetting issues. We evaluate the proposed ITL methods with two random ordering (*i.e.*, (1) {HK→UCL→ISBI→ISBI1.5→I2CVB}, and (2) {ISBI→ISBI1.5→I2CVB→HK→ UCL}). The results are shown in Appendix Table 5. We perform experiments using both ordering strategies and observe comparable performance.

Efficiency of ITL. We report the network size and memory costs in Appendix Table 6. We observe that ITL achieves competitive performance and utilizes less network parameters compared to isolated-site training (upper bound), which requires the new model when adding new site data. We also examine the required memory footprint at each incremental phase. We observe that ITL is significantly more memory-efficient than mixed-site training (upper bound), although the latter remains the same network size when adding a new training phase. These results further demonstrate the efficiency of our proposed ITL framework.

5   Conclusion

In this paper, we present a novel incremental transfer learning framework for incrementally tackling multi-site medical image segmentation tasks. We pose model-level and site-level incremental training strategies for better segmentation, generalization, and transfer performance, especially in limited clinical resource settings. Extensive experimental results on four different baseline architectures demonstrate the effectiveness of our approach, offering a strong starting point to encourage future work in these important practical clinical scenarios.

Appendix

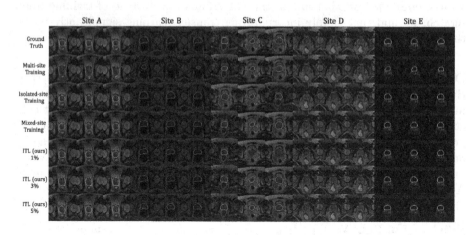

Fig. 2. Visualization of segmentation results on five benchmarks using ResNet-18 as the encoder. Different site results are shown in different colors.

Table 4. Segmentation decoder head architecture

Deocder	
Layer	Feature size
Upsample 1	48×48
Residual block 1	48×48
Upsample 2	96×96
Residual block 2	96×96
Upsample 3	192×192
Residual block 3	192×192
Upsample 4	384×384
Residual block 4	384×384
Output prediction	384×384

Table 5. Comparison of different ordering strategies using ResNet-18. We report mean and standard deviation across three random trials. Note that a larger DSC ($\uparrow$) and a smaller 95HD ($\downarrow$) indicate better performing ITL models.

Training sequence	DSC[%]	95HD[mm]
HK→UCL→ISBI→ISBI1.5→I2CVB	85.36 ± 0.33	11.38 ± 0.36
ISBI→ISBI1.5→I2CVB→HK→UCL	86.27 ± 0.27	12.01 ± 0.68

Table 6. Comparison of different training strategies using ResNet-18. We report mean and standard deviation across three random trials.

Scheme	DSC[%]	95HD[mm]	Model size(Mb)	Add new sites?	Memory cost
Isolated	90.95 ± 0.27	6.35 ± 0.68	$77.9 \times$ Site Num.	Linearly increase	New data
Mixed	89.29 ± 0.38	9.06 ± 0.84	77.9	Constant	Old data + New data
ITL	85.36 ± 0.33	11.38 ± 0.36	77.9	Constant	5% old data + new data

Table 7. Ablation of each component in the proposed ITL when using ResNet-18 under 5% exemplar portion. We report mean and standard deviation across three random trials. Note that a larger DSC ($\uparrow$) and a smaller 95HD ($\downarrow$) indicate better performing ITL models. The best results are in **bold**.

Backbone	Component	HK		UCL		ISBI		ISBI1.5		I2CVB		Avg. DSC	Avg. 95HD
		DSC[%]	95HD[mm]	DSC[%]	95HD[mm]	DSC[%]	95HD[mm]	DSC[%]	95HD[mm]	DSC[%]	95HD[mm]		
RES-18	Pretraining only	59.38	64.17	66.26	54.19	54.38	73.40	66.89	44.49	81.54	28.70	65.69 ± 1.51	52.99 ± 0.72
	$\mathcal{L}_{model}$ only	74.02	18.86	73.79	31.90	51.23	51.66	80.89	21.96	80.88	58.44	72.16 ± 0.38	36.56 ± 0.85
	Pretraining + $\mathcal{L}_{model}$	**81.81**	**5.50**	**84.45**	**13.95**	**84.52**	**15.65**	**89.32**	**10.11**	**86.72**	**11.70**	$\mathbf{85.36 \pm 0.33}$	$\mathbf{11.38 \pm 0.36}$

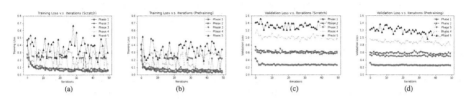

Fig. 3. Comparison of training from scratch against using pretraining. We use ResNet-18 on IMAGENET as the encoder. Under 5% exemplar portion, we plot (a) training loss (Scratch), (b) training loss (Pretraining), (c) validation loss (Scratch), (d) validation loss (Pretraining)

References

1. Aslani, S., Murino, V., Dayan, M., Tam, R., Sona, D., Hamarneh, G.: Scanner invariant multiple sclerosis lesion segmentation from MRI. In: ISBI. IEEE (2020)
2. Bloch, N., et al.: NCI-ISBI 2013 challenge: automated segmentation of prostate structures. Cancer Imaging Archive **370** (2015)
3. Chang, W.G., You, T., Seo, S., Kwak, S., Han, B.: Domain-specific batch normalization for unsupervised domain adaptation. In: CVPR (2019)
4. Chaudhry, A., Dokania, P.K., Ajanthan, T., Torr, P.H.: Riemannian walk for incremental learning: Understanding forgetting and intransigence. In: ECCV (2018)
5. Davidson, G., Mozer, M.C.: Sequential mastery of multiple visual tasks: networks naturally learn to learn and forget to forget. In: CVPR (2020)
6. Dosovitskiy, A., et al.: An image is worth 16x16 words: transformers for image recognition at scale. In: ICLR (2020)
7. Dou, Q., Liu, Q., Heng, P.A., Glocker, B.: Unpaired multi-modal segmentation via knowledge distillation. IEEE Trans. Med. Imaging **39**(7), 2415–2425 (2020)
8. Gibson, E., et al.: Inter-site variability in prostate segmentation accuracy using deep learning. In: Frangi, A.F., Schnabel, J.A., Davatzikos, C., Alberola-López, C., Fichtinger, G. (eds.) MICCAI 2018. LNCS, vol. 11073, pp. 506–514. Springer, Cham (2018). https://doi.org/10.1007/978-3-030-00937-3_58

9. He, K., Zhang, X., Ren, S., Sun, J.: Deep residual learning for image recognition. In: CVPR, pp. 770–778 (2016)

10. Jia, H., Song, Y., Huang, H., Cai, W., Xia, Y.: HD-Net: hybrid discriminative network for prostate segmentation in MR images. In: Shen, D., et al. (eds.) MICCAI 2019. LNCS, vol. 11765, pp. 110–118. Springer, Cham (2019). https://doi.org/10.1007/978-3-030-32245-8_13

11. Karani, N., Chaitanya, K., Baumgartner, C., Konukoglu, E.: A lifelong learning approach to brain MR segmentation across scanners and protocols. In: Frangi, A.F., Schnabel, J.A., Davatzikos, C., Alberola-López, C., Fichtinger, G. (eds.) MICCAI 2018. LNCS, vol. 11070, pp. 476–484. Springer, Cham (2018). https://doi.org/10.1007/978-3-030-00928-1_54

12. Lemaître, G., Martí, R., Freixenet, J., Vilanova, J.C., Walker, P.M., Meriaudeau, F.: Computer-aided detection and diagnosis for prostate cancer based on mono and multi-parametric MRI: a review. CBM **60**, 8–31 (2015)

13. Li, D., Zhang, J., Yang, Y., Liu, C., Song, Y.Z., Hospedales, T.M.: Episodic training for domain generalization. In: CVPR (2019)

14. Li, X., Yu, L., Chen, H., Fu, C.W., Heng, P.A.: Semi-supervised skin lesion segmentation via transformation consistent self-ensembling model. arXiv preprint arXiv:1808.03887 (2018)

15. Li, Z., Hoiem, D.: Learning without forgetting. IEEE Trans. Pattern Anal. Mach. Intell. **40**(12), 2935–2947 (2017)

16. Litjens, G., et al.: Evaluation of prostate segmentation algorithms for MRI: the PROMISE12 challenge. MIA **18**(2), 359–373 (2014)

17. Liu, P., Xiao, L., Zhou, S.K.: Incremental learning for multi-organ segmentation with partially labeled datasets. In: MICCAI (2021)

18. Liu, Q., Dou, Q., Heng, P.-A.: Shape-aware meta-learning for generalizing prostate MRI segmentation to unseen domains. In: Martel, A.L., et al. (eds.) MICCAI 2020. LNCS, vol. 12262, pp. 475–485. Springer, Cham (2020). https://doi.org/10.1007/978-3-030-59713-9_46

19. Liu, Q., Dou, Q., Yu, L., Heng, P.A.: MS-net: multi-site network for improving prostate segmentation with heterogeneous MRI data. IEEE Trans. Med. Imaging **39**(9), 2713–2724 (2020)

20. McCloskey, M., Cohen, N.J.: Catastrophic interference in connectionist networks: the sequential learning problem. In: Psychology of Learning and Motivation, vol. 24, pp. 109–165. Elsevier (1989)

21. Milletari, F., Navab, N., Ahmadi, S.A.: V-net: fully convolutional neural networks for volumetric medical image segmentation. In: 3DV, pp. 565–571. IEEE (2016)

22. Nie, D., Gao, Y., Wang, L., Shen, D.: ASDNet: attention based semi-supervised deep networks for medical image segmentation. In: Frangi, A.F., Schnabel, J.A., Davatzikos, C., Alberola-López, C., Fichtinger, G. (eds.) MICCAI 2018. LNCS, vol. 11073, pp. 370–378. Springer, Cham (2018). https://doi.org/10.1007/978-3-030-00937-3_43

23. Rebuffi, S.A., Kolesnikov, A., Sperl, G., Lampert, C.H.: iCaRL: incremental classifier and representation learning. In: CVPR (2017)

24. Rundo, L., et al.: Use-net: incorporating squeeze-and-excitation blocks into u-net for prostate zonal segmentation of multi-institutional MRI datasets. Neurocomputing **365**, 31–43 (2019)

25. Rundo, L., et al.: CNN-based prostate zonal segmentation on T2-weighted MR images: a cross-dataset study. In: Esposito, A., Faundez-Zanuy, M., Morabito, F.C., Pasero, E. (eds.) Neural Approaches to Dynamics of Signal Exchanges. SIST, vol.

151, pp. 269–280. Springer, Singapore (2020). https://doi.org/10.1007/978-981-13-8950-4_25

26. Shi, G., Xiao, L., Chen, Y., Zhou, S.K.: Marginal loss and exclusion loss for partially supervised multi-organ segmentation. Med. Image Anal. **70**, 101979 (2021)

27. Wu, Y., et al.: Large scale incremental learning. In: CVPR (2019)

28. Xiang, J., Shlizerman, E.: TKIL: tangent kernel approach for class balanced incremental learning. arXiv preprint arXiv:2206.08492 (2022)

29. Yang, L., et al.: NuSeT: a deep learning tool for reliably separating and analyzing crowded cells. PLoS Comput. Biol. **16**(9), e1008193 (2020)

30. Yao, Q., Xiao, L., Liu, P., Zhou, S.K.: Label-free segmentation of COVID-19 lesions in lung CT. IEEE Trans. Med. Imaging **40**(10), 2808–2819 (2021)

31. You, C., Dai, W., Staib, L., Duncan, J.S.: Bootstrapping semi-supervised medical image segmentation with anatomical-aware contrastive distillation. arXiv preprint arXiv:2206.02307 (2022)

32. You, C., Yang, J., Chapiro, J., Duncan, J.S.: Unsupervised Wasserstein distance guided domain adaptation for 3D multi-domain liver segmentation. In: Cardoso, J., et al. (eds.) IMIMIC/MIL3ID/LABELS -2020. LNCS, vol. 12446, pp. 155–163. Springer, Cham (2020). https://doi.org/10.1007/978-3-030-61166-8_17

33. You, C., et al.: Class-aware generative adversarial transformers for medical image segmentation. arXiv preprint arXiv:2201.10737 (2022)

34. You, C., Zhao, R., Staib, L., Duncan, J.S.: Momentum contrastive voxel-wise representation learning for semi-supervised volumetric medical image segmentation. arXiv preprint arXiv:2105.07059 (2021)

35. You, C., Zhou, Y., Zhao, R., Staib, L., Duncan, J.S.: SimCVD: simple contrastive voxel-wise representation distillation for semi-supervised medical image segmentation. IEEE Trans. Med. Imaging (2022)

36. Yu, L., Yang, X., Chen, H., Qin, J., Heng, P.A.: Volumetric convnets with mixed residual connections for automated prostate segmentation from 3D MR images. In: AAAI (2017)

37. Zhang, X., et al.: Automatic spinal cord segmentation from axial-view MRI slices using CNN with grayscale regularized active contour propagation. Comput. Biol. Med. **132**, 104345 (2021)

38. Zhang, X., Martin, D.G., Noga, M., Punithakumar, K.: Fully automated left atrial segmentation from MR image sequences using deep convolutional neural network and unscented Kalman filter. In: 2018 IEEE International Conference on Bioinformatics and Biomedicine (BIBM), pp. 2316–2323. IEEE (2018)

39. Zhang, X., Noga, M., Martin, D.G., Punithakumar, K.: Fully automated left atrium segmentation from anatomical cine long-axis MRI sequences using deep convolutional neural network with unscented Kalman filter. Med. Image Anal. **68**, 101916 (2021)

40. Zhang, X., Noga, M., Punithakumar, K.: Fully automated deep learning based segmentation of normal, infarcted and edema regions from multiple cardiac MRI sequences. In: Zhuang, X., Li, L. (eds.) MyoPS 2020. LNCS, vol. 12554, pp. 82–91. Springer, Cham (2020). https://doi.org/10.1007/978-3-030-65651-5_8

41. Zhang, Y., Yang, L., Chen, J., Fredericksen, M., Hughes, D.P., Chen, D.Z.: Deep adversarial networks for biomedical image segmentation utilizing unannotated images. In: Descoteaux, M., Maier-Hein, L., Franz, A., Jannin, P., Collins, D.L., Duchesne, S. (eds.) MICCAI 2017. LNCS, vol. 10435, pp. 408–416. Springer, Cham (2017). https://doi.org/10.1007/978-3-319-66179-7_47

42. Zheng, Y., Xiang, J., Su, K., Shlizerman, E.: BI-MAML: balanced incremental approach for meta learning. arXiv preprint arXiv:2006.07412 (2020)

43. Zhou, S.K., et al.: A review of deep learning in medical imaging: imaging traits, technology trends, case studies with progress highlights, and future promises. Proc. IEEE **109**(5), 820–838 (2021)
44. Zhu, J., Li, Y., Hu, Y., Ma, K., Zhou, S.K., Zheng, Y.: Rubik's Cube+: a self-supervised feature learning framework for 3D medical image analysis. Med. Image Anal. **64**, 101746 (2020)

FedAP: Adaptive Personalization in Federated Learning for Non-IID Data

Yousef Yeganeh[1(✉)], Azade Farshad[1], Johann Boschmann[1], Richard Gaus[1], Maximilian Frantzen[1], and Nassir Navab[1,2]

[1] Technical University of Munich, Munich, Germany
y.yeganeh@tum.de
[2] Johns Hopkins University, Baltimore, USA

Abstract. Federated learning (FL) is a distributed learning method that offers medical institutes the prospect of collaboration in a global model while preserving the privacy of their patients. Although most medical centers conduct similar medical imaging tasks, their differences, such as specializations, number of patients, and devices, lead to distinctive data distributions. Data heterogeneity poses a challenge for FL and the personalization of the local models. In this work, we investigate an adaptive hierarchical clustering method for FL to produce intermediate semi-global models, so clients with similar data distribution have the chance of forming a more specialized model. Our method forms several clusters consisting of clients with the most similar data distributions; then, each cluster continues to train separately. Inside the cluster, we use meta-learning to improve the personalization of the participants' models. We compare the clustering approach with classical FedAvg and centralized training by evaluating our proposed methods on the HAM10k dataset for skin lesion classification with extreme heterogeneous data distribution. Our experiments demonstrate significant performance gain in heterogeneous distribution compared to standard FL methods in classification accuracy. Moreover, we show that the models converge faster if applied in clusters and outperform centralized training while using only a small subset of data.

Keywords: Federated learning · Personalization · Meta-learning · Non-IID data

Y. Yeganeh, A. Farshad, J. Boschmann, R. Gaus and M. Frantzen—Equal Contribution.

Supplementary Information The online version contains supplementary material available at https://doi.org/10.1007/978-3-031-18523-6_2.

1   Introduction

Deep learning models outperform classic techniques for pathological diagnoses in medical imaging tasks [14]; however, their performance highly depends on the training data. Unavailability of medical imaging data due to privacy concerns, along with data heterogeneity, can negatively impact the representativity of the model. Federated learning (FL) tackles both of these challenges [12]. A federated setting consists of multiple clients and a server; local clients send their models to the server, and the server aggregates them and produces a global model [15]. Weighted aggregation in FL aims to improve performance in favor of a global model; in turn, parts of the data distribution that potentially have distinctive features are considered outliers, e.g., since hospitals often outweigh specialized centers in terms of the number of patients, the global model tends to represent hospitals' distribution, so the prospect of collaboration among institutes with similar data distribution is neglected. To improve personalization, we pose FL as a meta learning problem [8,16]. We demonstrate that clustering and applying a meta learning scheme improve personalization, preserve more specialized data, and enhance the convergence of the model. FedAvg (federated averaging) [15] was proposed as one of the first FL algorithms and has been used as a standard benchmark. Meta learning, or learning to learn [25], is learning how to efficiently solve new tasks from a set of known tasks [8]. FL clients can be interpreted as meta learning tasks since each client's data distribution equals a different problem; hence, meta learning ideas have been successfully applied to FL [5,6, 9,10]. Inspired by MAML [8], clients with similar distributions are grouped in clusters as a set of tasks, so each cluster is redefined a separate FL problem. This improves the homogeneity of the data between the clients in their corresponding clusters. Although in FL data is not explicitly accessible, we used the value differences of model parameters between the clients from the latest round and the global model as a similarity measure between those clients. Briggs *et al.* explores a hierarchical clustering technique to group similar models [4], and we utilized the same method for personalization of clients' models and combined it with our proposed Adaptive Personalization (FedAP) for the final training inside clusters. We kept the simplicity of FedAvg [9], but with two differences: 1) FedAP treats the aggregated global update as a meta-level gradient that can be used with a different optimizer to update the global model. Particularly, it introduces the new hyperparameter of a meta learning rate. 2) At the end of the training, FedAP personalizes the global model to each individual client. This can have a strong advantage in the context of FL [6,9]. An overview of our method is depicted in Fig. 1. The main contributions of this work are as follows: We propose FedAP, a new hierarchical clustering approach to perform adaptive personalization inside the clusters and each client for non-IID (not independent or identical) data. Our proposed method gains significant performance improvement in terms of classification accuracy and decreasing the accuracy variance between different clients.

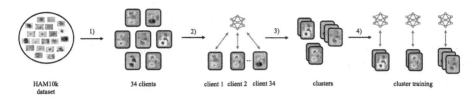

Fig. 1. Method overview. Our pipeline has four steps: 1) splitting the dataset, 2) training all clients with FedAvg for predefined rounds, 3) clustering the clients based on the latest model update, 4) performing FedAvg or FedAP on each separate cluster.

2   Related Work

A study on live data of millions of users shows that significant improvements can be achieved by personalizing the learning rate and batch size to clients [26]. FedOpt [17] extends the FedAvg algorithm and implements personalization by introducing adjustable gradient update strategies for each client and server. Employing weight decay over training rounds on the server-side is shown to be required to lower the error on non-i.i.d. data [13]. [1] proposes to learn base layers globally while keeping classification layers private on the client-side. FedMD [11] introduces a framework for individually designed by each client. The MOCHA [23] enables efficient meta-learning in the federated environment. Communication efficiency in federated learning is also addressed in [21] suggesting a compression protocol based on quantization. Non i.i.d. data is shown to impact both the convergence speed and the final performance of the FedAvg algorithm [13,21]. [13,30] tackle data heterogeneity by sharing a limited common dataset. IDA [28] proposes to stabilize and improve the learning process by weighting the clients' updates based on their distance from the global model. Motivated from classical machine learning techniques [12] introduces a weight regularization term to the local objective function to prevent the divergence between local and global models. Recently, a semi-supervised learning approach for federated learning on the ISIC skin lesion dataset was proposed [2,3]. Yue *et al.* [29] surveys on the data availability and heterogeneity in the medical domain, concluding that privacy restrictions and missing data pipelines block the full potential of deep Learning which requires big data sets. The described advances in the field of federated learning can help overcome the challenge of medical data privacy and disseminate machine learning techniques in healthcare [22]. Notably, data heterogeneity remains a significant hurdle to this development, so robust techniques towards non-IID data carry considerable future potential [18].

3   Method

In this section, we present our approach to tackling the problem of non-IID data distribution in federated learning. First, we describe the optimization process in a federated setting and its development in adaptive personalization. Then, we define the original federated averaging scenario. Later, we explain the entire pipeline of our proposed federated adaptive personalization method, followed by how hierarchical clustering can be embedded in our approach.

3.1 Definitions

The global data distribution is denoted by $\mathcal{D}$, while $\mathcal{S} \sim \mathcal{D}$ is the sampled data points and $s_1, ...s_N = \mathcal{S}$. The data points are distributed across M clients. Each client $i \in \{1, ..., M\}$ only sees its local dataset, which is a subset $\mathcal{S}_i \sim \mathcal{D}_i$ of the global data and $s_1, ..., s_{N_i} = \mathcal{S}_i$. $\mathcal{D}_i$ being the client's local data distribution. With the global model parameters θ_{global}, the overall optimization task can be defined as:

$$\min_{\theta_{global}} \mathcal{L}(\mathcal{S}) = \min_{\theta_{global}} \frac{1}{M} \sum_{i=1}^{M} l_{\theta_{global}}(\mathcal{S}_i) \tag{1}$$

where $\mathcal{L}$ is the global loss function and l the local loss function of each client. We hypothesize that, while each distribution $\mathcal{D}_i$ is different, they can be clustered by similarity. Following Briggs *et al.* [4], we introduce a distinct model θ_c for each resulting cluster $c \in C$, where C is the set of all clusters and θ_C is the set of all cluster model parameters.

We annotate the data distribution in each cluster by $\mathcal{D}_c$ with $\mathcal{S}_c \sim \mathcal{D}_c$ being the data points and $s_1, ..., s_{N_c} = \mathcal{S}_c$. Integrating these clusters into Eq. (1), we arrive at the following global and local loss function for each cluster c:

$$\min_{\theta_C} \mathcal{L}(\mathcal{S}) = \min_{\theta_C} \frac{1}{|C|} \sum_{c \in C} l_{\theta_c}(\mathcal{S}_c) \tag{2}$$

$$l_{\theta_c}(\mathcal{S}_c) = \frac{1}{|c|} \sum_{i \in c} l_{\theta_c}(\mathcal{S}_i) \tag{3}$$

Extending this model to a personalized version where each client has its own model results in Eq. (4):

$$\min_{(\theta_1, ..., \theta_M)} \mathcal{L}(\mathcal{S}) = \min_{(\theta_1, ..., \theta_n)} \frac{1}{M} \sum_{i=1}^{M} l_{\theta_i}(\mathcal{S}_i) \tag{4}$$

Equations (2) and (4) both introduce additional degrees of freedom which allow us to learn the sampled training data points from the respective distributions better than a single model as shown in Eq. (1). We can sum up the results in the following form:

$$\min_{\theta_{global}} \mathcal{L}(\mathcal{S}) \geq \min_{\theta_C} \mathcal{L}(\mathcal{S}) \geq \min_{(\theta_1, ..., \theta_M)} \mathcal{L}(\mathcal{S}) \tag{5}$$

While Eq. (5) introduces the idea of each client learning its own model to reduce the loss on its distribution, the amount of data available for training is reduced. As theoretical works in deep learning show, the generalization error of models grows if the number of training samples shrinks. This can also be observed in practice and is reflected by the overfitting phenomenon. To maintain a good generalization performance, we propose to train on all of the mentioned levels, gathering information about as many training samples as possible while reducing the problem complexity each model has to solve step by step. We start an initial training overall clients to find a global model θ_{global} which should learn basic features of the whole distribution. In the next step, we cluster the clients and begin with the training inside the clusters. The resulting cluster models θ_C are then personalized in the final step by performing local training on each client i, leading to the final personalized model θ_i for each client. Figure 1 visualizes the whole pipeline.

3.2 Federated Averaging

In the following, we analyze the federated averaging (FedAvg) algorithm in more detail. If we have M clients and $N_i = |\mathcal{D}_i|$ is the number of data samples of client i, the global and local loss functions take the following form:

$$f(\theta) = \sum_{i=1}^{M} \frac{N_i}{N} F_i(\theta) \quad \text{where} \quad F_i(\theta) = \frac{1}{N_i} \sum_{j} f_j(\theta) \tag{6}$$

where, $F_i(\theta)$ is the local objective of each client and $f(\theta)$ is the global objective averaged over all clients. Training with FedAvg consists of two main updating schemes. Firstly, the clients are training locally with an initially distributed model on their local data for a predefined amount of epochs e. For each communication round, a client i updates its model parameter θ_i, with learning rate α as follows,

$$\forall i, \ \theta_i^{t+1} \leftarrow \theta_i^t - \alpha \cdot \Delta\theta \tag{7}$$

In a second step, the server computes a weighted average based on the number of data points of each client i of all locally updated model parameters θ_i's:

$$\theta_{global}^{t+1} \leftarrow \sum_{i=1}^{M} \frac{N_i}{N} \theta_i^{t+1} \tag{8}$$

3.3 Federated Adaptive Personalization

Our methodology (Federated Adaptive Personalization or FedAP) begins with the initialization of the global model parameters θ_{global}. At the start of each of k federated rounds, they are transferred to a batch of n randomly selected clients, and local training is performed, yielding updated local model parameters θ_i in each client i. Next, θ is updated using an adaptive meta learning rate η based on the current round number. The adaptive meta learning rate decreases linearly throughout the training.

$$\theta_{global} \leftarrow \theta_{global} + \eta \sum_{i=1}^{n} \frac{N_i}{N} (\theta_i - \theta_{global}) \tag{9}$$

Following the last federated round, the local model parameters of all clients $i \in \{1, \ldots, M\}$ are personalized by performing a fixed number of gradient optimization epochs on the local training data.

3.4 Hierarchical Clustering

The personalization of the local models can benefit more from clients that share more similarities in their data with each specific client. Therefore, we propose to perform hierarchical clustering [4] after an initial phase of global federated learning, including all the clients. After performing FedAvg for a specified number of federated rounds, clients are clustered via hierarchical clustering according to their model updates in the current round. Each of the resultant client clusters is then treated as an isolated federated learning problem where either FedAvg or our proposed FedAP is employed. The full pipeline is visualized in Fig. 1.

4   Experiments and Results

In this section, we present the experimental setup and the results of our experiments. The dataset, data preprocessing, and the employed data split for federated learning are discussed in Sect. 4.1. We compare our proposed personalized clustered models to two baselines, a standard supervised model trained in the centralized setting and FedAvg [15]. Furthermore, we present the results of combining clustering and personalization with existing approaches on the HAM10k skin lesion dataset [24].

4.1   Experimental Setup

We employ a pretrained MobileNetV2 [19,20] on ImageNet as a base classifier for all the baselines and our proposed model. The hyperparameter tuning was performed using a validation set without any overlap with the test set for the centralized model. For all the federated learning experiments, hyperparameter optimization comprised two steps: First, all clients were generated using a fixed random seed, and the hyperparameters were optimized against the client's test sets. Then, we generated all clients anew for the evaluation using a different random seed, and a final learning curve was acquired using the previously fixed hyperparameter. The following hyperparameters were optimized: learning rate, batch size, and a number of local training epochs. The final values were reused in all of the experiments. The models were optimized with SGD optimizer, with learning rate 0.001, inner epochs $e = 1$, inner personalization epochs 7, inner batch size 16, initial and final meta-learning rate $\eta_0 = 1.0, \eta_k = 0.46$, total federated rounds $k = 220$, meta batch size $n = 5$. In FedAP, SGD is also used for global training so that the global update rule became $\theta \leftarrow \theta + \eta \cdot \Delta\theta$. Moreover, the adaptive weight decreases linearly with the number of federated rounds, from specified initial to final values. In the hierarchical clustering (HC) experiments, the models were trained with 20 cluster initialization rounds, Euclidean distance metric, ward linkage mechanism and maximum distance of 5.

Dataset and Preprocessing. The HAM10k dataset [24] is a collection of 10,015 dermatoscopic images of seven types of skin lesions. The ground truth labels in HAM10k are based on histopathology in over 50% of the cases and on follow-up examination, expert consensus, or in-vivo confocal microscopy. Our choice of HAM10k for evaluation of our method was due to this dataset's unbalanced and high non-IID nature. To address the problem of unbalancedness in the dataset, we utilized random undersampling [7]; *i.e.* at most 500 images from each lesion class were randomly sampled and used for training.

Federated Data Split. One of the common problems in clinical datasets that challenge machine learning methods is low statistical heterogeneity [27]. We modeled highly non-IID data distributions between our clients to represent this problem. Images within each class were partitioned into 35 groups, and the clients were randomly assigned two partitions from different classes until no partition pairs were left. This resulted in 34 clients, with 70 images assigned to each in total from two classes (see the supplementary material for the distribution heatmap). The 70 images were randomly split into training and test sets at an 80:20 ratio within each client.

4.2 Results and Discussions

In this section, we present the results of our experiments and the comparison of our proposed model to previous work. In order to take the number of personalization rounds in FedAP and initialization rounds in HC into account for our total training rounds, the reported accuracy values in Table 1 are based on the total number of training steps for all models.

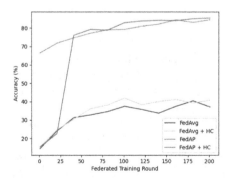

Fig. 2. Average test accuracy in different rounds. Classification accuracy averaged over all clients. This figure shows the increase in the convergence rate using both FedAP and HC.

Table 1. Results. comparison of our methods to the baselines on the non-IID HAM10k dataset. The reported values for federated models are based on the mean and std of all the clients.

Method	Accuracy (%)
Centralized	76.8
FedAvg [15]	41.1 ± 34.31
FedAvg + HC [4]	44.1 ± 20.86
FedAP (Ours)	84.1 ± 14.53
FedAP + HC (Ours)	**86.9 ± 12.81**

A standard **centralized** training setting was intended as a standard against which the more constrained federated learning experiments could be measured. For this experiment, a global training and test sets were created by pooling all clients' respective training and test data. Due to the availability of all clients' data to a single model, this model achieves much higher performance compared to FedAvg.

FedAvg achieves the worst performance across all methods. The learning curve shows a high degree of oscillation due to the fact that the single global model was not able to learn all necessary features from the different learning tasks imposed by different data distributions of the clients. Thus, this demonstrates the lack of robustness of *FedAvg* in a highly non-IID data setting, as indicated by preliminary evidence [13,21,30].

For the **FedAvg + HC** experiment, several FedAvg rounds (given by the hyperparameter "cluster initialization rounds") were performed before clustering. Following this, clients were clustered according to their local updates using hierarchical clustering (as in Briggs *et al.* [4]). Inside the individual clusters, conventional *FedAvg* training was performed. The global accuracy was obtained by simply averaging the test set accuracy of all clients. Hierarchical clustering increased the overall convergence speed of *FedAvg*. A sudden jump in the accuracy, as well as final model performance improvement, can be seen after clustering in Fig. 2. We assume that an approximation of a homogeneous learning setting is recovered inside the clusters, and indeed the model updates can be used to represent the data distribution. However, this approach still falls far behind the performance of *FedAP*, substantiating the crucial importance of model personalization in a highly non-IID data environment. similar to *FedAvg*, **FedAP** randomly samples a batch of n clients at each round. The evaluation of *FedAP* was performed in the same way as of FedAvg with the difference that, after the distribution of the global model, it was personalized to the clients by performing a number of gradient optimization steps on the local training sets. After this personalization, the model was evaluated on the test set, and again a global accuracy was calculated by averaging all local test set accuracies. The global model for *FedAP* was able to learn continuously, while the personalization step allowed the adaption to the different client distributions. Especially the extreme non-IID setting with simple underlying tasks allows the personalization to perform very well.

The **FedAP + HC** experiment was performed in the same way as the previous one, only that the adaptive personalization is performed after hierarchical clustering. As in the *FedAvg + HC* experiment, clusters were formed according to clients' model updates after initial 20 rounds of FedAvg. *FedAP + HC* shows the overall best performance compared to all other approaches. We observe the same learning curve behavior as in *FedAvg + HC*. It improves the convergence speed of the algorithm, shown again by the immediate jump in balanced accuracy after clustering depicted in Fig. 2. Despite achieving the best performance among the different mentioned variations of the federated setting, we observed that the FedAP + HC model suffers from overfitting in very long runs; *i.e.*

if we train both FedAP and FedAP + HC for around 500 more rounds, the performance stays the same or gains minimal improvement in FedAP, but the FedAP + HC starts deteriorating. We assume that this is an indication of the global model's higher adaptability to distinct tasks than the cluster models. The core idea of meta-learning roots in learning from many distinctive tasks. Indeed, clustering clients (representing the meta-learning task in a federated learning setting) reduces the diversity of tasks in each cluster to learn from. Therefore, this might be the reason behind FedAP + HC model's sensitivity to overfitting in more extended training.

5 Conclusion

In this work, we presented and analyzed an adaptive personalization approach along with hierarchical clustering of the clients to tackle the non-IID problem in federated learning. Our adaptive model parameter weighting with hierarchical clustering enables the better adaptation of the local models of clients to their distinctive data distribution while still taking advantage of the global aggregation of the different client model updates. The clients are clustered based on their similarity to local model updates and thus can approximate an IID setting in the respective clusters. Our experiments on the HAM10k dataset with the MobileNetV2 network show drastic improvements in classification accuracy over the standard supervised and over the FedAvg baseline. The lower standard deviation of our proposed method compared to previous work demonstrate that adaptive personalization of client models in the federated setting, inspired by meta-learning, yields higher generalizability of all clients models. In addition, hierarchical clustering increases the convergence speed and allows for better global models. Our experiments show that the models trained with FedAP and HC have the lowest standard deviation and highest average accuracy, demonstrating the proposed methods' effectiveness in reaching a reasonable and high accuracy performance in all clients. Despite the high performance gain of our proposed method, if the model is trained for too many rounds, the performance decreases, which shows its sensitivity to overfitting. Therefore, we plan to investigate this issue in future work.

Acknowledgements. We gratefully acknowledge the Munich Center for Machine Learning (MCML) with funding from the Bundesministerium für Bildung und Forschung (BMBF) under the project 01IS18036B.

References

1. Arivazhagan, M.G., Aggarwal, V., Singh, A.K., Choudhary, S.: Federated learning with personalization layers. arXiv:1912.00818 (2019)
2. Bdair, T., Navab, N., Albarqouni, S.: FedPerl: semi-supervised peer learning for skin lesion classification. In: de Bruijne, M. (ed.) MICCAI 2021. LNCS, vol. 12903, pp. 336–346. Springer, Cham (2021). https://doi.org/10.1007/978-3-030-87199-4_32

3. Bdair, T., Navab, N., Albarqouni, S.: Semi-supervised federated peer learning for skin lesion classification. Machine Learning for Biomedical Imaging 1(April 2022 issue), 1–10 (2022)
4. Briggs, C., Fan, Z., Andras, P.: Federated learning with hierarchical clustering of local updates to improve training on non-IID data (2020)
5. Chen, F., Luo, M., Dong, Z., Li, Z., He, X.: Federated meta-learning with fast convergence and efficient communication (2019)
6. Fallah, A., Mokhtari, A., Ozdaglar, A.: Personalized federated learning: a meta-learning approach (2020)
7. Fernández, A., García, S., Galar, M., Prati, R.C., Krawczyk, B., Herrera, F.: Learning from Imbalanced Data Sets. Springer, Cham (2018). https://doi.org/10.1007/978-3-319-98074-4
8. Finn, C., Abbeel, P., Levine, S.: Model-agnostic meta-learning for fast adaptation of deep networks. In: Precup, D., Teh, Y.W. (eds.) Proceedings of the 34th International Conference on Machine Learning. Proceedings of Machine Learning Research, vol. 70, pp. 1126–1135. PMLR, International Convention Centre, Sydney, Australia (2017). http://proceedings.mlr.press/v70/finn17a.html
9. Jiang, Y., Konecny, J., Rush, K., Kannan, S.: Improving federated learning personalization via model agnostic meta learning (2019)
10. Khodak, M., Balcan, M.F., Talwalkar, A.: Adaptive gradient-based meta-learning methods (2019)
11. Li, D., Wang, J.: FedMD: heterogenous federated learning via model distillation. arXiv:1910.03581 (2019)
12. Li, T., Sahu, A.K., Talwalkar, A., Smith, V.: Federated learning: challenges, methods, and future directions. IEEE Signal Proc. Mag. **37**(3), 50–60 (2020)
13. Li, X., Huang, K., Yang, W., Wang, S., Zhang, Z.: On the convergence of FedAvg on non-IID data. arXiv:1907.02189 (2020)
14. Madabhushi, A., Lee, G.: Image analysis and machine learning in digital pathology: challenges and opportunities. Medical Image Analysis **33**, 170–175 (2016). https://doi.org/10.1016/j.media.2016.06.037, https://www.sciencedirect.com/science/article/pii/S1361841516301141, 20th anniversary of the Medical Image Analysis journal (MedIA)
15. McMahan, B., Moore, E., Ramage, D., Hampson, S., y Arcas, B.A.: Communication-efficient learning of deep networks from decentralized data. In: Singh, A., Zhu, J. (eds.) Proceedings of the 20th International Conference on Artificial Intelligence and Statistics. Proceedings of Machine Learning Research, vol. 54, pp. 1273–1282. PMLR, Fort Lauderdale, FL, USA (2017). http://proceedings.mlr.press/v54/mcmahan17a.html
16. Nichol, A., Achiam, J., Schulman, J.: On first-order meta-learning algorithms (2018)
17. Reddi, S., et al.: Adaptive federated optimization. arXiv:2003.00295 (2020)
18. Rieke, N., et al.: The future of digital health with federated learning (2021)
19. Sae-Lim, W., Wettayaprasit, W., Aiyarak, P.: Convolutional neural networks using MobileNet for skin lesion classification. In: 2019 16th International Joint Conference on Computer Science and Software Engineering (JCSSE), pp. 242–247. IEEE (2019)
20. Sandler, M., Howard, A., Zhu, M., Zhmoginov, A., Chen, L.C.: MobileNetV2: Inverted residuals and linear bottlenecks. In: Proceedings of the IEEE conference on computer vision and pattern recognition, pp. 4510–4520 (2018)
21. Sattler, F., Wiedemann, S., Müller, K.R., Samek, W.: Robust and communication-efficient federated learning from non-IID data. arXiv:1903.02891 (2019)

22. Sheller, M.J., et al.: Federated learning in medicine: facilitating multi-institutional collaborations without sharing patient data. Sci. Report. **10**(1), 1–12 (2020)

23. Smith, V., Chiang, C.K., Sanjabi, M., Talwalkar, A.: Federated multi-task learning. arXiv:1705.10467 (2018)

24. Tschandl, P., Rosendahl, C., Kittler, H.: The HAM10000 dataset, a large collection of multi-source dermatoscopic images of common pigmented skin lesions. Sci. Data **5**(1), 1–9 (2018)

25. Vanschoren, J.: Meta-learning: a survey. arXiv preprint arXiv:1810.03548 (2018)

26. Wang, K., Mathews, R., Kiddon, C., Eichner, H., Beaufays, F., Ramage, D.: Federated evaluation of on-device personalization. arXiv:1910.10252 (2019)

27. Wynants, L., Riley, R., Timmerman, D., Van Calster, B.: Random-effects meta-analysis of the clinical utility of tests and prediction models. Stat. Med. **37**(12), 2034–2052 (2018)

28. Yeganeh, Y., Farshad, A., Navab, N., Albarqouni, S.: Inverse distance aggregation for federated learning with non-IID data. arXiv:2008.07665 (2020)

29. Yue, L., Tian, D., Chen, W., Han, X., Yin, M.: Deep learning for heterogeneous medical data analysis. World Wide Web **23**(5), 2715–2737 (2020). https://doi.org/10.1007/s11280-019-00764-z

30. Zhao, Y., Li, M., Lai, L., Suda, N., Civin, D., Chandra, V.: Federated learning with non-IID data. CoRR arxiv:abs/1806.00582 (2018)

Data Stealing Attack on Medical Images: Is It Safe to Export Networks from Data Lakes?

Huiyu Li$^{(\boxtimes)}$, Nicholas Ayache, and Hervé Delingette

Université Côte d'Azur, Inria, Epione Team, Sophia Antipolis, France
huiyu.li@inria.fr

Abstract. In privacy-preserving machine learning, it is common that the owner of the learned model does not have any physical access to the data. Instead, only a secured remote access to a data lake is granted to the model owner without any ability to retrieve the data from the data lake. Yet, the model owner may want to export the trained model periodically from the remote repository and a question arises whether this may cause is a risk of data leakage. In this paper, we introduce the concept of data stealing attack during the export of neural networks. It consists in hiding some information in the exported network that allows the reconstruction outside the data lake of images initially stored in that data lake. More precisely, we show that it is possible to train a network that can perform lossy image compression and at the same time solve some utility tasks such as image segmentation. The attack then proceeds by exporting the compression decoder network together with some image codes that leads to the image reconstruction outside the data lake. We explore the feasibility of such attacks on databases of CT and MR images, showing that it is possible to obtain perceptually meaningful reconstructions of the target dataset, and that the stolen dataset can be used in turns to solve a broad range of tasks. Comprehensive experiments and analyses show that data stealing attacks should be considered as a threat for sensitive imaging data sources.

Keywords: Data stealing attack · Privacy · Medical images

1 Introduction

A growing number of medical data warehouses or data lakes are been built within major hospitals or health organisations in order to exploit medical data. With those infrastructures, the access of health data such as medical images or health records is heavily restricted and regulated, and only a remote access to the training and test data is often granted to data scientists sitting outside those organizations. Any leakage of privacy sensitive medical data from those data lakes represents a serious threat to the reputation of the health organization holding the data lake, and it may also be used by cybercriminals to earn money through ransoms, or to cause harms [13].

S. Albarqouni et al. (Eds.): DeCaF 2022/FAIR 2022, LNCS 13573, pp. 28–36, 2022.
https://doi.org/10.1007/978-3-031-18523-6_3

Table 1. Attacks targeting the recovery of training data with the attacker knowledge about the trained model or the output of the model on the training data.

Attack	Adversary knowledge			
	Model		Output	
	Architecture	*Parameters*	*Final*	*Intermediate*
Inverting visual representations [5]	✓	✓	✗	✓
Model inversion attack [11]	✓	✓	✓	✗
Inverting gradients [7]	✓	✓	✗	✗
Data stealing attack	✓	✓	✗	✓

A number of AI-related cyber-attacks such as adversarial attacks [13] have been studied in the literature. In this paper, we are interested in attacks targeting the extraction of information from images available at the training stage. Indeed, previous studies have shown that trained models encapsulate some information about the training data, thus making them vulnerable to privacy attacks. A first group of attacks such as property inference [6] or reconstruction attacks [15] tries to retrieve some partial information about the training data. Membership inference attacks [9] identify whether a data sample is present in the dataset.

In Table 1, we list a second group of attacks that are aiming to reconstruct partially or entirely training set images from the knowledge of the complete model and some model output. Early work aimed at inverting visual representations [5] from some intermediate output. However, this leads to image reconstructions of limited quality and more sophisticated model inversion attacks have been proposed [4,8,16] based on GANs. Yet, these attacks generate images that look like the original ones but are not close copies. Also, they are restricted to solve classification tasks only. Finally, our study is also related to inverting gradient methods [7,10] that try to recover input images from model parameter gradient that are exchanged during training in federated learning framework.

In this paper, we introduce a new attack, the data stealing attack, allowing an attacker to recover training data from a remote data lake or in a federated learning setting. This attack is solely based on the export of a trained model and makes both limited and realistic assumptions. It consists in training an algorithm to perform lossy image compression and then to hide the image compression codes and the decoder into the exported neural network. Thus, the attacker can regenerate the training images with high perceptual quality outside the data lake by applying the decoder on the image codes. Besides, we show that a dedicated branch of the compression network can still solve a utility task such as segmenting an image, thus making it difficult to detect the nature of attack. To the best of our knowledge, this is the first work using learned image compression to develop such type of data attacks. Furthermore, we show that such attacks may be realistically deployed in the sensitive context of medical imaging.

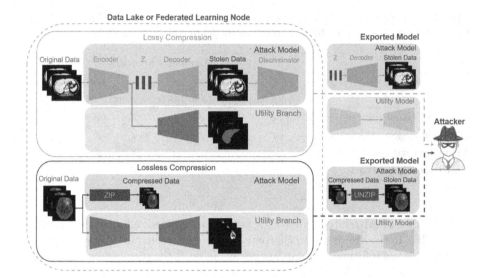

Fig. 1. Overview of the proposed data stealing attack. The attacker either uses the lossy compression (on top) or the lossless compression (on bottom) to compress the original data into compression codes. Then, the attacker recovers the original data with the exported model outside the data lake.

2   Data Stealing Attack

2.1   Attack Strategy

Attack Assumptions. We consider a practical setting where a data owner, usually an hospital or a medical center that controls a data lake, gives to a user, a remote access to some sensitive training data (see Fig. 1). This configuration is commonly encountered for instance when data scientists are remotely accessing health datasets in hospitals without the ability to retrieve locally the data for regulatory reasons. This is also the situation encountered in *federated learning* where the data lake corresponds to a participating node in a centralized or decentralized architecture. Inside the data lake the remote user has free access to some original imaging data that serve to solve a *utility task*. This task may be for example solving an image segmentation problem. Eventually, the remote user asks the data owner to retrieve the trained model in order to exploit it for its own purposes. In the case of federated learning, the locally trained model is periodically sent to a central server or another participating node in order to be aggregated into a global model.

Without sharing any data outside the data lake, this seems to be a robust privacy preserving framework, but what if the remote user acts as an attacker? The attacker may have stolen the identity of a trusted honest user with the motivations to create his or her own dataset for solving other tasks, or to cause harm to the reputation of the data owner, or to ransom the owner.

Attack Principle. The attack consists in exporting a neural network from the data lake that solves the utility task but also contains image codes allowing the attacker to reconstruct with or without losses images stored in the data lake. A limiting factor of the attack is the size of the exported network, since exporting a very large network may be suspicious to the data owner. Therefore the objective of the attacker is to maximize the number of stolen images while minimizing the disk size of the exported model.

To tackle this trade-off, the attacker may adopt either lossy or lossless compression approaches. In lossless compression (see Fig. 1 bottom), the attacker can apply a standard compression tool, such as *ZIP, or RAR* on images in the data lake and then store the compressed images inside the exported utility model. Yet, lossless image compression usually produces restricted compression ratio thus potentially limiting the number of images that can be stolen.

An interesting alternative is to develop lossy compression algorithms (see Fig. 1 top) reaching low bitrate but requiring a domain-specific encoder and decoder. For that purpose, we adopt in this paper the generative image compression model developed in [14] that combines GAN with learned compression techniques. It includes an encoder that transforms an image x into its latent code $y = E(x)$ and a decoder or generator which transforms the code y into an approximation of the original image, $x' = G(y) \approx x$, and a discriminator $D(x')$ to decide if the generated image is real or fake. In addition, a utility model solving for instance an image segmentation task must be devised in order to convince the data owner that the exported model is effective. To create a light utility model taking a limited amount of disk space, the attacker can use the encoder of the generative compression model as the feature extraction network, and train a decoding branch that is specialized in the utility task.

The proposed attack relies on an encoder E, generator G (a.k.a the decoder) and discriminator network D, thus in some ways mixing a GAN (with G and D) and an autoencoder (with E and G). This architecture is suitable for learned image compression with high quality data reconstruction. It differs from other attack models (such as model inversion) that rely on a GAN model with random noise as input. In data stealing attack, the exported model includes the generator G and the image codes generated by the encoder that are hidden in the neural network. The attacker can then generate the images outside the data lake by applying the decoder on the image codes.

Case of Centralized Federated Learning. In this setup, several aggregation steps are iteratively applied to send a local model from each participating node to a central server. Therefore, if the attacker controls the central server, each aggregation step may be an occasion to steal some more data from those local models. Since each node trains its own encoder, generator, and discriminator networks on the local dataset, the generator from each node may only be sent to the central server in the last aggregation step.

2.2   Attack Implementation

Training Pipeline. In the lossy compression case, the attacker starts to train the generative image compression model composed on the three E, G and D networks. The input of the encoder is a 2D 256×256 image with three channels, but to handle 3D medical images, specific preprocessing steps are detailed in Sect. 3.1. Once the compression model is trained, all images are encoded. Then the attacker freezes the parameters of the encoder network and trains the utility branch to solve the utility task. It is sufficient to obtain reasonable results for the utility task to convince the data owner to export the trained network.

Hiding Image Codes in Network Weight Files. In both cases, the data stealing attack assumes that image codes are hidden in network weight binary files. Indeed, those weights are commonly saved in HDF5 file formats where the weights of each layer are stored in a dictionary. Image codes may then be added as entries to the dictionary with dedicated keys making them easy to retrieve.

3   Experiments

3.1   Datasets and Models

We evaluate the effectiveness of our attack model on two public datasets. The former is the MICCAI 2017 Liver Tumor Segmentation (LiTS) Challenge dataset [2] that contains 130 CT cases for training and 70 CTs for testing. In this dataset, the utility task is to segment the liver parenchyma in a supervised manner. The second dataset is the BraTS 2021 challenge dataset [1] which includes 1251 skull-stripped brain images with multiple MR sequences for training and 219 cases for validation. The utility task is to segment the whole tumor based on FLAIR MR sequences.

On the LiTS (resp.BraTS 2021) dataset, we randomly partition the training set into 104/13/13 (resp. 1000/126/125) images that are used for training, validation, and testing of the utility task. Also, for testing the lossy compression network, we use the 70 (resp. 219) test images in the LiTS (resp. BraTS) dataset.

Table 2. Fidelity & compression results on LiTS and BraTS datasets. 'BPP_{input}/ BPP_{comp}': bit per pixel of input/compressed data, 'P_{ratio}': practical ratio.

Input	BPP_{input}	$\text{BPP}_{comp} \downarrow$	PSNR↑	MS_SSIM↑	$\text{P}_{ratio} \downarrow$
High$^{\text{LiTS}}_{\text{Training}}$	17.858 ± 1.791	0.221 ± 0.053	$\mathbf{40.322 \pm 0.793}$	0.992 ± 0.002	0.168 ± 0.019
Low$^{\text{LiTS}}_{\text{Training}}$	17.858 ± 1.791	$\mathbf{0.097 \pm 0.027}$	38.193 ± 0.444	0.987 ± 0.002	$\mathbf{0.017 \pm 0.002}$
High$^{\text{LiTS}}_{\text{Testing}}$	16.289 ± 1.899	0.125 ± 0.024	40.306 ± 1.096	$\mathbf{0.995 \pm 0.001}$	0.185 ± 0.023
Low$^{\text{LiTS}}_{\text{Testing}}$	16.289 ± 1.899	0.145 ± 0.029	33.424 ± 1.021	0.981 ± 0.004	0.021 ± 0.002
High$^{\text{BraTS}}_{\text{Training}}$	3.801 ± 0.285	$\mathbf{0.241 \pm 0.100}$	$\mathbf{37.842 \pm 1.687}$	$\mathbf{0.996 \pm 0.001}$	0.395 ± 0.024
High$^{\text{BraTS}}_{\text{Testing}}$	3.926 ± 0.282	0.250 ± 0.100	36.070 ± 2.280	0.995 ± 0.001	$\mathbf{0.387 \pm 0.025}$

Pre and Post-processing. Each slice of the LiTS CT images is of size 512 × 512 whereas the input size of the encoder network is 256 × 256 × 3. Two different approaches were tested corresponding to two different cost-quality compromises. The first method (Low) is to downsample each slice by a factor of 2 while the second (High) is to decompose each 512 × 512 slice into 3 × 3 overlapping patches that are separately encoded. Thus, the latter requires 9 times more image codes than the former to reconstruct an image. In the BraTS dataset, edge padding is applied since the slice resolution is only 240 × 240 pixels. Finally, a min-max intensity normalization is applied on the whole image, and each slice is surrounded by its upper and lower slices to fill the three input channels. For post-processing, the image intensity is mapped back to its original minimum and maximum range and upsampling with bilinear image blending is used to reconstruct the original slices for Low/High slice sampling.

Image Compression and Utility Models. Following [14], to speed-up training, the image compression model is first trained with rate and distortion losses only, then with all losses in a second stage. With lossy compression networks, the utility task is solved with a Utility Branch (UB) model connected to the last layer of the image encoder network. When lossless compression is chosen, we train from scratch an off-the-shelf model [3] coined as *Public Utility* (PU) model in the remainder. All models are optimized with Adam [12] and training continues until the validation loss has converged.

3.2 Effectiveness of Data Stealing Attacks

Compression-Fidelity Compromise. Table 2 reports the trade-off between image fidelity and compression ratio. The practical ratio is the ratio of the disk space needed to store the image codes of a volumetric image (lossy compression) to the disk space to store the ZIP compressed image (lossless compression). On the LiTS dataset, the low slice sampling approach leads to image codes 60 times smaller than an image compressed by ZIP. The high slice sampling approach requires 10 times more disk space but leads to higher image fidelity. On the BraTS dataset, the lossy compression gain is far smaller probably due to the large uniform background in the original images. Good fidelity reconstruction is obtained with a PSNR of nearly 40. A visual comparison between original and reconstructed images is available in Fig. 2 for both training and test sets.

Utility Task Performances. In Table 3, we report performances of the two utility models, branch (UB) and public (PU) models to solve the liver (resp. whole tumor) segmentation on the LiTS (resp. BraTS) dataset. Those models are trained on both the original images in the data lake and the lossy reconstructed (or stolen) version of the training set. The same unseen test image set is used for the three utility models and various metrics are used for comparison. We see that the performances of the public model are the same on the original and stolen data, showing that the image modifications due to image compression do

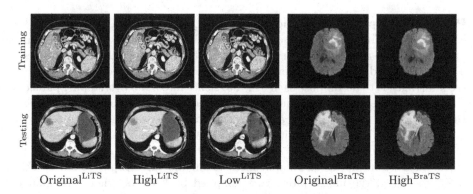

Fig. 2. Lossy image reconstructions on training and testing images from the LiTS and BraTS datasets. From left to right: original data, highly sampled reconstructions, under sampled reconstructions (LiTS dataset only).

not impact its generalization ability. The branch model is clearly less efficient since it is based on a frozen encoder branch. Yet, it leads to an average 0.93 Dice score, which makes it a plausible network to solve this task.

Table 3. Utility task results on LiTS and BraTS datasets. 'UB': the utility branch model, 'PU': the public utility model, 'stolen': the stolen dataset, 'VOE': volumetric overlap error, 'RVD': relative volume difference, 'ASSD': average symmetric surface distance, 'MSD': maximum surface distance, 'RMSD': root means square symmetric surface distance.

Methods	Dice↑	VOE↓	RVD↓	ASSD↓	MSD↓	RMSD↓
UB_{High}^{LiTS}	0.933 ± 0.04	0.123 ± 0.07	0.085 ± 0.12	1.757 ± 0.8	31.048 ± 21.9	3.665 ± 2.7
UB_{Low}^{LiTS}	0.923 ± 0.04	0.141 ± 0.07	0.032 ± 0.13	2.815 ± 3.4	51.690 ± 43.0	6.154 ± 8.5
PU_{High}^{LiTS}	0.948 ± 0.03	0.098 ± 0.05	0.053 ± 0.08	1.449 ± 0.7	38.275 ± 35.5	3.405 ± 2.29
PU_{Low}^{LiTS}	0.954 ± 0.03	0.087 ± 0.05	0.027 ± 0.07	1.404 ± 1.1	39.200 ± 28.8	3.768 ± 3.9
$PU_{High\ stolen}^{LiTS}$	0.958 ± 0.02	0.080 ± 0.04	0.033 ± 0.07	1.154 ± 0.6	37.876 ± 38.1	2.902 ± 2.0
$PU_{Low\ stolen}^{LiTS}$	$\mathbf{0.97 \pm 8e\text{-}3}$	$\mathbf{0.054 \pm 0.01}$	$\mathbf{0.001 \pm 0.02}$	$\mathbf{0.704 \pm 0.2}$	$\mathbf{28.16 \pm 19.5}$	$\mathbf{1.817 \pm 1.25}$
UB_{High}^{BraTS}	0.885 ± 0.07	0.200 ± 0.1	0.086 ± 0.2	1.087 ± 0.54	12.804 ± 5.27	1.876 ± 0.92
PU_{High}^{BraTS}	0.90 ± 0.07	0.168 ± 0.10	$\mathbf{0.046 \pm 0.17}$	0.884 ± 0.5	11.892 ± 5.6	1.641 ± 0.9
$PU_{High\ stolen}^{BraTS}$	$\mathbf{0.92 \pm 0.06}$	$\mathbf{0.149 \pm 0.09}$	0.083 ± 0.11	$\mathbf{0.735 \pm 0.45}$	$\mathbf{10.185 \pm 5.6}$	$\mathbf{1.375 \pm 0.85}$

Trade-Off Between Network Size and the Number of Stolen Images.
In Table 4, we estimate the disk size of three exported models (checkpoint files) involved in a data stealing attack on both the BraTS and LiTS datasets trying to steal 100 original images. In lossy compression, the decoder is very large (600 MB) but the generated image code per image is small: in average 2.2 MB (resp. 22 MB) for low (resp. high) slice sampling for LiTS CT dataset, and 0.9 MB for the BraTS dataset. With lossless compression, there is no need to export the decoder but the ZIP compressed images are fairly large to store: in average 134 MB for each CT scan in LiTS and 2.3 MB for BraTS. The branch utility

model has negligible disk size and the results in Table 4 suggest that an attacker willing to optimize the exported model disk size, would pick a lossy compression for CT images and lossless compression for MR skull-stripped images.

3.3 Mitigation of Data Stealing Attacks

To detect a data stealing attack, the data owner may check the size of the exported model considering large models as suspicious. In our test, the compression decoder is fairly large (598 MB) but has typically a similar size as a backbone such as VGG16 (576 MB). It is possible to largely decrease the disk size of such decoder by using for instance network quantization, or drop-out. Therefore, a robust mitigation to this type of attack is probably to certify that the code running in a data lake guarantees data privacy. Computational time may be another suspicious factor. For each training epoch, attack (A) model, utility (U) model (with shared encoder branch with A), and the public utility model (i.e. the baseline model) take 13.5 h/5 h, 14.5 h/3 h, and 24 h/8.5 h on LiTS/BraTS, respectively. Therefore, there is no significant impact of the attack (A+U) on the training time compared to the baseline (PU).

Table 4. Disk size needed to steal 100 images with various attack strategies. 'D': the decoder of attack model, 'UB'/'PU': the utility branch and public utility models, 'High/Low/ZIP': lossy or lossless compressed codes.

			Disk size (MB)		
Dataset	D	D + UB	D + UB+	D + UB+	PU+
			$100 \cdot \text{High}_{\text{Training}}$	$100 \cdot \text{Low}_{\text{Training}}$	$100 \cdot \text{ZIP}_{\text{Training}}$
LiTS	598	601	2800	**828**	13466
BraTS	598	601	692	/	**260**

4 Conclusion

In this paper, we have introduced a novel attack aiming to steal training data from a data lake or from participating nodes in federated learning. An attacker proceeds by using a learned generative lossy image compression network and exporting a decoder together with image codes. An alternative for stealing image annotation masks for instance is to use lossless compression with standard tools. We have shown that such attacks are feasible on two medical imaging datasets with a trade-off between the size of the exported network and the number of stolen images.

Acknowledgements. This work has been supported by the French government, through the 3IA Côte d'Azur Investments in the Future project managed by the National Research Agency (ANR) with the reference number ANR-19-P3IA-0002, and supported by the Inria Sophia Antipolis - Méditerranée, "NEF" computation cluster. HL is grateful to Yijian Wu for providing guidance and support.

References

1. Baid, U., et al.: The RSNA-ASNR-MICCAI BraTs 2021 benchmark on brain tumor segmentation and radiogenomic classification. arXiv preprint arXiv:2107.02314 (2021)
2. Bilic, P., et al.: The liver tumor segmentation benchmark (LITS). arXiv preprint arXiv:1901.04056 (2019)
3. Buda, M., Saha, A., Mazurowski, M.A.: Association of genomic subtypes of lower-grade gliomas with shape features automatically extracted by a deep learning algorithm. Comput. Biol. Med. **109**, 218–225 (2019)
4. Chen, S., Kahla, M., Jia, R., Qi, G.J.: Knowledge-enriched distributional model inversion attacks. In: Proceedings of the IEEE/CVF International Conference on Computer Vision, pp. 16178–16187 (2021)
5. Dosovitskiy, A., Brox, T.: Inverting visual representations with convolutional networks. In: Proceedings of the IEEE Conference on Computer Vision And Pattern Recognition, pp. 4829–4837 (2016)
6. Ganju, K., Wang, Q., Yang, W., Gunter, C.A., Borisov, N.: Property inference attacks on fully connected neural networks using permutation invariant representations. In: Proceedings of the 2018 ACM SIGSAC Conference on Computer and Communications Security, pp. 619–633 (2018)
7. Geiping, J., Bauermeister, H., Dröge, H., Moeller, M.: Inverting gradients-how easy is it to break privacy in federated learning? Adv. Neural. Inf. Process. Syst. **33**, 16937–16947 (2020)
8. Hitaj, B., Ateniese, G., Perez-Cruz, F.: Deep models under the gan: information leakage from collaborative deep learning. In: Proceedings of the 2017 ACM SIGSAC Conference on Computer and Communications Security, pp. 603–618 (2017)
9. Hu, H., Salcic, Z., Dobbie, G., Zhang, X.: Membership inference attacks on machine learning: a survey. arXiv preprint arXiv:2103.07853 (2021)
10. Jin, X., Chen, P.Y., Hsu, C.Y., Yu, C.M., Chen, T.: CAFE: catastrophic data leakage in vertical federated learning. Adv. Neural. Inf. Process. Syst. **34**, 994–1006 (2021)
11. Kaissis, G.A., Makowski, M.R., Rückert, D., Braren, R.F.: Secure, privacy-preserving and federated machine learning in medical imaging. Nat. Mach Intell. **2**(6), 305–311 (2020)
12. Kingma, D.P., Ba, J.: Adam: a method for stochastic optimization. arXiv preprint arXiv:1412.6980 (2014)
13. Levy, M., Amit, G., Elovici, Y., Mirsky, Y.: The security of deep learning defences for medical imaging. arXiv preprint arXiv:2201.08661 (2022)
14. Mentzer, F., Toderici, G.D., Tschannen, M., Agustsson, E.: High-fidelity generative image compression. Adv. Neural. Inf. Process. Syst. **33**, 11913–11924 (2020)
15. Panchendrarajan, R., Bhoi, S.: Dataset reconstruction attack against language models. In: CEUR Workshop (2021)
16. Zhang, Y., Jia, R., Pei, H., Wang, W., Li, B., Song, D.: The secret revealer: generative model-inversion attacks against deep neural networks. In: Proceedings of the IEEE/CVF Conference on Computer Vision and Pattern Recognition, pp. 253–261 (2020)

Can Collaborative Learning Be Private, Robust and Scalable?

Dmitrii Usynin[1,2,3], Helena Klause[1], Johannes C. Paetzold[3],
Daniel Rueckert[1,3], and Georgios Kaissis[1,2(✉)]

[1] Artificial Intelligence in Medicine and Healthcare, Technical University of Munich,
Munich, Germany
[2] Institute of Diagnostic and Interventional Radiology,
Technical University of Munich, Munich, Germany
`g.kaissis@tum.de`
[3] Department of Computing, Imperial College London, London, UK

Abstract. In federated learning for medical image analysis, the safety
of the learning protocol is paramount. Such settings can often be com-
promised by adversaries that target either the private data used by the
federation or the integrity of the model itself. This requires the medical
imaging community to develop mechanisms to train collaborative models
that are private and robust against adversarial data. In response to these
challenges, we propose a practical open-source framework to study the
effectiveness of combining differential privacy, model compression and
adversarial training to improve the robustness of models against adversarial samples under train- and inference-time attacks. Using our framework, we achieve competitive model performance, a significant reduction
in model's size and an improved empirical adversarial robustness without
a severe performance degradation, critical in medical image analysis.

Keywords: Collaborative learning · Federated learning · Medical
image analysis · Differential privacy · Adversarial training · Model
compression

1 Introduction

Collaborative machine learning (CML), and in particular collaborative medical image analysis, can significantly benefit from A) having access to large,
well-descriptive datasets, which are often highly sensitive and hence difficult to
obtain and B) deep machine learning models, which can require significant computational resources during training [21,23]. Such models are often trained in
a distributed manner, allowing a federation of clients to obtain a joint model
without the need to share the data directly, often at the cost of an additional

---

Supplementary Information The online version contains supplementary material
available at https://doi.org/10.1007/978-3-031-18523-6_4.

communication burden being put on the federation [20]. The existing methods of collaborative training, such as federated learning, are also particularly vulnerable to inference as well as model poisoning attacks [25], additionally requiring formal means of privacy and integrity protection [11]. One such scenario was demonstrated by [10], showing that without carefully selected privacy parameters, the adversary in the context of multi-institutional federated learning on pneumonia classification data was able to reconstruct the private chest X-ray data. Current methods that aim to resolve these issues can pose additional challenges to the federation as they can be difficult to implement in practice (such as model compression, which often requires a public dataset that comes from the same distribution as the training data for calibration), rely on unobvious additional hyper-parameters (such as ε in DP) or only mitigate a subset of attacks (such as adversarial training that improves model robustness, but does not mitigate any inference attacks). In this work we propose a framework for training and evaluation of ML models, which can help the medical imaging community to A) reduce the communication overhead, B) formally preserve privacy and C) achieve better adversarial robustness. We investigate this by studying model poisoning attacks [7] and their mitigations through the utilisation of differentially private training (DP) [4], model quantization and adversarial training. We investigate two main threat models, which include inference-time and train-time attackers on collaborative learning. Our contributions can be summarised as follows:

- We determine how techniques for private and scalable ML (such as DP and model compression) training can be combined to improve adversarial robustness in CML;
- We evaluate the most commonly used (e.g. projected gradient descent or PGD) as well as the state-of-the-art (e.g. fast adaptive boundary or FAB) adversarial attacks in these settings and show that the combination of these techniques can provide sufficient protection against utility-oriented adversaries;
- We propose an updated view on the relationship between these mechanisms and threat modelling, providing recommendations for achieving improved adversarial robustness using these techniques;
- Finally, we propose a framework (namely *PSREval*[1]) for private training and evaluation of image classification models trained in low-trust environments.

2   Related Work

Several studies have studied the applications of model compression against adversarial samples in CML [5,9,12,14,28], however, there is no prior *unified* perspective on whether quantization techniques improve adversarial robustness against **all** utility-based attacks. Authors of [15] discover that when the trained model is subjected to train-time attacks (e.g. backdoor attacks), model compression can significantly reduce robustness. Additionally, the work of [8] highlights, that as

---

[1] Code available at https://github.com/dimasquest/PSREval.

there exists a number of quantisation strategies (e.g. discretisation, distillation assisted quantization), a large number of such strategies provide the participants with a semblance of robustness. However, authors of [12] and [19] discover that for a number of inference-time poisoning attacks, model compression reduces the effectiveness of most adversaries. This is due to a smaller set of values that the model can utilise compared to its full-precision counterpart, making the attacker use a significantly higher perturbation budget to affect the decision of the model. Originally, [13] deployed DP as a method to provably certify ML models against adversarial samples of known perturbation budgets. However, this discussion was limited as the noise was applied directly to the training data or to the output of the first model layer, without considering the arguably most widely used application of DP in deep learning, namely DP-SGD [1]. Various other works [2,18] discussed how DP-SGD can be augmented or combined with adversarial training for better model robustness, yet none of them made links to model compression before or considered a train-time attacker, which we address in this work. Finally, adversarial training is considered to be one of the most successful empirical defence mechanisms against malicious samples [6,22], but similarly to model compression, its effects when combined with other robustness enhancement methods have not been studied in sufficient detail.

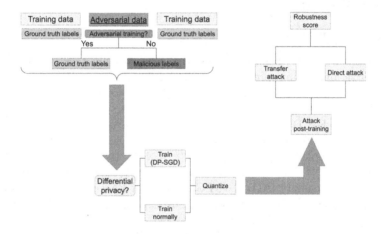

Fig. 1. Overview of our *PSREval* framework, which we describe in Sect. 3.

3   Methods

We present an overview of our methodology in Fig. 1. In this work we generate an adversarial dataset that is used over the course of collaborative training: This dataset can be either used for adversarial training or used to attack the model at train time. We then train two models: One using a normal training procedure and the other using DP-SGD. If the adversary is an active train-time attacker, they would use their malicious data at train time, otherwise the adversary only targets the model at inference-time. Once the models are trained, we then quantize them using the validation dataset (public) to tune the quantization parameters. In this study we perform a *static* model quantization (i.e. post-training quantization of both the weights and the activations), where we replace the full-precision 32-bit floating point parameters in the model with signed 8-bit integer parameters. Finally, we perform one of the two attacks to validate the robustness of the model. In the first setting, the adversary has full access (white-box or WB) to the trained model before it is deployed and thus is able to utilise it to generate the adversarial data directly. In the second setting, the adversary is attacking a similar (same architecture, different weights) model that has previously been deployed elsewhere, while only having WB access to the model they obtained during training (partial WB). This setting is termed the *transfer* attack. Our framework provides the robustness scores (in this case accuracies) for both adversarial settings. Note that our framework allows the user to train the models individually and perform model aggregation using their preferred aggregation algorithm (in this study we used federated averaging, where the data was split between 2 clients, one of which was an adversary).

4 Experiments

4.1 Experimental Setting

In this study we perform two collaborative classification tasks on CIFAR-10 and paediatric pneumonia prediction (PPPD) (adapted from [10]) datasets. We utilise ResNet-9 and ResNet-18 architectures. We employ ReLU as our activation function and replace the batch norm layers with group norm layers for compatibility with DP. For DP training we utilise the opacus library [27] with three privacy regimes (representing different end on the privacy-utility spectrum): Concretely, we implemented settings for ($\varepsilon = 1.7$), ($\varepsilon = 3.4$) and ($\varepsilon = 7.0$). For PPPD $\delta = 1e^{-4}$ and for CIFAR-10 $\delta = 1e^{-5}$. We utilise three adversarial attacks methods, namely PGD [16], FGSM [7] and FAB [3]. When performing train time attacks and adversarial training, we experiment with different proportions of adversarial data, namely 10%, 20%, 30% or 40% of the training dataset. By default, each attack (if required) is ran for 10 steps, with a perturbation budget of 8/255 and a step size (the limit of perturbation during a single step) of 2/255. We deliberately chose a high perturbation budget (in comparison to the frequently used budget of 2/255 [3]) to represent the worst-case scenarios, when the adversary has an ability to significantly affect the training process. We repeat the attacks 10 times for each setting and report the average values.

4.2 Performance Overview

We begin by discussing the performance comparison between a normally trained model as well as its DP and quantized counterparts. We present a summary of the standard accuracies for each setting in the Supplementary Material. We note that after the compression procedure, the sizes of ResNet-9 and ResNet-18 were reduced by 74.4% and 76.6% respectively. The accuracy of the model post-quantization step has not been significantly altered and stayed within ±1% of the original value.

4.3 Different Privacy Regimes Under Quantization

We experiment with three distinct privacy settings, defined by the values of ε, where lower value represents the "stronger" notion of privacy as there is a stricter bound on the release of information content (Sect. 4.1). This allows us to establish a more clear relationship between the DP-SGD and its ability to affect adversarial robustness when subjected to partial WB attacks. In general, for partial WB attacks, we did not find the DP-trained model to be significantly more robust than the original ones (within ±2%), regardless of the privacy regime. When adding post-training quantization, we found that robustness of the model can be improved by up to 5% for smaller models and by up to 20% in larger models (Fig. 2). This seemingly small post-training adaptation allows the federation to achieve a significantly higher adversarial robustness as well as significantly reduce the model size.

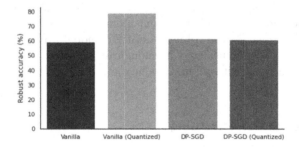

Fig. 2. Transfer attack comparison (generators are the WB models for both, PPPD, ResNet-18, $\varepsilon = 7.0$). Higher is better. Here we observe that quantization does not affect adversarial robustness of privatised models as much as it affects the non-private models under inference-time attacks.

From Fig. 3, we see that the overall loss of accuracy for DP-trained models (when the adversary uses a model trained with DP-SGD to generate the adversarial samples) is significantly larger than for its non-private counterparts under transfer or partial WB attacks. In fact, we found that the adversary is, in some cases, able to attack a DP-trained model that has the same architecture with almost 100% accuracy, which they are unable to do if the generating model is non-private. The opposite is partially true: If a non-private model is used as a generator, DP-SGD retains a robust accuracy of 30% in comparison to 5% for the original model. Additionally, while for smaller architectures,

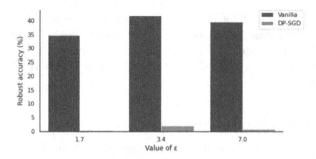

Fig. 3. Transfer attack comparison (generators are the WB models for both, PPPD, ResNet-18, $\varepsilon = 1.7$). Higher is better. This experiment shows that DP models (of various privacy levels) published online can be used to generate adversarial images for private models of identical architectures with high fidelity.

both the original and the DP models showed a severe lack of robustness, larger models and datasets were significantly more vulnerable only when trained with DP-SGD. This result holds for all three attack implementations and raises questions about the "safety" of the publication of private models, because while they provide theoretical guarantees with regards to the privacy of the training data, they can be used as perfect adversarial sample generators, potentially violating the integrity of other learning contexts relying on similar data or architectures. We finally note, that this finding is even more important under the light of the recent publications on the robustness of DP models, as this attack vector has previously not been considered in enough detail, resulting in a semblance of robustness associated with a blind application of DP-SGD without a careful threat model selection.

4.4   Using Adversarial Training

One method that has been particularly effective against utility-based attacks is adversarial training. We analyse three methods of generating the adversarial samples and compare the results to identify the method that is A) effective against malicious adversaries, B) does not result in a significant performance overhead and C) does not interfere with the learning process. We note that FAB was an ineffective method that both severely degraded the performance (a ×20 increase in training time) and the utility (down to 20% accuracy in all settings) of the trained model. We see (from Fig. 4) that adversarial training can significantly improve the robustness of the trained model in all settings. We also note, however, that this robustness can come at a severe utility cost, which is typically associated with such training process augmentation (reducing the overall accuracy by up to 13% for ResNet-18). Similarly to [2] we found that adversarial training can be effectively combined with DP training, significantly improving the robustness of the model as well as suffering a much smaller utility penalty when compared to a non-private learning setting. We show exemplary results for a high-privacy (low ε) regime in Fig. 4 and more in the Supplementary Material. We found PGD to be the optimal sample generation method in a private setting, allowing the federation to mitigate both the privacy-oriented and the utility-oriented attacks. It must be noted, however, that PGD results in a significantly longer training time when compared to FGSM (up to 8 times longer training for 40% of adversarial samples). In general, we find that there is no "optimal" amount of adversarial data that can be used irrespective of the learning context, but using 20% of adversarial data typically resulted in highest robustness across most settings.

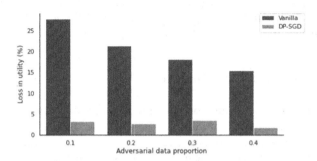

Fig. 4. Accuracy loss under a partially WB attack with adversarial training (generators are the WB models for both, CIFAR-10, ResNet-9, $\varepsilon = 1.7$). Lower is better. Here we see that DP can effectively mitigate a train-time attacker even when they control 40% of the training data.

4.5 Train- and Inference-Time Attacks

While a number of previous works typically considers an adversary who has a WB access to a pre-trained model, we believe that it is important to evaluate the learning settings against an adversary who actively interferes with the training process itself. As described in our Sect. 4.1, the adversary controls different proportions of the training data and we study how this can affect the federation. Overall, as seen in Fig. 5 (as well as in the Supplementary Material), we find that any train time attack can pose a significant risk to a non-private learning setting, irrespective of the dataset or the architecture of the shared model. However, we also found that DP training can **severely** reduce this risk even for adversaries that control 40% of the training data, as the contributions of the outlier samples are greatly reduced under DP-SGD. This, alongside with the application of adversarial training, leads us to recommend a wider use of DP-SGD against WB attackers. We additionally note that both of these approaches are fully compatible with quantization techniques, allowing the federation to train private and robust models at scale.

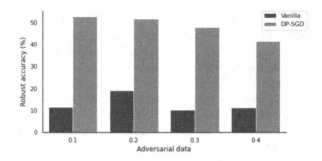

Fig. 5. Robust accuracy under a train-time attacker (CIFAR-10, ResNet-9, $\varepsilon = 3.4$). Higher is better. The result here corresponds to the setting above, showing that we can expect this behavior to hold even under a weaker privacy regime.

5   Discussion and Conclusion

In this work we propose a framework for training and evaluation of image analysis models, combining differentially private training, model compression and adversarial training against model poisoning attacks. Our framework allowed us to determine that for the strongest insider adversary, post-training quantization did not have a significant impact on the results of the attack. The opposite is true for partial WB attacks, where the federation enjoys an improvement in robustness of up to 20% in certain contexts compared to an uncompressed setting. In general, we found DP-SGD to be detrimental in partially WB settings, which is primarily due to a significantly lower accuracy of the DP-trained models after training. Our framework revealed that DP-trained models can be more susceptible to transferable adversarial samples. This finding can be surprising, given a **greatly** higher robustness of DP-trained models (particularly at train time). In essence, DP models are very sensitive to the threat model that the adversary chooses to employ, therefore not allowing a concrete overall conclusion about the effectiveness of this method. However, there also exist a number of factors that can potentially have an influence on the results of our evaluations that are not explicitly covered. Firstly, similarly to [24], we discovered that the accuracy of the trained model can have a significant impact on the results of the attack. This is due to the fact that the adversarial labels (i.e. those used by the train-time adversary) are inferred from model predictions and these depend on how well the model is able to distinguish between different classes, affecting the attack. This, in turn, makes it more challenging for us to disentangle how the individual factors that influence model accuracy can affect adversarial robustness. Secondly, in this work, we relied on the post-training quantization, as we find this approach to be the most *practical* (or low-effort and foolproof), as it only requires a single calibration round and a replacement of a small number of operations during model initialisation. Other approaches can be applicable when discussing robustness of collaboratively trained models, such as train-time quantization or quantization-aware training. However, these methods require a larger number of setup steps and adaptations of the training process, making them less practical. Finally, there exists a number of contexts that we have not covered in *PSREval*, which go beyond the scope of this work. We are planning to expand our framework with other robustness-enhancement methods, such as adversarial regularisation, knowledge distillation [17] and feature squeezing [26], all of which were previously shown to mitigate utility-oriented adversaries in CML. We used a simple federated averaging aggregated method in our work, therefore leaving more advanced aggregation techniques (some of which can come with additional adversarial robustness) as part of the future work. Additionally, we are aiming to produce a more context-agnostic study, including attacks on image segmentation and object detection tasks, so that the research community can evaluate their model in a much larger number of clinical settings, resulting in a wider adoption of private, robust and scalable training.

Acknowledgements. G.K. received funding from the Technical University of Munich, School of Medicine Clinician Scientist Programme (KKF), project reference H14. D.U. received funding from the Technical University of Munich/Imperial College London Joint Academy for Doctoral Studies. This research was supported by the UK Research and Innovation London Medical Imaging and Artificial Intelligence Centre for Value Based Healthcare. J.C.P. was supported by the DCoMEX project (16HPC010), co-financed by the Federal Ministry of Education and Research of Germany and the EuroHPC JU. The funders played no role in the design of the study, the preparation of the manuscript or the decision to publish.

References

1. Abadi, M., Chu, A., Goodfellow, I., McMahan, H.B., Mironov, I., Talwar, K., Zhang, L.: Deep learning with differential privacy. In: Proceedings of the 2016 ACM SIGSAC Conference on Computer and Communications Security, pp. 308–318 (2016)
2. Bu, Z., Li, P., Zhao, W.: Practical adversarial training with differential privacy for deep learning (2021)
3. Croce, F., Hein, M.: Minimally distorted adversarial examples with a fast adaptive boundary attack (2019). https://doi.org/10.48550/ARXIV.1907.02044
4. Dwork, C., Roth, A.: The algorithmic foundations of differential privacy. Found. Trend. Theor. Comput. Sci. **9**(3–4), 211–407 (2013). https://doi.org/10.1561/0400000042
5. Feng, Y., Chen, B., Dai, T., Xia, S.T.: Adversarial attack on deep product quantization network for image retrieval. In: Proceedings of the AAAI Conference on Artificial Intelligence, vol. 34, pp. 10786–10793 (2020)
6. Ganin, Y., et al.: Domain-adversarial training of neural networks. J. Mach. Learn. Res. **17**(1), 2030–2096 (2016)
7. Goodfellow, I.J., Shlens, J., Szegedy, C.: Explaining and harnessing adversarial examples (2014). https://doi.org/10.48550/ARXIV.1412.6572
8. Gupta, K., Ajanthan, T.: Improved gradient based adversarial attacks for quantized networks. arXiv preprint arXiv:2003.13511 (2020)
9. Hong, S., Panaitescu-Liess, M.A., Kaya, Y., Dumitras, T.: Qu-anti-zation: Exploiting quantization artifacts for achieving adversarial outcomes. Advances in Neural Information Processing Systems 34 (2021)

10. Kaissis, G., et al.: End-to-end privacy preserving deep learning on multi-institutional medical imaging. Nat. Mach. Intell. **3**(6), 473–484 (2021)

11. Kaissis, G.A., Makowski, M.R., Rückert, D., Braren, R.F.: Secure, privacy-preserving and federated machine learning in medical imaging. Nat. Mach. Intell. **2**(6), 305–311 (2020)

12. Khalid, F., et al.: QuSecNets: Quantization-based defense mechanism for securing deep neural network against adversarial attacks. In: 2019 IEEE 25th International Symposium on On-Line Testing and Robust System Design (IOLTS), pp. 182–187. IEEE (2019)

13. Lecuyer, M., Atlidakis, V., Geambasu, R., Hsu, D., Jana, S.: Certified robustness to adversarial examples with differential privacy. In: 2019 IEEE Symposium on Security and Privacy (SP), pp. 656–672. IEEE (2019)

14. Lin, J., Gan, C., Han, S.: Defensive quantization: when efficiency meets robustness. arXiv preprint arXiv:1904.08444 (2019)

15. Ma, H., et al.: Quantization backdoors to deep learning models. arXiv preprint arXiv:2108.09187 (2021)

16. Madry, A., Makelov, A., Schmidt, L., Tsipras, D., Vladu, A.: Towards deep learning models resistant to adversarial attacks (2017). https://doi.org/10.48550/ARXIV.1706.06083

17. Papernot, N., McDaniel, P.: Extending defensive distillation. arXiv preprint arXiv:1705.05264 (2017)

18. Phan, H., Thai, M.T., Hu, H., Jin, R., Sun, T., Dou, D.: Scalable differential privacy with certified robustness in adversarial learning. In: International Conference on Machine Learning, pp. 7683–7694. PMLR (2020)

19. Rakin, A.S., Yi, J., Gong, B., Fan, D.: Defend deep neural networks against adversarial examples via fixed and dynamic quantized activation functions. arXiv preprint arXiv:1807.06714 (2018)

20. Reisizadeh, A., Mokhtari, A., Hassani, H., Jadbabaie, A., Pedarsani, R.: Fedpaq: A communication-efficient federated learning method with periodic averaging and quantization. In: International Conference on Artificial Intelligence and Statistics, pp. 2021–2031. PMLR (2020)

21. Rieke, N., et al.: The future of digital health with federated learning. NPJ Digit. Med. **3**(1), 1–7 (2020)

22. Shafahi, A., et al.: Adversarial training for free! Advances in Neural Information Processing Systems 32 (2019)

23. Sheller, M.J., et al.: Federated learning in medicine: facilitating multi-institutional collaborations without sharing patient data. Sci. Report. **10**(1), 1–12 (2020)

24. Usynin, D., Rueckert, D., Passerat-Palmbach, J., Kaissis, G.: Zen and the art of model adaptation: low-utility-cost attack mitigations in collaborative machine learning. Proc. Priv. Enhan. Technol. **2022**(1), 274–290 (2022)

25. Usynin, D., et al.: Adversarial interference and its mitigations in privacy-preserving collaborative machine learning. Nat. Mach. Intell. **3**(9), 749–758 (2021)

26. Xu, W., Evans, D., Qi, Y.: Feature squeezing: Detecting adversarial examples in deep neural networks. arXiv preprint arXiv:1704.01155 (2017)

27. Yousefpour, A., et al.: Opacus: User-friendly differential privacy library in pytorch. arXiv preprint arXiv:2109.12298 (2021)

28. Zheng, T., Chen, C., Ren, K.: Is PGD-adversarial training necessary? alternative training via a soft-quantization network with noisy-natural samples only (2018)

Split-U-Net: Preventing Data Leakage in Split Learning for Collaborative Multi-modal Brain Tumor Segmentation

Holger R. Roth$^{(\boxtimes)}$, Ali Hatamizadeh, Ziyue Xu, Can Zhao, Wenqi Li, Andriy Myronenko, and Daguang Xu

NVIDIA, Bethesda, USA
`hroth@nvidia.com`

Abstract. Split learning (SL) has been proposed to train deep learning models in a decentralized manner. For decentralized healthcare applications with vertical data partitioning, SL can be beneficial as it allows institutes with complementary features or images for a shared set of patients to jointly develop more robust and generalizable models. In this work, we propose "Split-U-Net" and successfully apply SL for collaborative biomedical image segmentation. Nonetheless, SL requires the exchanging of intermediate activation maps and gradients to allow training models across different feature spaces, which might leak data and raise privacy concerns. Therefore, we also quantify the amount of data leakage in common SL scenarios for biomedical image segmentation and provide ways to counteract such leakage by applying appropriate defense strategies.

Keywords: Split learning · Vertical federated learning · Multi-modal brain tumor segmentation · Data inversion

1 Introduction

Collaborative and decentralized techniques to train artificial intelligence (AI) models have been gaining popularity, especially in healthcare applications where data sharing to build centralized datasets is particularly challenging due to patient privacy and regulatory concerns [20]. Federated learning (FL) [16] and split learning (SL) [7] are two approaches that can be useful depending on the nature of the data partitioning [32]. In the healthcare and biomedical imaging sector, data is often "horizontally" partitioned such that each participating site, i.e., a hospital, possesses some data/features and optionally corresponding labels for their set of patients. Horizontal FL (HFL) algorithms like federated averaging [16] typically train models initialized from a current "global" model independently on each participant and frequently update the global model with the model gradients sent by each site. In contrast, so-called "vertical" data partitioning allows sites with complementary features but from an overlapping set of patients to collaborate [32]. This vertical FL (VFL) scenario could be useful

S. Albarqouni et al. (Eds.): DeCaF 2022/FAIR 2022, LNCS 13573, pp. 47–57, 2022.
https://doi.org/10.1007/978-3-031-18523-6_5

where different sites possess features that need to be securely combined in order to train a joined AI model, e.g., one hospital has imaging while the other one has lab results or the diagnoses for the same set of patients. Here, SL can be used to train models when using deep learning (DL) methods for VFL. During training, SL splits the forward pass of a DL model into two or more parts and exchanges intermediate features or activation maps and gradients between participating sites to complete a training step. Therefore features from different sites can be combined in later parts of the network and the model can be trained across institutional boarders [28].

In biomedical image segmentation, VFL could be useful to combine different image modalities of the same patient in order to train joined segmentation models collaboratively. This scenario is what we explore in this work by studying SL as a collaborative technique to learn a tumor segmentation model for multi-model MRI images. For this purpose, we propose "Split-U-Net", a modification to the popular U-Net [21] architecture, to allow its use in a VFL setup. Figure 1 illustrates the situation where four sites would like to jointly train a multi-modal segmentation model given their corresponding images. Only one site possesses the label mask and computes the loss to be optimized. Previous works on SL in

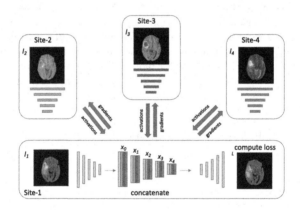

Fig. 1. Split learning set up with Split-U-Net.

healthcare applications have focused on classification and regression tasks [8,19, 28]. One example of splitting U-Net for single modality semantic segmentation was described in [18], but to the best of our knowledge, our work is the first to apply SL in a multi-modal vertical data partitioning scenario for biomedical image segmentation across multiple parties.

We show that SL can be used successfully for this task and also investigate potential security implications that arise from sharing intermediate features between collaborating sites by implementing an effective inversion attack. Prior works on inversion attacks in SL were mainly focused on images of small sizes (MNIST or CIFAR-10) [5,11,12,17] and are theoretical in nature. However, it is important for the medical imaging community to understand the potential benefits and security considerations for applying SL in healthcare applications.

Our inversion attack not only shows the potential risks but can be used to quantify and inform appropriate defense strategies against it. In this work, we explore both dropout [25] and differential privacy (DP) [4] to prevent data leakage during SL. Our contributions can be summarized as follows.

- We propose "Split-U-Net" and successfully apply SL for biomedical image segmentation for multi-institutional collaboration.
- We develop a successful inversion attack to measure and quantify data leakage in SL.
- We propose and evaluate defense measures (dropout and DP) to prevent data leakage.

2   Methods

2.1   Split-U-Net

The basis of our network is a common implementation of U-Net [21] with $L = 4$ down- and up-sampling levels. The default number of output features at each level are configured as shown in Table 1. To turn this network $F(x)$ into Split-U-Net $F(x) = g(f(x))$ used for multi-modal collaborative SL, we divided the number of encoder features by the number of sites/modalities K involved in training. The number of features in the decoder stays the same as in the default network. Figure 1 shows an example setup with $K = 4$. In this example, the "split" is done at the bottleneck. All encoder layers participate in SL, and only the site with label images has the decoder for segmentation. During training, each site k computes the forward pass $\{x_0^k, x_1^k, \ldots, x_L^k\} = f^k(I_k)$ where I_k is a mini-batch of size B of input images with modality k and x_i^k is the feature map of layer i of L. Corresponding batch indices are communicated to each site before each training step. The site k with label images then takes the activation maps from all other participating sites and concatenates them at the appropriate feature levels (see Fig. 1). It then computes the loss and backward pass to obtain a gradient

$$\nabla \leftarrow \mathcal{L}_{seg}\left(g(\{x_0^k, x_1^k, \ldots, x_L^k\}), labels\right) \tag{1}$$

and performs an optimizer update on its part of the network $g(x)$. The gradient ∇ at the split level is then communicated back to all $f^k(x)$ to complete the backward pass and update their parts of the model (the encoder branches $f^k(x)$), and the process is iterated until convergence. Note that in SL, a larger batch size can be used to reduce the total number of communication steps needed [24]. We assume that at each iteration, a random set of batch indices b_i is selected such that each client uses the same patients' data and augmentation to build their mini-batch I_k. Furthermore, each site might apply additional spatial normalization steps, e.g., using non-linear image registration to bring their images from different modalities into a common data space to help the network better encode common anatomical features across modalities [3,30].

Table 1. U-Net and Split-U-Net features for brain tumor segmentation.

Level i	In	0	1	2	3	4	5	6	7	8	Out
U-Net (default) $F(x)$	4	32	32	64	128	256	128	64	32	32	4
Split-U-Net Encoder (per site) $f^k(x)$	1	8	8	16	32	64	-	-	-	-	-
Split-U-Net Decoder $g(x)$	-	-	-	-	-	-	128	64	32	32	4

2.2   Measuring Data Leakage by Inversion Attack

In SL, activation maps are shared to complete each iteration step [7]. Therefore, a potential malicious actor, e.g., Site-1 in Fig. 1, receiving the activation maps from other sites may invert them to recover the underlying private data. Such attacks used to recover the data are called "inversion attacks" [27]. In the following, we explain how our inversion attack is executed and how its result can be used to measure the data leakage in order to inform an appropriate defense strategy. Our attack tries to optimize a randomly initialized C-channel input $\tilde{I}_i$ such that the activations $\tilde{x}_i$ at the forward layer of the attacker model $\tilde{f}_i(x)$ become the same as the intercepted activations x_i. In this work, we assume the attacker has access to the current state of the model used by the client to generate the forward pass. Therefore $\tilde{f}_i^k(x) \equiv f_i^k(x)$ given the same input x. This setting is typically referred to as a "white-box" attack [11]. In practical implementations of SL, this could be the case if a common network is used to initialize $f^k(x)$ on each participating client. The main loss used to align both activation maps is a L^2-norm. Furthermore, we employ two common image prior losses often used in inversion attacks [6,33], namely total variation [22] (TV) and L^2-norm of the recovered image $\tilde{I}$. The main loss for the inversion attack hence becomes

$$\mathcal{L}_{\text{inv}}\left(x_i^k, \tilde{x}_i^k, \tilde{I}_i^k\right) = \alpha_{\text{act}}||x_i^k - \tilde{x}_i^k||_2 + \alpha_{\text{tv}}TV(\tilde{I}_i^k) + \alpha_{l_2}||\tilde{I}_i^k||_2. \tag{2}$$

Therefore, the final inversion attack to recover an image $\tilde{I}_i$ from activation x_i at level i of Split-U-Net can be formulated as

$$\tilde{I}_i = \underset{\tilde{I}}{\text{argmin}} \ \mathcal{L}_{\text{inv}}\left(x_i^k, \tilde{x}_i^k, \tilde{I}_i^k\right), \tag{3}$$

where $\tilde{I}_i \in \mathbf{R}^{B,C,H,W}$ with B, C, H, W being the batch size, number of channels, height and width of the image, respectively. Note that the inversion can be run on large batch sizes B or independently for each activation in a mini-batch, depending on the compute resources of the attacker. The data inversions from intercepted activation maps can be seen in Fig. 2. To measure the amount of data leakage, we compute a common similarity metric between the recovered image $\tilde{I}_i$ and the original image I used to produce the activation x_i. Structural Similarity index (SSIM) [29] aims to provide a more intuitive and interpretable metric compared to other commonly used metrics like root-mean-squared error or peak signal-to-noise ratio. We, therefore, use SSIM in our analysis, but including other metrics would be possible.

2.3 Defenses

A straightforward defense strategy is to not send feature activation maps from early layers (x_0, x_1, and x_2) which are likely to leak more data (see Fig. 2 and Fig. 4). We also investigate dropout [25] as an effective tool against inversion attacks. Each layer of the encoder can randomly drop the activations from neurons of the network with a probability of p_{dropout}. Another effective tool often used in the FL literature [10,13,15,31], is differential privacy (DP). DP in its simplest form adds some calibrated random noise to any shared values in order to preserve the privacy of individual data entries. Here, we use a Gaussian mechanism [31] to add random noise sampled from a normal distribution $N\left(0,\ \sigma^2\right)$ to each activation mask x_i^k before sharing it with the next participant.

3 Experiments and Results

Data: In our study, we assume a collaborative model training setup where four institutes, here referred to as "sites", jointly train a multi-modal image segmentation model using split learning. We use the *Medical Segmentation Decathlon* MSD[1] brain tumor segmentation dataset (Task 1) to simulate this setup. Each 3D volume in the dataset contains four MRI modalities, namely T1-weighted, post-Gadolinium contrast T1-weighted, T2-weighted, and T2 Fluid-Attenuated Inversion Recovery volumes [23]. For the purpose of this study, we extract one axial slice from each volume through the center of the tumor and formulate the task as a 2D semantic segmentation problem, resulting in a total of 484 images with ground truth annotation masks. We randomly split the data into 338 training, 49 validation, and 97 testing images, corresponding to 70%, 10%, 20% of the data, respectively. The segmentation task is to predict the brain tumor sub-regions, i.e., edema, enhancing, and non-enhancing tumor. Therefore, our network predicts four output classes, including the background, using a final softmax activation. Given the $K = 4$ MRI input modalities, we simulate the Split-U-Net to be trained collaboratively among four sites, as shown in Fig. 1. Each site possesses the images for all patients but for just one modality. Site-1 is assumed to also have the annotation masks and can therefore compute the objective function using a combined Dice loss and cross-entropy loss.

---

[1] http://medicaldecathlon.com.

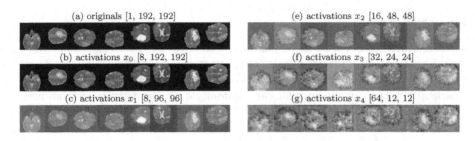

Fig. 2. Inversions from activations sent from different layers of the Split-U-Net encoder of Site-4 possessing one MRI modality when training with a mini-batch size of 8. Activations from earlier layers from the encoder are more likely to leak data, i.e., $x_0 \sim x_2$. The inversions from other sites and modalities are of the same quality.

Data leakage of shared activation maps: First, we investigate how much data the activation map at each layer can leak when sharing them during Split-U-Net training. We invert all activation maps of a mini-batch from layers x_0, x_1, x_2, x_3, x_4, respectively. One can observe that the amount of data leakage reduces with the depth of the network and the resolution of the share activation map. The first level x_0 with a resolution similar to the input image is practically non-distinguishable from the original augmented images fed to the encoder networks during training. All inversions computed in this work used $\alpha_{\mathrm{act}} = 1e - 3$, $\alpha_{\mathrm{tv}} = 1e - 4$, and $\alpha_{l_2} = 1e - 5$ (see Eq. 2). We used the Adam optimizer to solve Eq. 3 using a cosine learning rate decay with an initial rate of 0.1^2.

Collaborative multi-modal image segmentation: To evaluate the effectiveness of Split-U-Net, we compare it to a baseline U-Net model taking the four MRI modalities directly as input (see the default setup in Table 1). In Table 2, we show Split-U-Net performs on par with its centralized counterpart (U-Net). The performance is comparable[3] to the MSD challenge results reported for 3D tumor segmentation [2].

---

[2] *Implementation:* We utilize components from MONAI (https://monai.io/) and NVIDIA FLARE (https://developer.nvidia.com/flare) to implement our SL simulation. In particular, we utilize MONAI's *BasicUNet* as basis for Split-U-Net. All experiments were run on NVIDIA V100 GPUs with 16 GB memory.

[3] The current leading entry - `Swin_UNETR` [9] achieves an average Dice score of 0.647 for the three foreground tumor classes.

Table 2. Comparison of a centralized U-Net and different Split-U-Net settings with different privacy-preserving measures (dropout and differential privacy (DP)). The setting "w" and "w/o" indicates the performance of Split U-Net with and without skip connections, respectively; "x_3, x_4 only" indicates the performances when only activations from later layers are being shared. The best Dice score achieved with Split-U-Net for each data subset is highlighted in **bold**.

Dice	Training (n=338)	Validation (n=49)	Testing (n=97)
U-Net	*0.732*	*0.701*	*0.698*
Split-U-Net (w/o skip)	0.743	0.619	0.599
Split-U-Net (w skip)	**0.882**	0.663	0.693
Split-U-Net (x_3, x_4 only)	0.821	0.675	0.650
Split-U-Net (p_{dropout}=0.1)	0.818	0.648	0.681
Split-U-Net (p_{dropout}=0.2)	0.843	0.658	0.683
Split-U-Net (p_{dropout}=0.5)	0.766	0.637	0.665
Split-U-Net (p_{dropout}=0.8)	0.719	0.643	0.650
Split-U-Net (DP σ=1)	0.865	0.671	0.691
Split-U-Net (DP σ=2)	0.797	0.669	**0.695**
Split-U-Net (DP σ=3)	0.821	0.658	0.666
Split-U-Net (DP σ=5)	0.811	**0.684**	0.687
Split-U-Net (DP σ=50)	0.543	0.394	0.393

Effectiveness of defenses: Adding dropout and Gaussian noise during training can be an effective defense (Fig. 3). The SSIM scores between originals and inversions go down with higher p_{dropout} or σ as shown in Fig. 4. The model performance is less affected when adding DP and even benefits from it during training, as seen in Table 1 for $\sigma = 2.0$ in contrast to using dropout as a defense.

4   Discussion

To the best of our knowledge, our work was the first to apply SL to a multi-modal image segmentation task. We showed competitive results of Split-U-Net for 2D brain tumor segmentation on a relatively small dataset (only one slice per original volume). Further hyperparameter tuning and data augmentation might improve the performance. It should be investigated if weight sharing between the encoder branches could allow for further performance boosts [26]. An extension of Split-U-Net to 3D semantic segmentation tasks would be straightforward.

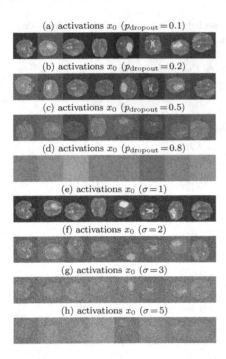

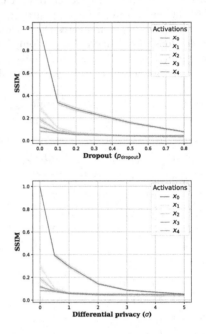

Fig. 3. Dropout (a-d) and differential privacy (e-h) as a defense against inversion attacks.

Fig. 4. Structural SIMilarity index (SSIM) [29] between the original images and inversions of each activation.

A major focus of this work is on the security aspect when applying SL. As shown in our results, depending on the depth of activation layers inside Split-U-Net, the data inversion attack can be successful, generating inversions that are visually indistinguishable from the original images (SSIM close to 1.0). This is the case, especially for the first layer (x_0). Finding an appropriate defense strategy against such inversion attacks is very important. It can be assumed that the same defense settings are effective for each modality used in Split-U-Net training. Therefore, a recommendation would be for the site possessing both images and labels to study the data leakage vulnerabilities using our proposed data inversion and data leakage metrics to establish a secure setting that each collaborator can use. Of course, this assumes a level of trust in this site but might help protect against a potentially malicious server that coordinates the split learning. At the same time, each site could utilize public datasets with images and labels, as we have done in this study, to measure the data leakage risks of the network architecture they would like to train in real-world SL. Our results indicate that the dangers come from the architecture itself rather than the particular dataset used for training (see Fig. 2 where the inversion quality is not affected by different samples in the batch). This is in contrast to other studies in horizontal FL, where certain images in the batch are more likely to leak data [10,33].

Our study also has some limitations. For example, the inversion attack assumes to have access to the current state of the model that the data site uses to compute its forward pass $(f^k(X))$. This setting is typically referred to as a "white-box" attack [11] and assumes the attacker has knowledge about the state of the model during training. This could be true in some implementations of SL where one of the participants sends an initialization for all participants. As the training continues, this initial model will become less and less useful to the attacker. At the same time, our finding shows that a potential avenue for more secure implementations of SL is to not use a common initialization but let each participant randomly initialize their part of the model. A "black-box" attack [11] where the inversion needs to optimize for both the inputs and the current state of the model could be implemented next to better measure the data leakage risks in such a scenario. Furthermore, we assumed the participating sites to have a common anonymous identifier used to build mini-batches with images of corresponding patients. In real-world scenarios, a pre-processing step to securely compute the intersecting set of patients between sites has to be performed [1]. Also, some synchronization of data augmentation across different modalities should be incorporated in the communication protocols. An additional privacy risk in SL is the inversion of label sets from the shared model gradients. A similar attack to the one presented in this work could be applied to match gradients during SL to recover the label masks. However, we assumed that tumor segmentation masks are less likely to leak patient-identifiable information and therefore focused on the data/image recovery in this work. In this work, we simulated a multi-site FL study using pre-registered multi-modal MRI scans. In reality, more variations that are potentially critical to model performance would need to be considered before performing similar collaborative model training, including temporal and spatial misalignment across images of the same patient and mismatch between image and annotation masks. Finally, cryptographic techniques like homomorphic encryption [34] or secure multi-party computation [14] could be employed to reduce the risk of data leakage in SL. Those techniques typically come with higher computation costs but should be explored, especially for medical image analysis tasks where patient privacy is of utmost concern.

In conclusion, we provided strong evidence that SL can be useful for biomedical image segmentation tasks when taking the appropriate security considerations into account. A real-world implementation of SL will provide clinical collaborators the chance to jointly leverage all available data to train more robust and generalizable AI models.

References

1. Angelou, N., et al.: Asymmetric private set intersection with applications to contact tracing and private vertical federated machine learning. arXiv preprint arXiv:2011.09350 (2020)
2. Antonelli, M., et al.: The medical segmentation decathlon. arXiv preprint arXiv:2106.05735 (2021)

3. Studholme, C., Hill, D.L.G., Hawkes, D.J.: Automated 3D registration of MR and pet brain images by multi-resolution optimisation of voxel similarity measures. Med. Phys. **24**(1), 25–35 (1997)
4. Dwork, C., McSherry, F., Nissim, K., Smith, A.: Calibrating noise to sensitivity in private data analysis. In: Theory of cryptography conference, pp. 265–284. Springer (2006). https://doi.org/10.1007/11681878_14
5. Erdogan, E., Kupcu, A., Cicek, A.E.: Unsplit: data-oblivious model inversion, model stealing, and label inference attacks against split learning. arXiv preprint arXiv:2108.09033 (2021)
6. Geiping, J., Bauermeister, H., Dröge, H., Moeller, M.: Inverting gradients-how easy is it to break privacy in federated learning? Adv. Neural Info. Proc. Syst. **33**, 16937–16947 (2020)
7. Gupta, O., Raskar, R.: Distributed learning of deep neural network over multiple agents. J. Netw. Comput. Appl. **116**, 1–8 (2018)
8. Ha, Y.J., Lee, G., Yoo, M., Jung, S., Yoo, S., Kim, J.: Feasibility study of multi-site split learning for privacy-preserving medical systems under data imbalance constraints in covid-19, x-ray, and cholesterol dataset. Sci. Report. **12**(1), 1–11 (2022)
9. Hatamizadeh, A., Nath, V., Tang, Y., Yang, D., Roth, H., Xu, D.: Swin UNETR: swin transformers for semantic segmentation of brain tumors in MRI images. arXiv preprint arXiv:2201.01266 (2022)
10. Hatamizadeh, A., et al.: Do gradient inversion attacks make federated learning unsafe? arXiv preprint arXiv:2202.06924 (2022)
11. He, Z., Zhang, T., Lee, R.B.: Model inversion attacks against collaborative inference. In: Proceedings of the 35th Annual Computer Security Applications Conference, pp. 148–162 (2019)
12. Jin, X., Chen, P.Y., Hsu, C.Y., Yu, C.M., Chen, T.: Catastrophic data leakage in vertical federated learning. In: Advances in Neural Information Processing Systems 34 (2021)
13. Kaissis, G., et al.: End-to-end privacy preserving deep learning on multi-institutional medical imaging. Nat. Mach. Intell. **3**(6), 473–484 (2021)
14. Kaissis, G.A., Makowski, M.R., Rückert, D., Braren, R.F.: Secure, privacy-preserving and federated machine learning in medical imaging. Nat. Mach. Intell. **2**(6), 305–311 (2020)
15. Li, W., et al.: Privacy-preserving federated brain tumour segmentation. In: Suk, H.-I., Liu, M., Yan, P., Lian, C. (eds.) MLMI 2019. LNCS, vol. 11861, pp. 133–141. Springer, Cham (2019). https://doi.org/10.1007/978-3-030-32692-0_16
16. McMahan, B., Moore, E., Ramage, D., Hampson, S., y Arcas, B.A.: Communication-efficient learning of deep networks from decentralized data. In: Artificial intelligence and statistics, pp. 1273–1282. PMLR (2017)
17. Pasquini, D., Ateniese, G., Bernaschi, M.: Unleashing the tiger: inference attacks on split learning. In: Proceedings of the 2021 ACM SIGSAC Conference on Computer and Communications Security, pp. 2113–2129 (2021)
18. Poirot, M.G.: Split learning in health care: multi-center deep learning without sharing patient data. Master's thesis, University of Twente (2020)
19. Poirot, M.G., Vepakomma, P., Chang, K., Kalpathy-Cramer, J., Gupta, R., Raskar, R.: Split learning for collaborative deep learning in healthcare. arXiv preprint arXiv:1912.12115 (2019)
20. Rieke, N., et al.: The future of digital health with federated learning. NPJ Digital Med. **3**(1), 1–7 (2020)

21. Ronneberger, O., Fischer, P., Brox, T.: U-Net: convolutional networks for biomedical image segmentation. In: Navab, N., Hornegger, J., Wells, W.M., Frangi, A.F. (eds.) MICCAI 2015. LNCS, vol. 9351, pp. 234–241. Springer, Cham (2015). https://doi.org/10.1007/978-3-319-24574-4_28

22. Rudin, L.I., Osher, S., Fatemi, E.: Nonlinear total variation based noise removal algorithms. Phys. D: Nonlinear Phenom. **60**(1–4), 259–268 (1992)

23. Simpson, A.L., et al.: A large annotated medical image dataset for the development and evaluation of segmentation algorithms. arXiv preprint arXiv:1902.09063 (2019)

24. Singh, A., Vepakomma, P., Gupta, O., Raskar, R.: Detailed comparison of communication efficiency of split learning and federated learning. arXiv preprint arXiv:1909.09145 (2019)

25. Srivastava, N., Hinton, G., Krizhevsky, A., Sutskever, I., Salakhutdinov, R.: Dropout: a simple way to prevent neural networks from overfitting. J. Mach. Learn. Res. **15**(1), 1929–1958 (2014)

26. Thapa, C., Chamikara, M.A.P., Camtepe, S., Sun, L.: Splitfed: when federated learning meets split learning. arXiv preprint arXiv:2004.12088 (2020)

27. Usynin, D., et al.: Adversarial interference and its mitigations in privacy-preserving collaborative machine learning. Nat. Mach. Intell. **3**(9), 749–758 (2021)

28. Vepakomma, P., Gupta, O., Swedish, T., Raskar, R.: Split learning for health: distributed deep learning without sharing raw patient data. arXiv preprint arXiv:1812.00564 (2018)

29. Wang, Z., Bovik, A.C., Sheikh, H.R., Simoncelli, E.P.: Image quality assessment: from error visibility to structural similarity. IEEE Trans. Image Proc. **13**(4), 600–612 (2004)

30. Xu, Z., et al.: Efficient multi-atlas abdominal segmentation on clinically acquired CT with SIMPLE context learning. Med. Image Anal. **24**(1), 18–27 (2015)

31. Yang, M., Lyu, L., Zhao, J., Zhu, T., Lam, K.Y.: Local differential privacy and its applications: a comprehensive survey. arXiv preprint arXiv:2008.03686 (2020)

32. Yang, Q., Liu, Y., Chen, T., Tong, Y.: Federated machine learning: concept and applications. ACM Trans. Intell. Syst. Technol. (TIST) **10**(2), 1–19 (2019)

33. Yin, H., Mallya, A., Vahdat, A., Alvarez, J.M., Kautz, J., Molchanov, P.: See through gradients: image batch recovery via gradinversion. In: Proceedings of the IEEE/CVF Conference on Computer Vision and Pattern Recognition, pp. 16337–16346 (2021)

34. Zhang, C., Li, S., Xia, J., Wang, W., Yan, F., Liu, Y.: BatchCrypt: efficient homomorphic encryption for {Cross-Silo} federated learning. In: 2020 USENIX Annual Technical Conference (USENIX ATC 20), pp. 493–506 (2020)

Joint Multi Organ and Tumor Segmentation from Partial Labels Using Federated Learning

Chen Shen[1], Pochuan Wang[2], Dong Yang[3], Daguang Xu[3], Masahiro Oda[1], Po-Ting Chen[4], Kao-Lang Liu[4], Wei-Chih Liao[4], Chiou-Shann Fuh[2], Kensaku Mori[1], Weichung Wang[2(✉)], and Holger R. Roth[3]

[1] Nagoya University, Nagoya, Japan
[2] National Taiwan University, Taipei, Taiwan
wwang@math.ntu.edu.tw
[3] NVIDIA Corporation, Santa Clara, USA
[4] National Taiwan University Hospital, Taipei, Taiwan

Abstract. Segmentation studies in medical image analysis are always associated with a particular task scenario. However, building datasets to train models to segment multiple types of organs and pathologies is challenging. For example, a dataset annotated for the pancreas and pancreatic tumors will result in a model that cannot segment other organs, like the liver and spleen, visible in the same abdominal computed tomography image. The lack of a well-annotated dataset is one limitation resulting in a lack of universal segmentation models. Federated learning (FL) is ideally suited for addressing this issue in the real-world context. In this work, we show that each medical center can use training data for distinct tasks to collaboratively build more generalizable segmentation models for multiple segmentation tasks without the requirement to centralize datasets in one place. The main challenge of this research is the heterogeneity of training data from various institutions and segmentation tasks. In this paper, we propose a multi-task segmentation framework using FL to learn segmentation models using several independent datasets with different annotations of organs or tumors. We include experiments on four publicly available single-task datasets, including MSD liver (w/ tumor), MSD spleen, MSD pancreas (w/ tumor), and KITS19. Experimental results on an external validation set to highlight the advantages of employing FL in multi-task organ and tumor segmentation.

Keywords: Federated learning · Segmentation · Partial labels

1 Introduction

Fully automated segmentation of organs and tumors from computed tomography (CT) volumes is essential for medical image analysis. Numerous studies have

---

C. Shen and P. Wang—Equal contribution.

S. Albarqouni et al. (Eds.): DeCaF 2022/FAIR 2022, LNCS 13573, pp. 58–67, 2022.
https://doi.org/10.1007/978-3-031-18523-6_6

concentrated on single specialized task segmentation throughout the last few decades [1,4,15,17]. For instance, the pancreas regions and pancreatic tumors will be included in the annotations if we want to develop an automated segmentation model for pancreatic cancer. However, this model cannot segment other organs and pathologies, like the liver and liver tumors. In a real-world clinical scenario, a generalized segmentation model for various organ types and associated malignancies is desired to develop comprehensive computer-aided diagnostic (CAD) systems.

The main challenge for achieving such generalized models is the lack of substantial datasets for multi-task organ segmentation. Most datasets are solely intended for a few very specialized segmentation tasks [5,18]. It is also tough to get annotated datasets for multi-task scenarios from multiple institutions to cover a large and diverse patient population and different scanner types and acquisition protocols. To simultaneously annotate various organ and tumor types demands extensive medical expertise as well as time.

In order to address these issues, several studies have attempted to build a generalized segmentation using multiple partially annotated datasets [2,6,21]. However, they centralized all training datasets locally. In real-world clinical situations, sharing the datasets among different institutions presents numerous technological, legal, and privacy concerns and might be therefore infeasible.

Federated learning (FL) is inherently suited for solving this problem [10,13]. Recently, combining FL methods with other deep learning techniques has grown in favor. A rising number of studies have been conducted using the FL method in segmentation tasks in the medical field. Li et al. [9] applied FL to brain tumor segmentation in practical for preserving data privacy. Wang et al. [19] carried out the real-world pancreas and pancreatic tumor segmentation using FL between two institutions across different nations. This work shows that FL considerably enhances the model performance of organ and tumor segmentation when compared to local standalone training. Additionally, recent real-world studies have shown that the FL approach is beneficial in many applications such as brain tumor segmentation [16], mammography classification [14], and COVID-19 prediction [3,11]. However, the main goal of these studies is to enhance the effectiveness of a single particular task. Some studies proposed to handle the multiple datasets using FL for classification task [8], but research on segmentation models for medical imaging is lacking.

In this work, we suggested a multi-task segmentation framework that makes use of FL to increase the generalizability of segmentation models using several partially annotated datasets. We explored the efficacy of the FedAvg model aggregation approach across several different segmentation tasks. We employed the MSD liver (w/ tumor), MSD spleen, MSD pancreas (w/ tumor) [18], and KITS19 [5] datasets, which are publicly accessible for single-task segmentation. Examples of axial CT slices of four partial labeled datasets for different segmentation tasks are shown in Fig. 1. Experimental results revealed that the FL framework boosted the segmentation performance of jointly trained task-specific models. Additionally, we evaluated our models on an unseen external dataset, and the segmentation results were satisfactory. To our knowledge, this is the

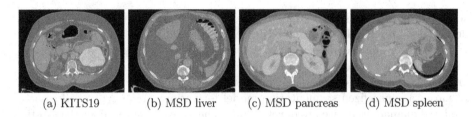

| (a) KITS19 | (b) MSD liver | (c) MSD pancreas | (d) MSD spleen |

Fig. 1. Samples of (a) KITS19 (b) MSD liver (c) MSD pancreas and (d) MSD spleen. The kidney and kidney tumor are pink and brown, respectively; the liver and liver tumor are red and green, respectively; the pancreas and pancreatic tumor are yellow and aquamarine, respectively; and the spleen is blue. (Color figure online)

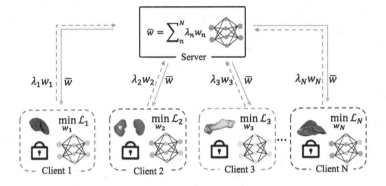

Fig. 2. An overview of the federated learning framework for multi-task medical image segmentation from partial labels. The training model is shared by each client for different segmentation tasks, and the model is aggregated by the server.

first work on multi-organ and tumor segmentation from partial labels for medical imaging using FL.

2   Methods

2.1   Federated Learning

FL [10] is a prominent distributed learning technique applied in many fields. In the area of medical image analysis, there is growing interest in FL techniques [13, 19,20]. The key advantage of FL is that it can learn from various datasets without the necessity for centralizing all datasets locally. An FL framework consists of a server and several clients. The server manages the whole FL process, and each client tackles their own task independently. The models are trained on the clients using local datasets, and they only exchange the learned parameters with the server; the server does not possess any data. The server only aggregates the model after receiving new parameters from a minimum number of clients specified and then sends an updated global model back to each client. In a new FL round, each client receives the global model from the server and refines it using their local dataset. An overview of our federated learning framework is shown in Fig. 2. In this study, each client trains on a different segmentation task.

2.2 Federated Averaging for Learning from Partial Labels

Federated averaging (FedAvg) is an effective aggregation method widely used in FL [10]. In FedAvg, the server aggregates the parameters shared by clients after each client trains trains on their local data using gradient-based optimization. In each round of FL, the following objective is being optimized:

$$\mathcal{L} = min \sum_{k}^{N} \eta_k \mathcal{L}_k, \tag{1}$$

where $\mathcal{L}_k$ represents the k-th client's local loss function out of the N clients. Each client trainers to optimize its $\mathcal{L}_k$ independently. The weight of each client is denoted as η_k, and the total weight of all clients in a round equals to 1. Using all clients for stochastic gradient updates in real-world FedAvg usage is costly in terms of both time and communication. At each round, a subset of N clients, which can be represented as K, can be selected for server model updates. Each client's weight is determined by the percentage of training data, with a total of n. We have $n = \sum_{k}^{K} n_k$, where n_k is the number of training data in client k. The weight of client η_k is $\eta_k = \frac{n_k}{n}$. When updating the global model using FedAvg, the client with more training data contributes more during the aggregation.

To avoid conflict of background labels between each client, we use sigmoid as the output activation function, and $\mathcal{L}_k$ for each client is the average Dice of all output channels except the background.

$$\mathcal{L}_k = \frac{1}{C} \sum_{c=2}^{C} \mathcal{L}_{Dice}(\mathcal{F}(x)_c, y_c) \tag{2}$$

where $\mathcal{F}$ is the model and C is the number of total classes, in this work $C = 8$, the corresponding organ for indices 1 to 8 are background, liver, liver tumor, spleen, pancreas, pancreas tumor, kidney, kidney tumor.

3   Experimental Details and Results

3.1   Datasets

Four publicly accessible datasets were used in this experiment. The server only collects the model parameters provided by the client and does not possess any data. Each client trained the model with a single dataset among distinct segmentation tasks. There are four types of different segmentation tasks, including the segmentation of the liver and liver tumor (**Task 1**); the pancreas and pancreatic tumor (**Task 2**); the kidney and kidney tumor (**Task 3**); the spleen (**Task 4**).

Table 1. Number of images used in the experiments. Each dataset was randomly divided into training, validation, and testing sets in the equal amounts.

	Training	Validation	Testing	Total
Task 1 (MSD liver)	79	26	26	131
Task 2 (MSD pancreas)	169	56	56	281
Task 3 (Kits19)	126	42	42	210
Task 4 (MSD spleen)	25	8	8	41

The dataset for **Task 1** is from Medical Segmentation Decathlon (MSD) liver task [18]. We only kept the 131 training cases with liver and liver tumor labels here. All the volumes are contrast-enhanced and the resolutions of volumes are (0.5–1.0, 0.5–1.0, 0.45–6.0) mm. For **Task 2**, we used 281 MSD pancreas task cases collected from patients undergoing pancreatic mass resection [18]. These CT volumes are in portal-venous phases. For **Task 3**, we utilized 210 cases from the KITS19 Challenge (Kits19) [5]. The CT volumes are in the late-arterial phase. For **Task 4**, 41 cases of portal venous phase CT from the MSD spleen task were used [18]. We randomly split the datasets into training, validation, and testing sets in the proportions of 60%, 20%, and 20%, respectively. The details of data divisions are shown in Table 1.

We employ another open dataset, MICCAI Multi-Atlas Labeling Beyond the Cranial Vault challenge (BTCV) [7], as an external validation dataset. This dataset contains 30 portal venous phase CT images with segmentation mask of 13 abdomen organs. We only kept the liver, pancreas, kidney, spleen segmentation mask in our testing as they overlap with the partial labels from tasks used during training.

3.2 Implementation Details

We use NVIDIA Federated Learning Application Runtime Environment (*NVIDIA FLARE*)[1] [12] as the backend of the FL framework. Our implementation is base on PyTorch Lighting[2]. We use a single NVIDIA GPU (Tesla V100 with 32GB) for each client in all experiments. We resampled all the volumes to $1 \times 1 \times 1mm^3$ isotropic spacing to guarantee the CT volumes had the same resolution. The intensity of the Hounsfield unit (HU) was clipped to the range [−500, 500] and normalized to [0, 1], which encompasses most of the abdominal organs. A random intensity shift augmentation was applied on training volumes with a probability of 0.8. The offset factor of it is 0.1 under the MONAI implementation[3]. We reset the orientation close to RAS+ so that all the CT volumes are in the same orientation. The input size of our model is $96 \times 96 \times 96$ with a batch size of 8.

---

[1] https://nvidia.github.io/NVFlare/.

[2] https://www.pytorchlightning.ai/.

[3] https://monai.io/.

Table 2. Comparison of Dice Score for the four different segmentation tasks on *standalone model* trained from scratch on single dataset; on *FL global best model* on server side; and *FL local best model* on client side.

Dice (%)	Task 1		Task 2		Task 3		Task 4	Avg.
	Liver	Tumor	Pancreas	Tumor	Kidney	Tumor	Spleen	
SL	67.4%	13.3%	64.2%	19.6%	93.1%	30.2%	48.7%	63.5%
FL global model (server)	0.0%	0.0%	66.9%	30.4%	90.6%	39.3%	0.0%	44.6%
FL local model (client)	**84.4%**	**33.8%**	**74.3%**	**38.4%**	**94.9%**	**63.7%**	**72.9%**	**86.7%**

The network architecture we utilized was obtained from the coarse-to-fine network architecture search (C2FNAS), which already demonstrates strong generalizability on organs and tumors segmentation in multiple different medical image segmentation tasks [20]. We training using the loss formulated in Eq. 2. For validation and testing we threshold the output values by 0.5 and calculate the Dice score for each channel separately. Clients train locally in the FL and communicate the learned parameters to the server at every 500 iterations. A total of 60 rounds were completed on the server, and the minimum client number to aggregate the model is 4.

3.3   Experimental Results

Our experimental results include the standalone training model (SL) trained with each partially labeled dataset, the FL client model on the local client, and the FL global best model aggregated by FedAvg on the server.

Table 2 compares the Dice score on four different segmentation tasks with standalone training (SL) models, FL global model on the server, and FL local model on each client. Comparing FL local models to SL models, the average Dice score for each client increases by 23.3%. The highest improvement, which is 33.5%, is in the segmentation of kidney tumors. The Dice score of the FL global model is not ideal. The FL global model fails on the liver, liver tumor, and spleen segmentation.

We present the axial visualizations of the four segmentation tasks in Fig. 4. The segmentation of organs and tumors performs best when using the local client model for specialized to each task during FL.

3.4   Validation on External Dataset

To verify the generalizability of our FL model for multi-organ segmentation, we validate the ensemble of the local models on the BTCV [7], which is a completely unseen dataset in this work. Table 3 shows our evaluation Dice scores for the spleen, kidney, pancreas, and liver organs. We compared the results of the FL global model, the ensembled local models and the ensembled results with extra post processing. The ensemble method we used is to combine corresponding output channels of the four local models. Since the final activation is sigmoid, the

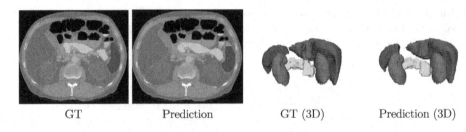

| GT | Prediction | GT (3D) | Prediction (3D) |

Fig. 3. The segmentation visualization of an external dataset in axial slice and 3D rendering using FL local model with post-processing. On this entirely new dataset, the major organ segmentation performs satisfactorily.

Table 3. Testing results on external dataset of the ensemble of four FL local models and FL global model.

Dice (%)	Task 1	Task 2	Task 3	Task 4	Avg.
	Liver	Pancreas	Kidney	Spleen	
SL	65.8%	57.5%	70.7%	44.6%	60.0%
FL global model	0.0%	62.9%	54.5%	0.0%	29.4%
FL local model (ensemble)	87.7%	71.8%	**80.5%**	69.9%	77.5%
FL local model (processed)	**91.6%**	**75.4%**	80.2%	**73.1%**	**80.1%**

output of the global model and the ensembled model may overlap. To overcome the overlapping issue we first take the largest connected components from each channel and discard any smaller objects. Then we fuse the output channels from corresponding models in the order of liver, liver tumor, spleen, pancreas, pancreas tumor, kidney and kidney tumor. Note, the later label might override a former label but we did not notice this to be problematic. The visualization of post processed results are presented in Table 3.

4   Discussion

As seen in Table 2, federated learning considerably improved the segmentation performance on the local model of each client compared to the results of standalone training. The average Dice score of the four segmentation tasks increased by 23.3%. By employing the task-specialized FL local models, there is a noticeable improvement in the segmentation of both tumors and organs. Although the training data on each client only contains annotations for one of the different segmentation tasks, the learned global parameters are beneficial for all other segmentation tasks. The FL local models were improved by adjusting the parameters obtained from the server to fit the particular segmentation task for the local dataset. However, the heterogeneity between different client datasets and annotation tasks causes the averaged global to not perform well, especially on **Task 1** and **Task 3** (liver and spleen).

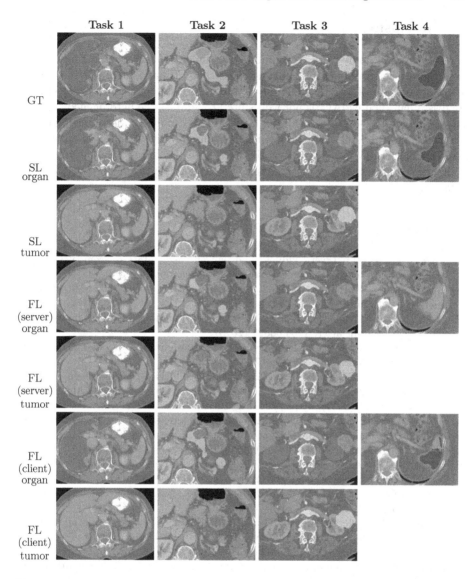

Fig. 4. Examples of segmentation results of four tasks including liver and tumor (**Task 1**); pancreas and tumor (**Task 2**); kidney and tumor (**Task 3**); spleen (**Task 4**) on ground truth (GT), standalone model (SL), and FL model on server-site and client-site.

Nevertheless, we validate the ensemble of local segmentation models on an external dataset. Both qualitative and quantitative evaluation results demonstrate the robustness of our FL local models. The segmentation performance of the ensemble models on the corresponding organs is satisfactory and shows how a successful ensemble model can be trained using FL with only partially annotated datasets.

5 Conclusion

In this study, we apply the FL techniques for multi-task organs and tumors segmentation. The experimental results suggest that FL has a favorable impact on the segmentation of organs and tumors, although the datasets on other clients are dissimilar. The FedAvg is not well-suited to address the heterogeneous problems of multi-task datasets. Hence the FL global model underperformed. We confirmed the robustness of the local model ensemble with external validation using an unseen dataset. Future work is required to address the heterogeneity challenge in multi-task organs and tumor segmentation from partially labeled datasets.

References

1. Altini, N., et al.: Liver, kidney and spleen segmentation from CT scans and MRI with deep learning: a survey. Neurocomputing **490**, 30–53 (2022). https://doi.org/10.1016/j.neucom.2021.08.157, https://www.sciencedirect.com/science/article/pii/S0925231222003149
2. Chen, S., Ma, K., Zheng, Y.: Med3D: transfer learning for 3d medical image analysis. arXiv preprint arXiv:1904.00625 (2019)
3. Dayan, I., et al.: Federated learning for predicting clinical outcomes in patients with Covid-19. Nat. Med. **27**(10), 1735–1743 (2021)
4. Heller, N., et al.: The state of the art in kidney and kidney tumor segmentation in contrast-enhanced CT imaging: Results of the KITS19 challenge. Med. Image Anal. **67**, 101821 (2021). https://doi.org/10.1016/j.media.2020.101821
5. Heller, N., et al.: The KITS19 challenge data: 300 kidney tumor cases with clinical context, CT semantic segmentations, and surgical outcomes (2019). https://doi.org/10.48550/ARXIV.1904.00445, https://arxiv.org/abs/1904.00445
6. Huang, R., Zheng, Y., Hu, Z., Zhang, S., Li, H.: Multi-organ segmentation via co-training weight-averaged models from few-organ datasets. In: Martel, A.L., et al. (eds.) MICCAI 2020. LNCS, vol. 12264, pp. 146–155. Springer, Cham (2020). https://doi.org/10.1007/978-3-030-59719-1_15
7. Landman, B., et al.: 2015 MICCAI multi-atlas labeling beyond the cranial vault - workshop and challenge (2015). https://doi.org/10.7303/syn3193805
8. Li, Q., He, B., Song, D.: Model-contrastive federated learning. In: Proceedings of the IEEE/CVF Conference on Computer Vision and Pattern Recognition, pp. 10713–10722 (2021)
9. Li, W., et al.: Privacy-preserving federated brain tumour segmentation. In: Suk, H.I., Liu, M., Yan, P., Lian, C. (eds.) Machine Learning in Medical Imaging, pp. 133–141. Springer, Cham (2019)
10. McMahan, H.B., Moore, E., Ramage, D., Hampson, S., y Arcas, B.A.: Communication-efficient learning of deep networks from decentralized data. In: AISTATS (2017)
11. Nguyen, D.C., Ding, M., Pathirana, P.N., Seneviratne, A., Zomaya, A.Y.: Federated learning for covid-19 detection with generative adversarial networks in edge cloud computing. IEEE Internet of Things J. **9**, 10257–10271 (2021)
12. Nvidia Corporation: Nvidia FLARE, June 2022. https://doi.org/10.5281/zenodo.6780567,https://github.com/NVIDIA/nvflare

13. Rieke, N., et al.: The future of digital health with federated learning. NPJ Digit. Med. **3**(1), 1–7 (2020)

14. Roth, H.R., et al.: Federated learning for breast density classification: a real-world implementation. In: Domain Adaptation and Representation Transfer, and Distributed and Collaborative Learning, pp. 181–191. Springer, Cham (2020). https://doi.org/10.1007/978-3-030-60548-3

15. Seo, H., Huang, C., Bassenne, M., Xiao, R., Xing, L.: Modified U-Net (mU-Net) with incorporation of object-dependent high level features for improved liver and liver-tumor segmentation in CT images. IEEE Trans. Med. Imaging **39**(5), 1316–1325 (2020). https://doi.org/10.1109/TMI.2019.2948320

16. Sheller, M.J., et al.: Federated learning in medicine: facilitating multi-institutional collaborations without sharing patient data. Sci. Rep. **10**(1), 1–12 (2020)

17. Shen, C.: Multi-task federated learning for heterogeneous pancreas segmentation. In: Oyarzun Laura, C., et al. (eds.) DCL/PPML/LL-COVID19/CLIP -2021. LNCS, vol. 12969, pp. 101–110. Springer, Cham (2021). https://doi.org/10.1007/978-3-030-90874-4_10

18. Simpson, A.L., et al.: A large annotated medical image dataset for the development and evaluation of segmentation algorithms. CoRR abs/1902.09063 (2019). http://arxiv.org/abs/1902.09063

19. Wang, P., et al.: Automated pancreas segmentation using multi-institutional collaborative deep learning. In: Albarqouni, S., et al. (eds.) DART/DCL -2020. LNCS, vol. 12444, pp. 192–200. Springer, Cham (2020). https://doi.org/10.1007/978-3-030-60548-3_19

20. Yu, Q., et al.: C2FNAS: coarse-to-Fine neural architecture search for 3D medical image segmentation. In: 2020 IEEE/CVF Conference on Computer Vision and Pattern Recognition (CVPR), December 2019

21. Zhang, J., Xie, Y., Xia, Y., Shen, C.: DodNet: learning to segment multi-organ and tumors from multiple partially labeled datasets. In: Proceedings of the IEEE/CVF Conference on Computer Vision and Pattern Recognition (CVPR), pp. 1195–1204, June 2021

GAN Latent Space Manipulation and Aggregation for Federated Learning in Medical Imaging

Matteo Pennisi[1], Federica Proietto Salanitri[1(✉)], Simone Palazzo[1],
Carmelo Pino[1,2], Francesco Rundo[2], Daniela Giordano[1],
and Concetto Spampinato[1]

[1] PeRCeiVe Lab, University of Catania, Catania, Italy
`federica.proiettosalanitri@phd.unict.it`
[2] STMicrolectronics, ADG Central R&D, Catania, Italy
`http://www.perceivelab.com/`

Abstract. Federated learning aims at improving data privacy by training local models on distributed nodes and at integrating information on a central node, without data sharing. However, this calls for effective integration methods that are currently missing as existing strategies, e.g., averaging model gradients, are unable to deal with data multimodality due to different distributions at multiple nodes. In this work, we tackle this problem by having multiple nodes that share a synthetic version of their own data, built in a way to hide patient-specific visual cues, with a central node that is responsible for training a deep model for medical image classification. Synthetic data are generated through an aggregation strategy consisting in: 1) learning the distribution of original data via a Generative Adversarial Network (GAN); 2) projecting private data samples in the GAN latent space; 3) clustering the projected samples and generating synthetic images by interpolating the cluster centroids, thus reducing the possibility of collision with latent vectors corresponding to real samples and a consequent leak of sensitive information. The proposed approach is tested over two X-ray datasets for Tuberculosis classification to simulate a realistic scenario with two different nodes and non-i.i.d. data. Experimental results show that our approach yields performance comparable to, or even outperforming, training on the full joint dataset. We also show quantitatively and qualitatively that images synthesized with our approach are significantly different from original images, thus limiting the possibility to recover original data through attacks.

Keywords: Federated learning · Generative models · Privacy preserving

1 Introduction

The recent success of deep learning in the medical domain has shown it to be a promising tool to support medical diagnosis and treatment, but large amounts of

---

M. Pennisi and F. Proietto Salanitri—These authors contributed equally to this work.

S. Albarqouni et al. (Eds.): DeCaF 2022/FAIR 2022, LNCS 13573, pp. 68–78, 2022.
https://doi.org/10.1007/978-3-031-18523-6_7

training data are still needed to build models able to achieve good accuracy and generalization. However, medical institutions generally curate their own datasets and keep them private for privacy concerns. Due to their small size, models trained on private datasets tend to overfit, introduce biases and generalize badly on other data sources that address the same task [27].

A viable solution for increasing the size and diversity of data is to employ a collaborative learning strategy, where multiple distributed nodes support the training of a model for a shared task [26]. Federated Learning [16,21], in particular, has emerged as a training paradigm where each node trains a copy of a shared model on its private data and sends the local updates to a central server, where model parameters are tuned based on aggregated local updates. However, aggregating gradients or weights from multiple nodes does not deal with the non-i.i.d. nature of distributed data. Furthermore, gradient integration raises privacy issues as training data might be reconstructed, to a certain degree, starting from the shared gradients as demonstrated in [6,30,31].

In this work, we propose a generative approach where each distributed node generates, and shares, a synthetic version of its own data through manipulation and aggregation of latent spaces learned by a Generative Adversarial Network (GAN). In particular, our synthetic samples are drawn from the same distribution as the original ones, but are designed to prevent the inclusion of patient-specific visual patterns. Sharing the manipulated images, rather than the generation model, prevents the reconstructions of real data through attacks to the model and circumvents the gradient/weight aggregation problem.

We tested our approach on the task of tuberculosis classification from X-ray images of two different datasets, namely, the Montgomery County X-ray Set and Shenzhen Hospital X-ray Set [2,9,10]. Our experiments simulate a multi-node multimodal data scenario, where each dataset is located on a different node. It achieves 75% and 60% in classification accuracy on the Shenzhen and the Montgomery datasets, respectively, whereas standard centralized training on the dataset union (i.e., not in a federated learning setting) yields 78% and 43%. The capabilities of our approach to synthesize images visually distant from the real ones are measured quantitatively by evaluating LPIPS distance [29] between real images and samples generated through latent space optimization on a standard (non-privacy-preserving) GAN and by the proposed approach. Qualitatively, we also show several examples of generated images with corresponding closest match in the real dataset, demonstrating significant differences that prevent tracing back to the original real distribution.

2   Related Work

Federated learning (FL) embraces a family of privacy-preserving distributed learning strategies that allow nodes to keep training data private, while supporting the creation of a shared model. Typically, a central server sends a model to a set of client nodes; local model updates are aggregated by the server, which sends the new model to the clients in an iterative process. In FedAvg [16], the server computes model averaging combining local stochastic gradient descent updates of each client. FedProx [14] is a generalization and re-parametrization of FedAvg proving theoretically convergence guarantee when training over non-identical distributed data (statistical heterogeneity). FedMA [23] builds a shared global in a layer-wise manner by matching and averaging hidden elements with similar feature extraction signatures. All these methods attempt to train a central model using the gradients gathered from multiple models trained on local private data.

FL particularly suits medical field applications, where data privacy is a critical concern. Li et al. [15] present the first FL system for medical image analysis, employing FedAvg and differential privacy [1] for brain tumor segmentation. Roy et al. [20] also apply FL for whole-brain segmentation in MRI. Recently, several other collaborative learning methods [4,5,18] have been proposed, especially because of the emergency need raised by the COVID-19 pandemic, in order to harness multiple data sources to promptly react to emergency scenarios.

However, gradient aggregation does not seem to guarantee the required level of data privacy, as it has been demonstrated that network inputs can be recovered from gradient updates [6,24,31]. Differential privacy [1,8,13] attempts to reduce this issue by obfuscating gradients through noise. Zhu et al. [31], for instance, add Gaussian/Laplacian noise to gradients and compress the model with gradient pruning. However, adding noise to the gradients significantly compromises model's performance.

In this work, we tackle the problem of federated learning from a data-perspective: rather than sharing weights/updates, which can be attacked, we share a synthetic version of private data—generated through a GAN—that retains visual content to support distributed training, but improves privacy by hiding specific visual patterns of patients. GANs have been also employed in federated learning regime, but always in the view of aggregating parameters to create a general model. In GS-WGAN [3], a gradient-sanitized Wasserstein GAN improves differential privacy, by carefully distorting gradient information in a way that reduces loss of information and generates more informative samples. Federated CycleGAN [22] is designed to perform unsupervised image translation; however, they still share local gradients, which may introduce the above privacy concerns. FedDPGAN [28] designs a distributed DPGAN [25] trained in a FL framework, to train models for COVID-19 diagnosis from chest X-ray images, without data sharing. In [19], the authors propose a framework to extend a large family of GANs to a FL setting utilizing a centralized adversary.

3   Method

3.1   Overview

In our approach, shown in Fig. 1, a set of distributed nodes create synthetic images and share them with a central node, where a model is trained using the received data. Specifically, each node trains a GAN to transform its own private dataset into a privacy-preserved one where patient information leak is minimized. The visual features of the privacy-preserved dataset still come from the same distribution of the real private one (as per GAN training) in order to support the training of the centralized model.

Although we do not perform a formal security analysis of our approach, for the sake of readability we will refer to it as "privacy-preserving", to distinguish it from the cases where no precaution is taken to prevent patient information leak in the sharing and learning process (referred to as "non privacy-preserving").

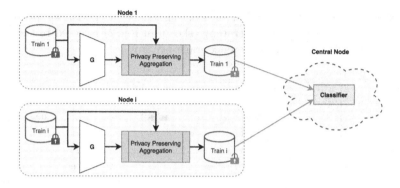

Fig. 1. The proposed federated learning framework

3.2 Generative Adversarial Network

Generative Adversarial Networks (GANs) [7] consist of two networks, a generator model and a discriminator model: the former is trained to generate realistic images, while the latter is trained to distinguish between real and synthetic samples. In the conditional settings, where the generation process is controlled by a label to synthesize samples for a specific class, the two models are alternately trained to minimize the following losses, respectively:

$$L_D = \mathbb{E}_{x,y}[\log(D(x,y))] + \mathbb{E}_{z,y}[\log(1 - D(G(z,y),y))] \qquad (1)$$

$$L_G = \mathbb{E}_{z,y}[\log(D(G(z,y),y))] \qquad (2)$$

where (x,y) is sampled from the real data distribution $\mathcal{D}$, z is sampled from a latent distribution $\mathcal{Z}$ (mapped by generator G to the real distribution for class y) and D is the discriminator model that predicts the likelihood of the input being real, given the target label. During training, the better D becomes at recognizing fake samples, the more G has to improve its generation capabilities, thus increasing the realism of synthetic data.

In this work, our GAN architecture is based on StyleGAN2 [12], where an auxiliary network maps a class-conditioned latent vector z to an intermediate latent vector $w \in \mathcal{W}$, which helps to improve generation quality and simplifies the projection of real images in $\mathcal{D}$ to the latent space $\mathcal{W}$. Indeed, given a real image x of class y, it is then possible to find an intermediate latent point $\hat{w}$ such that $G(\hat{w}) \approx x$, by optimizing the LPIPS distance loss [29] between x and $G(\hat{w})$ with respect to $\hat{w}$, which measures the similarity of activations by a pre-trained model. Of course, this projection property negatively affects the sought privacy in FL, as the generated synthetic distribution may contain visual patterns highly similar to those of the original samples.

3.3 Privacy-Preserving Aggregation

To address the privacy limitation of existing GAN methods, we propose a *Privacy-Preserving Aggregation* strategy (shown in Fig. 2) injected in the GAN training during data generation to encourage privacy.

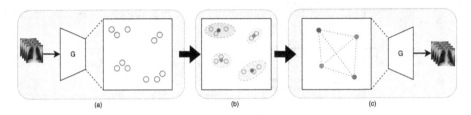

Fig. 2. Privacy Preserving Aggregation: a) a generator G is trained for each node using its own private dataset. Training images are then projected in the generator latent space; b) projected latent vectors are clustered through spectral clustering, based on pairwise LPIPS distance between corresponding images; c) linear interpolation among cluster centroids produces new latent vectors, which are used to generate synthetic samples that are sent to the central node.

Let $\hat{W} = \{\hat{w}_1, \hat{w}_2, ..., \hat{w}_N\}$ be a set of points obtained by projecting N images onto the GAN latent space, for a given dataset class. We carry out spectral clustering [17] based on LPIPS distances between the images corresponding to $\hat{W}$ projections. Cluster centroids $\hat{W}^c = \{\hat{w}_1^c, \hat{w}_2^c, ..., \hat{w}_M^c\}$, representing latent aggregations with similar visual features in terms of LPIPS distance, are then employed as a starting point for data synthesis. Working with centroids allows us to capture shared patterns between dataset samples while improving privacy, since the resulting latent vectors cannot be traced back to specific patients. To create enough synthetic samples to allow model's training, we then carry out an augmentation procedure based on linearly interpolating the $\hat{W}^c$ centroids in the latent space and generating training samples using points along the trajectories between them. This is also beneficial for increasing dataset variability, as it allows to produce samples that combine patterns of groups of patients (e.g., interpolating clusters with lesions on left/right lung may produce synthetic images with lesions on both lungs), leading to better generalization capabilities. Note that clustering and interpolation are carried out independently for each dataset class, by exploiting the conditional generation capabilities of the generator. This ensures that sampled latent vectors are assigned a well-defined label, making the corresponding synthetic images suitable for training the central node classifier. Clusters with only one sample are discarded in the process.

4 Experiments and Results

We test the proposed approach on the task of tuberculosis classification from X-ray images in a non-i.i.d. federated learning setting, where different datasets are used for each node, to simulate a more realistic training scenario. Each node generates synthetic X-ray images by applying our aggregation approach on its private dataset; images generated by each node are shared with a central node and used to train a classification model.

4.1 Datasets and Training Procedure

We employ the Montgomery County X-ray Set and the Shenzhen Hospital X-ray set[1] [2,9,10]. The Montgomery Set contains 138 frontal chest X-ray images (80 negatives and 58 positives), captured with a Eureka stationary machine (CR) at 4020×4892 or 4892×4020 pixel resolution. The Shenzhen dataset was collected using a Philips DR Digital Diagnostic system. It includes 662 frontal chest X-ray images (326 negatives and 336 positives), with a variable resolution of approximately 3000×3000 pixels. In our federated learning setting, each dataset is associated to a node. We employ 80% of each dataset to train a GAN and generate synthetic images using the proposed approach. The remaining 20% of each dataset is used for testing the model trained on the central node. Test labels are balanced: 65 positives and 65 negatives on the Shenzhen dataset, and 15 positives and 15 negatives on the Montgomery dataset.

We use StyleGAN2-ADA [11] for image generation on each node, because of its suitability in low-data regimes and its intrinsic latent projection mechanism. GANs are trained in a label-conditioned setting and yield a Fréchet inception distance (FID) of 21.36 and 55.38 on the Shenzhen and Montgomery datasets, respectively. Latent space projection is carried out as in [12] for 500 iterations. Spectral clustering is carried out using 20 clusters on the Shenzhen Dataset and 10 on Montgomery one, due to the difference in sizes. Centroid interpolation computes 9 intermediate points for each pair of centroids. The resulting synthetic datasets include 1,730 samples per class on Shenzen and 415 samples per class on Montgomery. On the central node, we use a ResNet-50 classifier, trained by minimizing a cross-entropy loss with mini-batch gradient descent using the Adam optimizer for a total of 1,000 epochs; mini-batch size is set to 64 and the learning rate is 10^{-6}. All images are resized to 256×256, and data augmentation is carried out with random horizontal flip and random 90-degree rotations. Experiments are performed on an NVIDIA GeForce RTX 3090, using PyTorch.

4.2 Experimental Results

We evaluate the performance of our approach by considering three different data usage scenarios:

---

[1] This dataset was released by National Library of Medicine, National Institute Of health, Bethesda, USA.

1. **Real data:** the central server trains a classifier on the original joint dataset using images of all nodes (this is the standard supervised centralized setting).
2. **Synthetic (non privacy-preserving) data:** each node generates a synthetic training set by sampling from a GAN trained on the real data; synthetic samples are then used to train on the central server. No privacy-preserving mechanism is enforced: sampled images are drawn from the original distribution as learned by the GAN.
3. **Synthetic privacy-preserving data:** the training set for the central server is created by employing our privacy-preserving generation procedure (see Sect. 3.3).

Table 1 reports the test accuracy on each dataset under the above three scenarios. On the Shenzhen dataset, our approach is close to centralized training using all data, respectively 0.75 and 0.78 classification accuracy. Interestingly, the non-privacy-preserving synthetic setting achieves even higher performance, which is explained by the larger number of training samples (662 real samples in Shenzhen, compared to 3,460 synthetic samples), confirming that sample synthesis helps making up for data scarcity—although in this case no precautions are taken to improve privacy. This phenomenon is even more evident on the smaller Montgomery dataset (138 samples), where the usage of synthetic data yields significantly improved accuracy (0.43 on the original dataset vs 0.60 on the synthetic one).

Table 1. Classification accuracy on the test set of each dataset, in different training scenarios.

Dataset	Training data	Accuracy
Shenzhen	Real	0.78
	Synthetic (non privacy-preserving)	0.82
	Synthetic (privacy-preserving)	0.75
Montgomery	Real	0.43
	Synthetic (non privacy-preserving)	0.60
	Synthetic (privacy-preserving)	0.60

Privacy-preserving capabilities of the proposed approach are measured quantitatively by computing the LPIPS distance between real training images and a) their projected counterparts using StyleGAN2, and b) the most similar samples from the pool of images generated by our strategy. Ideally, we would expect that, when using a standard StyleGAN2 network, the latent projection procedure should be able to recover an image that the model has used at training time—which is undesirable, since knowledge of the model would allow an attacker to reconstruct original samples; we also expect that images synthesized through generative aggregation should be significantly dissimilar to any real sample. Indeed, LPIPS distance histograms in Fig. 3 show that a distribution shift can be observed between the two sets of measured distances: latent space projection of real images tends to produce samples with significantly smaller distances than those obtained with most similar synthetic images generated by our approach. This effect can be also appreciated qualitatively in the samples reported in Fig. 4, showing six images randomly sampled from the Shenzhen Dataset (top row) compared to their projection in the generator latent space (middle row) and the closest image in the aggregated dataset (bottom row).

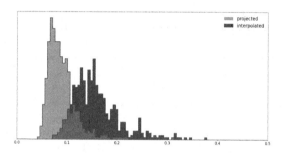

Fig. 3. In red, LPIPS distance histogram between real images and the corresponding images obtained through latent space projection. In blue, LPIPS distance histogram between real images and the closest images generated with the proposed approach. (Color figure online)

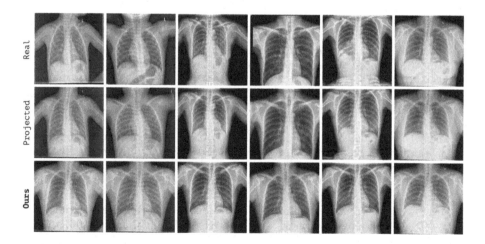

Fig. 4. Top: real images from Shenzhen Dataset; middle: images generated by latent projection; bottom: most similar synthetic images obtained with the proposed method.

5 Conclusion

In this study we propose a synthetic data aggregation approach as an alternative to classic federated learning with gradient aggregation, which is subject to privacy concerns due to the risk of reconstructing the original inputs. Rather than training a central model by aggregating gradients from individual nodes, we propose to generate a synthetic dataset for each node and use the union of these datasets to train the central model. We tested our approach in a realistic scenario, using two X-Rays datasets for Tuberculosis classification, simulating a system with two nodes and non-i.i.d. data. The results demonstrated the validity of our approach, which obtains comparable performance to those obtained when training on the union of all datasets. Moreover, we showed, both quantitatively and qualitatively, that the generated images exhibit visual features typical of the original data, while being significantly different from any actual real image, thus preventing to trace them back to individual patients. Still, this is a preliminary work: future developments will investigate its validity in the presence of more nodes or in the presence of i.i.d. distributions.

Acknowledgements. This research was supported by the following grants: 1) Rehastart funded by PO FESR 2014-2020 Sicilia, Azione 1.1.5; project number 08ME6201000222, CUP: G79J18000610007); 2) the "Adaptive Brain-Derived Artificial Intelligence Methods for Event Detection" - BrAIn funded by the "Programma per la ricerca di ateneo UNICT 2020-22 linea 3".

Matteo Pennisi is a PhD student enrolled in the National PhD in Artificial Intelligence, XXXVII cycle, course on Health and life sciences, organized by Università Campus Bio-Medico di Roma.

References

1. Abadi, M., et al.: Deep learning with differential privacy. In: Proceedings of the 2016 ACM SIGSAC Conference on Computer and Communications Security, pp. 308–318 (2016)
2. Candemir, S., et al.: Lung segmentation in chest radiographs using anatomical atlases with nonrigid registration. IEEE Trans. Med. Imaging **33**(2), 577–590 (2013)
3. Chen, D., Orekondy, T., Fritz, M.: GS-WGAN: a gradient-sanitized approach for learning differentially private generators. Adv. Neural. Inf. Process. Syst. **33**, 12673–12684 (2020)
4. Dayan, I., et al.: Federated learning for predicting clinical outcomes in patients with COVID-19. Nat. Med. **27**(10), 1735–1743 (2021)
5. Feki, I., Ammar, S., Kessentini, Y., Muhammad, K.: Federated learning for COVID-19 screening from chest x-ray images. Appl. Soft Comput. **106**, 107330 (2021)
6. Geiping, J., Bauermeister, H., Dröge, H., Moeller, M.: Inverting gradients-how easy is it to break privacy in federated learning? Adv. Neural. Inf. Process. Syst. **33**, 16937–16947 (2020)
7. Goodfellow, I., et al.: Generative adversarial nets. In: Advances in Neural Information Processing Systems, vol. 27 (2014)
8. Guo, S., Zhang, T., Xu, G., Yu, H., Xiang, T., Liu, Y.: Topology-aware differential privacy for decentralized image classification. IEEE Trans. Circuits Syst. Video Technol. (2021)

9. Jaeger, S., Candemir, S., Antani, S., Wáng, Y.X.J., Lu, P.X., Thoma, G.: Two public chest x-ray datasets for computer-aided screening of pulmonary diseases. Quant. Imaging Med. Surg. **4**(6), 475 (2014)
10. Jaeger, S., et al.: Automatic tuberculosis screening using chest radiographs. IEEE Trans. Med. Imaging **33**(2), 233–245 (2013)
11. Karras, T., Aittala, M., Hellsten, J., Laine, S., Lehtinen, J., Aila, T.: Training generative adversarial networks with limited data. Adv. Neural. Inf. Process. Syst. **33**, 12104–12114 (2020)
12. Karras, T., Laine, S., Aittala, M., Hellsten, J., Lehtinen, J., Aila, T.: Analyzing and improving the image quality of StyleGAN. In: Proceedings of the IEEE/CVF Conference on Computer Vision and Pattern Recognition, pp. 8110–8119 (2020)
13. Lecuyer, M., Atlidakis, V., Geambasu, R., Hsu, D., Jana, S.: Certified robustness to adversarial examples with differential privacy. In: 2019 IEEE Symposium on Security and Privacy (SP), pp. 656–672. IEEE (2019)
14. Li, T., Sahu, A.K., Zaheer, M., Sanjabi, M., Talwalkar, A., Smith, V.: Federated optimization in heterogeneous networks. Proc. Mach. Learn. Syst. **2**, 429–450 (2020)
15. Li, W., et al.: Privacy-preserving federated brain tumour segmentation. In: Suk, H.-I., Liu, M., Yan, P., Lian, C. (eds.) MLMI 2019. LNCS, vol. 11861, pp. 133–141. Springer, Cham (2019). https://doi.org/10.1007/978-3-030-32692-0_16
16. McMahan, B., Moore, E., Ramage, D., Hampson, S., Arcas, B.A.: Communication-efficient learning of deep networks from decentralized data. In: Artificial Intelligence and Statistics, pp. 1273–1282. PMLR (2017)
17. Ng, A., Jordan, M., Weiss, Y.: On spectral clustering: analysis and an algorithm. In: Advances in Neural Information Processing Systems, vol. 14 (2001)
18. Pang, J., Huang, Y., Xie, Z., Li, J., Cai, Z.: Collaborative city digital twin for the COVID-19 pandemic: a federated learning solution. Tsinghua Sci. Technol. **26**(5), 759–771 (2021)
19. Rajotte, J.F., et al.: Reducing bias and increasing utility by federated generative modeling of medical images using a centralized adversary. In: Proceedings of the Conference on Information Technology for Social Good, pp. 79–84 (2021)
20. Roy, A.G., Siddiqui, S., Pölsterl, S., Navab, N., Wachinger, C.: Braintorrent: a peer-to-peer environment for decentralized federated learning. arXiv preprint arXiv:1905.06731 (2019)
21. Sheller, M.J., Reina, G.A., Edwards, B., Martin, J., Bakas, S.: Multi-institutional deep learning modeling without sharing patient data: a feasibility study on brain tumor segmentation. In: Crimi, A., Bakas, S., Kuijf, H., Keyvan, F., Reyes, M., van Walsum, T. (eds.) BrainLes 2018. LNCS, vol. 11383, pp. 92–104. Springer, Cham (2019). https://doi.org/10.1007/978-3-030-11723-8_9
22. Song, J., Ye, J.C.: Federated CycleGAN for privacy-preserving image-to-image translation. arXiv preprint arXiv:2106.09246 (2021)
23. Wang, H., Yurochkin, M., Sun, Y., Papailiopoulos, D., Khazaeni, Y.: Federated learning with matched averaging. arXiv preprint arXiv:2002.06440 (2020)
24. Wang, Z., Song, M., Zhang, Z., Song, Y., Wang, Q., Qi, H.: Beyond inferring class representatives: user-level privacy leakage from federated learning. In: IEEE INFOCOM 2019-IEEE Conference on Computer Communications, pp. 2512–2520. IEEE (2019)
25. Xie, L., Lin, K., Wang, S., Wang, F., Zhou, J.: Differentially private generative adversarial network. arXiv preprint arXiv:1802.06739 (2018)
26. Yang, Q., Liu, Y., Chen, T., Tong, Y.: Federated machine learning: concept and applications. ACM Trans. Intell. Syst. Technol. (TIST) **10**(2), 1–19 (2019)

27. Zech, J.R., Badgeley, M.A., Liu, M., Costa, A.B., Titano, J.J., Oermann, E.K.: Variable generalization performance of a deep learning model to detect pneumonia in chest radiographs: a cross-sectional study. PLoS Med. **15**(11), e1002683 (2018)
28. Zhang, L., Shen, B., Barnawi, A., Xi, S., Kumar, N., Wu, Y.: FedDPGAN: federated differentially private generative adversarial networks framework for the detection of COVID-19 pneumonia. Inf. Syst. Front. **23**(6), 1403–1415 (2021)
29. Zhang, R., Isola, P., Efros, A.A., Shechtman, E., Wang, O.: The unreasonable effectiveness of deep features as a perceptual metric. In: Proceedings of the IEEE Conference on Computer Vision and Pattern Recognition, pp. 586–595 (2018)
30. Zhao, B., Mopuri, K.R., Bilen, H.: iDLG: improved deep leakage from gradients. arXiv preprint arXiv:2001.02610 (2020)
31. Zhu, L., Liu, Z., Han, S.: Deep leakage from gradients. In: Advances in Neural Information Processing Systems, vol. 32 (2019)

A Specificity-Preserving Generative Model for Federated MRI Translation

Onat Dalmaz[1,2(✉)], Usama Mirza[1,2], Gökberk Elmas[1,2], Muzaffer Özbey[1,2], Salman U. H. Dar[1,2], and Tolga Çukur[1,2]

[1] Department of Electrical and Electronics Engineering, Bilkent University, Ankara, Turkey
onat@ee.bilkent.edu.tr
[2] National Magnetic Resonance Research Center (UMRAM), Bilkent University, Ankara, Turkey

Abstract. MRI translation models learn a mapping from an acquired source contrast to an unavailable target contrast. Collaboration between institutes is essential to train translation models that can generalize across diverse datasets. That said, aggregating all imaging data and training a centralized model poses privacy problems. Recently, federated learning (FL) has emerged as a collaboration framework that enables decentralized training to avoid sharing of imaging data. However, FL-trained translation models can deteriorate by the inherent heterogeneity in the distribution of MRI data. To improve reliability against domain shifts, here we introduce a novel specificity-preserving FL method for MRI contrast translation. The proposed approach is based on an adversarial model that adaptively normalizes the feature maps across the generator based on site-specific latent variables. Comprehensive FL experiments were conducted on multi-site datasets to show the effectiveness of the proposed approach against prior federated methods in MRI contrast translation.

Keywords: Federated learning · Site-specificity · MRI · Translation · Heterogeneity

1 Introduction

Multi-contrast MRI enables non-invasive diagnostic assessment of anatomy and accumulates complementary information via examination of multiple tissue contrasts [2,26]. Yet, multi-contrast protocols have time and economic costs that can prevent collection of all desired contrasts in an MRI exam [18,34]. This limitation can be addressed by contrast translation, which is the imputation of missing sequences in a protocol from the acquired sequences [15]. Deep models have made remarkable progress in this area, enabling centralized models to significantly improve MRI translation performance. [8,36,39]. Unfortunately, learning generalizable models for medical imaging tasks requires training on diverse datasets. However, compiling such datasets at a central institution would inevitably compromise patient privacy [17].

© The Author(s), under exclusive license to Springer Nature Switzerland AG 2022
S. Albarqouni et al. (Eds.): DeCaF 2022/FAIR 2022, LNCS 13573, pp. 79–88, 2022.
https://doi.org/10.1007/978-3-031-18523-6_8

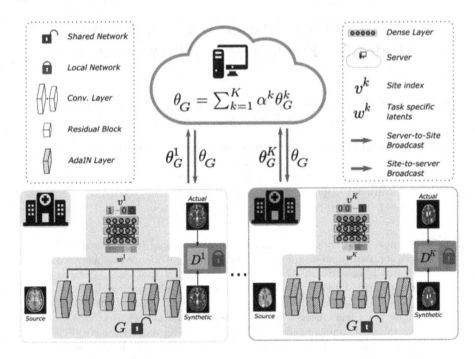

Fig. 1. SPFL-Trans is a decentralized contrast translation method based on federated learning of a conditional adversarial model. AdaIN layers along with site-specific latents produced by a subnetwork effectively modulate feature maps in order to cope with data heterogeneity across different sites.

Federated learning (FL) is a powerful framework to address this major limitation based on decentralized model training across multiple institutions [9,21,23,29,30,33]. In this framework, a server aggregates locally optimized models to compute a shared global model [24,35]. Aggregated models can be impaired by the heterogeneity in the data distribution naturally evident for multi-institutional datasets [29,32] due to different scanners, acquisition parameters etc. Previous studies on FL-based medical imaging have introduced several prominent approaches to cope with data heterogeneity in segmentation [5,22,23,27,31,38], classification [3,22,40], and reconstruction [10,11] tasks. However, influence of data heterogeneity on FL-based MRI contrast translation remains understudied.

Here, we introduce a novel Specificity-Preserving Federated Learning method for MRI Translation (SPFL-Trans). In contrast to previous approaches, the proposed method embodies a site-aware architecture that effectively addresses the inherent data heterogeneity in multi-institutional datasets. SPFL-Trans is based on a generator backbone equipped with Adaptive Instance Normalization layers (AdaIN) to adaptively tune the statistics of feature maps for improved generalization across sites. FL experiments conducted on multi-contrast MRI datasets indicate the superiority of the proposed approach against prior FL-based translation methods.

2   Theory

2.1   MRI Translation with Adversarial Models

Conditional generative adversarial networks (cGANs) have emerged as a gold-standard for MRI contrast translation in recent years due to their exceptional recovery for high-frequency textural details in medical images [4,7,8,20]. cGANs perform adversarial learning via a pair of generator (G) and discriminator (D) subnetworks [8]. G predicts a synthetic target-contrast image $(\hat{x}_t)$ given as input an acquired source-contrast image (x_s), whereas the D tries to distinguish actual (x_t) and synthetic target-contrast images. To learn image translation, cGANs are typically trained to minimize an aggregate loss function composed of adversarial and pixel-wise terms:

$$\mathcal{L} = \mathbb{E}_{x_s,x_t}[-(D(x_s,x_t)-1)^2 - D(x_s,G(x_s))^2 + \lambda_{pix}||x_t - G(x_s)||_1], \quad (1)$$

where $\mathbb{E}$ denotes expectation, and λ_{pix} is the relative weighing term for the pixel-wise loss.

2.2   Specificity-Preserving Federated Learning of MRI Translation

Network Architecture. The proposed model is a conditional adversarial architecture that takes as input the source image along with site-specifying information (Fig. 1). The first component of the generator is a latent producing block (LPS) to form site-specific latents w^k given one-hot encoding of site index $v^k \in \mathbb{R}^K$:

$$w^k = LPS(v^k) \quad (2)$$

The generator architecture is inspired by the ResNet model [8,13] with a residual bottleneck between a convolutional encoder and a convolutional decoder. To mitigate heterogeneity reflected in the statistics of derived feature maps, an AdaIN layer is inserted after each convolutional layer in the encoder/decoder, and each residual block in the bottleneck. At the output of the ith layer of the generator, the mean and standard deviation of output feature maps $g_i \in \mathbb{R}^{F_i, H_i, W_i}$ are modulated. To do this, site-specific latents w^k are first transformed into scale and bias vectors $\gamma_i, \beta_i \in \mathbb{R}^{F_i}$:

$$\gamma_i = Q_i^\gamma w^k + b_i^\gamma; \quad \beta_i = Q_i^\beta w^k + b_i^\beta \quad (3)$$

where $Q_i^{\gamma,\beta} \in \mathbb{R}^{F_i, J}$ and $b_i^{\gamma,\beta} \in \mathbb{R}^{F_i}$ are learnable linear transformations. The AdaIN layer then modulates the first- and second-order statistics of each channel [14]:

$$g_i' = \text{AdaIN}(g_i, \gamma_i, \beta_i) = \begin{bmatrix} \gamma_i[1]\frac{g_i[1]-\mu(g_i[1])\mathbf{1}}{\sigma(g_j[1])} + \beta_i[1]\mathbf{1} \\ \gamma_i[2]\frac{g_i[2]-\mu(g_i[2])\mathbf{1}}{\sigma(g_j[2])} + \beta_i[2]\mathbf{1} \\ \vdots \end{bmatrix} \quad (4)$$

where $\mathbf{1} \in \mathbb{R}^{H_j, W_j}$ is a matrix of ones, μ, σ compute the mean and standard deviation of individual channels $g_i[j] \in \mathbb{R}^{H_i, W_i}$, and g_i' is the input to the next network layer $i+1$.

Algorithm 1: Training of SPFL-Trans

    Data: $\{\mathcal{D}^1, \cdots, \mathcal{D}^K\}$ from K sites
    Input: P: number of communication rounds
    $\alpha^1, \cdots, \alpha^K$: averaging weights for K sites
    G: global generator with parameters θ_G
    $D^1, \cdots, D^K$: local discriminators with $\theta_{D^1}, \cdots, \theta_{D^K}$
    $Opt()$: optimizer for parameter updates
    Output: θ_G^* Optimized global generator

1   Randomly initialize θ_G and $\theta_{D^1}, \cdots, \theta_{D^K}$
2   **for** $p = 1$ *to* P **do**
3   **for** $k = 1$ *to* K **do**
4   **for** *one epoch* **do**
5              $\theta_G^k \leftarrow \theta_G$ // Broadcast global generators to the sites
6   Calculate $\nabla_{\theta_G^k}\mathcal{L}^k(\mathcal{D}^k)$ and $\nabla_{\theta_D^k}\mathcal{L}^k(\mathcal{D}^k)$ based on Eq. 1
7              $\theta_G^k \leftarrow \theta_G^k - Opt(\nabla_{\theta_G^k}\mathcal{L}^k(\mathcal{D}^k)); \ \theta_D^k \leftarrow \theta_D^k - Opt(\nabla_{\theta_D^k}\mathcal{L}^k(\mathcal{D}^k))$

8      $\theta_G = \sum_{k=1}^K \alpha^k \theta_G^k,$ // Aggregate locally trained generators

---

Federated Training. To train SPFL-Trans, a decentralized learning procedure takes place for a total of P communication rounds between the FL server and individual sites (see Fig. 1, Algorithm 1) [25]. Throughout the procedure, generators are shared across sites, though discriminators are kept unshared for enhanced privacy preservation [12,28]. During local training, models are optimized on the training sets from individual sites according to the aggregate cGAN loss function as expressed in Eq. 1.

3 Methods

3.1 Datasets

Demonstrations were performed on four public datasets taken to represent four different sites in the FL framework: IXI (https://brain-development.org/ixi-dataset/), BRATS [1], MIDAS [6], and OASIS [19]. Multi-contrast brain MRI data including T_1- and T_2-weighted images were analyzed. A total of 53 healthy subjects were selected from the IXI dataset, and data were split into 25 training, 10 validation, 18 test subjects. A total of 55 glioma patients were selected from the BRATS dataset, and data were split into 25 training, 10 validation, 20 test subjects. A total of 66 healthy subjects were selected from the MIDAS dataset, and data were split into 48 training, 5 validation, 13 test subjects. Lastly, a total of 48 healthy subjects were selected from the OASIS dataset, and data were split into 22 training, 9 validation, 17 test subjects. In each subject, nearly 100 axial cross-sections centrally located within the volume were included.

Table 1. Performance of centralized and federated translation models in $T_1 \rightarrow T_2$ and $T_2 \rightarrow T_1$ tasks. Higher PSNR, SSIM scores and lower FID score indicate improved performance. Bold font indicates the top performing federated model for each task.

		IXI		BRATS		MIDAS		OASIS	
		$T_1 \rightarrow T_2$	$T_2 \rightarrow T_1$	$T_1 \rightarrow T_2$	$T_2 \rightarrow T_1$	$T_1 \rightarrow T_2$	$T_2 \rightarrow T_1$	$T_1 \rightarrow T_2$	$T_2 \rightarrow T_1$
Centralized	PSNR	28.6 ± 1.3	27.9 ± 1.1	26.1 ± 0.9	24.5 ± 1.9	28.1 ± 0.5	25.9 ± 1.2	25.2 ± 0.6	21.2 ± 0.8
	SSIM	94.3 ± 1.3	94.4 ± 1.2	93.0 ± 1.1	92.5 ± 1.1	91.9 ± 0.9	87.0 ± 2.1	83.7 ± 2.4	76.8 ± 1.9
	FID	7.4	27.3	24.9	14.2	9.7	11.9	18.1	18.6
SPFL-Trans	PSNR	$\mathbf{28.0\pm1.4}$	$\mathbf{27.6\pm1.0}$	$\mathbf{26.0\pm0.9}$	$\mathbf{24.7\pm1.6}$	$\mathbf{27.9\pm0.5}$	$\mathbf{26.0\pm1.1}$	$\mathbf{24.7\pm0.5}$	$\mathbf{20.9\pm0.7}$
	SSIM	$\mathbf{94.1\pm1.2}$	$\mathbf{94.1\pm1.2}$	$\mathbf{92.8\pm1.1}$	$\mathbf{92.5\pm1.0}$	$\mathbf{91.8\pm0.9}$	$\mathbf{86.4\pm2.1}$	$\mathbf{82.1\pm2.0}$	$\mathbf{75.0\pm2.6}$
	FID	$\mathbf{9.0}$	31.3	$\mathbf{26.8}$	16.9	$\mathbf{9.4}$	$\mathbf{11.1}$	32.0	24.5
FedGAN	PSNR	26.6 ± 1.1	26.4 ± 0.8	25.2 ± 1.2	22.9 ± 0.7	27.0 ± 0.5	24.6 ± 0.9	21.7 ± 0.5	20.8 ± 1.4
	SSIM	91.8 ± 1.7	92.8 ± 1.1	91.1 ± 1.3	88.8 ± 1.0	89.6 ± 1.4	81.5 ± 2.2	67.7 ± 3.5	74.3 ± 3.5
	FID	14.7	39.2	45.2	47.0	13.3	20.6	43.7	37.7
FedMRI	PSNR	27.5 ± 1.0	27.4 ± 1.1	25.7 ± 0.7	24.7 ± 1.2	27.6 ± 0.6	25.9 ± 1.2	23.6 ± 0.5	20.7 ± 1.0
	SSIM	93.6 ± 1.3	94.0 ± 1.2	92.6 ± 1.1	91.6 ± 0.9	91.3 ± 1.0	85.4 ± 2.1	80.6 ± 2.1	72.1 ± 2.6
	FID	11.2	35.6	34.9	19.4	12.2	12.3	33.2	27.2
FedMedGAN	PSNR	25.6 ± 1.2	24.9 ± 0.7	24.7 ± 1.2	20.9 ± 0.8	26.8 ± 0.5	22.5 ± 0.6	21.5 ± 0.4	20.5 ± 1.3
	SSIM	91.7 ± 1.8	91.6 ± 1.2	90.8 ± 1.3	86.5 ± 0.8	89.9 ± 0.9	82.3 ± 1.9	62.9 ± 3.8	72.6 ± 3.5
	FID	19.8	48.3	36.1	58.6	16.8	84.8	59.1	35.3

3.2 Competing Methods

We demonstrated the proposed approach against a centrally-trained translation model [8], and FL-based translation models including FedGAN [28], FedMRI [11] and FedMedGAN [37]. The centralized model and FedGAN was implemented with matching architecture to the proposed model, except for the AdaIN layers that were excluded. FedMRI was implemented with a U-Net backbone, where encoders were shared while decoders were kept site-specific as originally proposed in [11]. The loss function of the proposed model was adopted for fair comparison. FedMedGAN was implemented with a U-Net backbone as originally proposed in [37]. However, the loss function of the proposed model was used in FedMedGAN as opposed to cycle-consistency loss for fair comparison in the paired translation tasks reported here. FL-based models followed the same federated optimization procedure as the proposed approach. Hyperparameter selection was performed for each model in order to maximize the performance in the validation set. Shared generators across sites and site-specific local discriminators were adopted for all FL models considered here.

3.3 Experiments

SPFL-Trans was implemented with an *LPS* with 6 dense layers to produce latent variables. The encoder in the generator had three convolutional layers of kernel size $7, 3, 3$. The bottleneck contained 9 residual blocks of kernel size 3. The decoder had three convolutional layers of kernel size $3, 3, 7$. Discriminators for all competing methods were based on the PatchGAN architecture [16]. Network weights were learned via the Adam optimizer run at $\beta_1 = 0.5$ and $\beta_2 = 0.999$. Training was continued for $P = 150$ rounds. A fixed learning rate was selected as

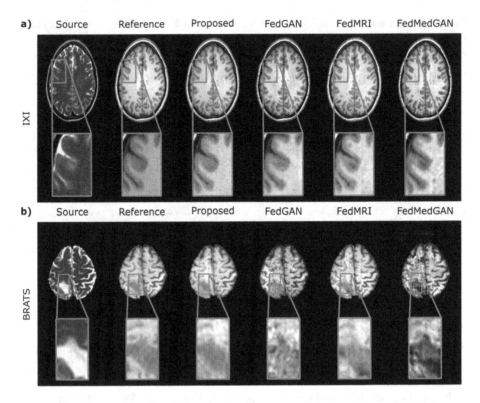

Fig. 2. Synthesized images in IXI and BRATS for the $T_2 \rightarrow T_1$ task. Results are shown for all competing methods, and they are displayed along with the source images and the reference target images.

0.0002 during the first 75 rounds, and it was linearly decayed to 0 during the last 75 rounds. The relative weight of the pixel-wise loss was selected as $\lambda_{pix} = 100$. Modeling was performed via Pytorch framework.

We considered learning two individual one-to-one translation tasks ($T_1 \rightarrow T_2$, $T_2 \rightarrow T_1$ where the mapping is denoted as *source* $\rightarrow$ *target*) in an FL setup with 4 sites. Translation performance was evaluated via PSNR, SSIM, and Fretchet Inception Distance (FID) metrics. PSNR and SSIM were measured between synthetic and reference target-contrast images for individual cross-sections, and averaged across the volume. Results were reported as mean and standard deviation across test subjects within each individual dataset.

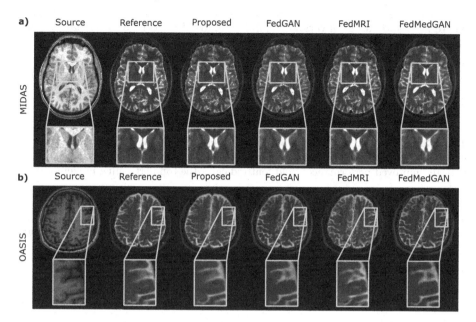

Fig. 3. Synthesized images in MIDAS and OASIS for the $T_1 \rightarrow T_2$ task. Results are shown for all competing methods, and they are displayed along with the source images and the reference target images.

4 Results

To demonstrate the effectiveness of the proposed approach in federated learning of multi-contrast MRI translation, we compared it against state-of-the-art FL-based translation models and a centrally-trained model as a performance baseline. Quantitative performance metrics for the competing methods in each dataset and in each task are listed in Table 1. The proposed approach yields the highest performance across tasks and across sites. On average, SPFL-Trans achieves 1.3 dB higher PSNR, 3.3 % higher SSIM, and 13.5 point lower FID over competing methods. Representative target images from all competing methods are shown in Fig. 3 for the $T_1 \rightarrow T_2$ task in MIDAS and OASIS datasets. Representative results are shown in Fig. 2 for the $T_2 \rightarrow T_1$ task in IXI and BRATS datasets. SPFL-Trans yields superior translation performance in regions where competing models have inaccurate tissue depiction, especially near gray matter and pathology. Overall, SPFL-Trans generates images with fewer artifacts and lower noise levels compared to baselines. These quantitative and qualitative assessments indicate that site-specific modulation of feature statistics in SPFL-Trans enhances translation performance compared to competing federated models.

We also conducted an ablation study to investigate the benefits of the statistical modulation mechanism achieved by AdaIN layers in federated learning of MRI synthesis. To do this, we compared SPFL-Trans with an ablated variant where LPS and AdaIN layers were jointly removed (w/o LPS and AdaIN) from the generator. Quantitative performance metrics for SPFL-Trans and w/o LPS and AdaIN models are listed in Table 2. The proposed method outperforms the ablated variant across all sites and tasks except for SSIM. These results signals the performance gain brought by the LPS subnetwork and AdaIN layers in SPFL-Trans.

Table 2. Performance of SPFL-Trans and a variant ablated of LPS and AdaIN layers in $T_1 \rightarrow T_2$ and $T_2 \rightarrow T_1$ tasks. Higher PSNR, SSIM scores and lower FID score indicate improved performance. Bold font indicates the top performing model for each task.

		IXI		BRATS		MIDAS		OASIS	
		$T_1 \rightarrow T_2$	$T_2 \rightarrow T_1$	$T_1 \rightarrow T_2$	$T_2 \rightarrow T_1$	$T_1 \rightarrow T_2$	$T_2 \rightarrow T_1$	$T_1 \rightarrow T_2$	$T_2 \rightarrow T_1$
SPFL-Trans	PSNR	**28.0±1.4**	**27.6 ± 1.0**	**26.0 ± 0.9**	**24.7 ± 1.6**	**27.9 ± 0.5**	**26.0 ± 1.1**	**24.7 ± 0.5**	**20.9 ± 0.7**
	SSIM	**94.1 ± 1.2**	**94.1 ± 1.2**	**92.8 ± 1.1**	**92.5 ± 1.0**	**91.6 ± 0.9**	**86.4 ± 2.1**	**82.1 ± 2.0**	75.0 ± 2.6
	FID	**9.0**	**31.3**	**26.8**	**16.9**	**9.4**	**11.1**	**32.0**	**24.5**
w.o. LPS and AdaIN	PSNR	26.4±1.2	26.5±0.8	25.6±0.9	23.2±0.9	27.1±0.4	24.3±0.8	22.0±0.5	20.8±1.3
	SSIM	90.9±2.1	93.1±1.3	90.1±1.6	89.5±0.9	89.6±1.3	80.9±2.4	65.3±3.9	**77.2 ± 3.0**
	FID	14.8	43.2	42.4	48.0	12.9	19.8	43.6	39.3

5 Discussion and Conclusion

Federated MRI translation involves multi-site imaging data collected under different settings, so it has to operate reliably under distributional heterogeneity [22]. In this context, the proposed approach offers a site specificity-preserving global MRI translation model for multi-institutional collaborations. Experiments on public multi-site brain MRI data demonstrate that SPFL-Trans offers competitive performance to a centralized baseline model, while significantly outperforming alternative federated baselines both visually and quantitatively. Our results suggest that SPFL-Trans can improve generalizability and flexibility in multi-site collaborations by enabling training on imaging data from diverse sites and protocols. Improved generalization against domain shifts in the distribution of MRI data renders SPFL-Trans a promising candidate for multi-site training of MRI contrast translation models. In the future, the proposed approach might also be adopted for cross-modal image translation tasks.

References

1. Bakas, S., et al.: Identifying the best machine learning algorithms for brain tumor segmentation, progression assessment, and overall survival prediction in the BRATS challenge. arXiv:1811.02629 (2019)
2. Bakas, S., et al.: Advancing the cancer genome atlas glioma MRI collections with expert segmentation labels and radiomic features. Sci. Data 4, 1–13 (2017)
3. Bdair, T., Navab, N., Albarqouni, S.: FedPerl: semi-supervised peer learning for skin lesion classification. In: de Bruijne, M., et al. (eds.) MICCAI 2021, Part III. LNCS, vol. 12903, pp. 336–346. Springer, Cham (2021). https://doi.org/10.1007/978-3-030-87199-4_32

4. Beers, A., et al.: High-resolution medical image synthesis using progressively grown generative adversarial networks. arXiv:1805.03144 (2018)

5. Bercea, C.I., Wiestler, B., Rueckert, D., Albarqouni, S.: FedDis: disentangled federated learning for unsupervised brain pathology segmentation (2021). https://doi.org/10.48550/ARXIV.2103.03705. https://arxiv.org/abs/2103.03705

6. Bullitt, E., et al.: Vessel tortuosity and brain tumor malignancy. Acad. Radiol. **12**, 1232–40 (2005). https://doi.org/10.1016/j.acra.2005.05.027

7. Dalmaz, O., Yurt, M., Çukur, T.: ResViT: residual vision transformers for multimodal medical image synthesis. IEEE Trans. Med. Imaging 1 (2022). https://doi.org/10.1109/TMI.2022.3167808

8. Dar, S.U., Yurt, M., Karacan, L., Erdem, A., Erdem, E., Çukur, T.: Image synthesis in multi-contrast MRI with conditional generative adversarial networks. IEEE Trans. Med. Imaging **38**(10), 2375–2388 (2019). https://doi.org/10.1109/TMI.2019.2901750

9. Dayan, I., et al.: Federated learning for predicting clinical outcomes in patients with COVID-19. Nat. Med. **27**, 1–9 (2021). https://doi.org/10.1038/s41591-021-01506-3

10. Elmas, G., et al.: Federated learning of generative image priors for MRI reconstruction. arXiv:2202.04175 (2022)

11. Feng, C.M., Yan, Y., Fu, H., Xu, Y., Shao, L.: Specificity-preserving federated learning for MR image reconstruction. arXiv:2112.05752 (2021)

12. Han, T., et al.: Breaking medical data sharing boundaries by using synthesized radiographs. Sci. Adv. **6**(49), eabb7973 (2020)

13. He, K., Zhang, X., Ren, S., Sun, J.: Deep residual learning for image recognition. In: Comput. Vis. Pattern Recognit, pp. 770–778 (2016)

14. Huang, X., Belongie, S.: Arbitrary style transfer in real-time with adaptive instance normalization. In: ICCV (2017)

15. Iglesias, J.E., Konukoglu, E., Zikic, D., Glocker, B., Van Leemput, K., Fischl, B.: Is synthesizing MRI contrast useful for inter-modality analysis? In: Medical Image Computing and Computer-Assisted Intervention, pp. 631–638 (2013)

16. Isola, P., Zhu, J.Y., Zhou, T., Efros, A.A.: Image-to-image translation with conditional adversarial networks. In: Computer Vision and Pattern Recognition, pp. 1125–1134 (2017)

17. Kaissis, G.A., Makowski, M.R., Rüeckert, D., Braren, R.F.: Secure, privacy-preserving and federated machine learning in medical imaging. Nat. Mach. Intell. **2**(6), 305–311 (2020)

18. Krupa, K., Bekiesińska-Figatowska, M.: Artifacts in magnetic resonance imaging **80**, 93–106 (2015)

19. LaMontagne, P.J., et al.: OASIS-3: longitudinal neuroimaging, clinical, and cognitive dataset for normal aging and Alzheimer disease. medRxiv (2019). https://doi.org/10.1101/2019.12.13.19014902. https://www.medrxiv.org/content/early/2019/12/15/2019.12.13.19014902

20. Lee, D., Kim, J., Moon, W.J., Ye, J.C.: CollaGAN: collaborative GAN for missing image data imputation. In: Computer Vision and Pattern Recognition, pp. 2487–2496 (2019)

21. Li, W., et al.: Privacy-preserving federated brain tumour segmentation. In: Suk, H.-I., Liu, M., Yan, P., Lian, C. (eds.) MLMI 2019. LNCS, vol. 11861, pp. 133–141. Springer, Cham (2019). https://doi.org/10.1007/978-3-030-32692-0_16

22. Li, X., Jiang, M., Zhang, X., Kamp, M., Dou, Q.: FedBN: federated learning on non-IID features via local batch normalization. In: International Conference on Learning Representations (2021). https://openreview.net/pdf?id=6YEQUn0QICG

23. Liu, Q., Chen, C., Qin, J., Dou, Q., Heng, P.: FedDG: federated domain generalization on medical image segmentation via episodic learning in continuous frequency space. In: CVPR, pp. 1013–1023 (2021)

24. McMahan, H.B., Moore, E., Ramage, D., Hampson, S., Arcas, B.A.: Communication-efficient learning of deep networks from decentralized data. In: AISTATS (2017)

25. McMahan, H.B., Moore, E., Ramage, D., Hampson, S., Arcas, B.A.: Communication-efficient learning of deep networks from decentralized data (2016)

26. Moraal, B., et al.: Multi-contrast, isotropic, single-slab 3D MR imaging in multiple sclerosis. Neuroradiol. J. **22**, 33–42 (2009)

27. Pati, S., et al.: The federated tumor segmentation (FeTS) challenge (2021). https://doi.org/10.48550/ARXIV.2105.05874. https://arxiv.org/abs/2105.05874

28. Rasouli, M., Sun, T., Rajagopal, R.: FedGAN: federated generative adversarial networks for distributed data. arXiv:2006.07228 (2020)

29. Rieke, N., et al.: The future of digital health with federated learning. NPJ Digit. Med. **3**(1), 119 (2020). https://doi.org/10.1038/s41746-020-00323-1

30. Roth, H.R., et al.: Federated learning for breast density classification: a real-world implementation. In: DART, DCL, pp. 181–191 (2020)

31. Roth, H.R., et al.: Federated whole prostate segmentation in MRI with personalized neural architectures. In: de Bruijne, M., et al. (eds.) MICCAI 2021. LNCS, vol. 12903, pp. 357–366. Springer, Cham (2021). https://doi.org/10.1007/978-3-030-87199-4_34

32. Sheller, M., et al.: Federated learning in medicine: facilitating multi-institutional collaborations without sharing patient data. Sci. Rep. **10** (2020). https://doi.org/10.1038/s41598-020-69250-1

33. Sheller, M.J., Reina, G.A., Edwards, B., Martin, J., Bakas, S.: multi-institutional deep learning modeling without sharing patient data: a feasibility study on brain tumor segmentation. In: Crimi, A., Bakas, S., Kuijf, H., Keyvan, F., Reyes, M., van Walsum, T. (eds.) BrainLes 2018. LNCS, vol. 11383, pp. 92–104. Springer, Cham (2019). https://doi.org/10.1007/978-3-030-11723-8_9

34. Thukral, B.: Problems and preferences in pediatric imaging **25**, 359–364 (2015)

35. Wang, J., et al.: A field guide to federated optimization (2021)

36. Wei, W., et al.: Fluid-attenuated inversion recovery MRI synthesis from multi-sequence MRI using three-dimensional fully convolutional networks for multiple sclerosis **6**(1), 014005 (2019)

37. Xie, G., et al.: FedMed-GAN: federated domain translation on unsupervised cross-modality brain image synthesis (2022)

38. Yang, D., et al.: Federated semi-supervised learning for COVID region segmentation in chest CT using multi-national data from China, Italy, Japan. Med. Image Anal. **70**, 101992 (2021). https://doi.org/10.1016/j.media.2021.101992. https://www.sciencedirect.com/science/article/pii/S1361841521000384

39. Yu, B., Zhou, L., Wang, L., Shi, Y., Fripp, J., Bourgeat, P.: Ea-GANs: edge-aware generative adversarial networks for cross-modality MR image synthesis. IEEE Trans. Med. Imaging **38**(7), 1750–1762 (2019). https://doi.org/10.1109/TMI.2019.2895894

40. Zhou, S., Landman, B.A., Huo, Y., Gokhale, A.: Communication-efficient federated learning for multi-institutional medical image classification. In: Deserno, T.M., Park, B.J. (eds.) Medical Imaging 2022: Imaging Informatics for Healthcare, Research, and Applications, vol. 12037, pp. 6–12. International Society for Optics and Photonics. SPIE (2022). https://doi.org/10.1117/12.2611654

Content-Aware Differential Privacy with Conditional Invertible Neural Networks

Malte Tölle[1,3,4(✉)], Ullrich Köthe[2,3], Florian André[1,3,4], Benjamin Meder[1,3,4], and Sandy Engelhardt[1,3,4]

[1] Department of Internal Medicine III, Heidelberg University Hospital, Heidelberg, Germany
`malte.toelle@med.uni-heidelberg.de`
[2] Visual Learning Lab, Ruprecht-Karls University Heidelberg, Heidelberg, Germany
[3] Informatics for Life Institute, Ruprecht-Karls University Heidelberg, Heidelberg, Germany
[4] DZHK (German Centre for Cardiovascular Research), Partner Site Heidelberg/Mannheim, Heidelberg, Germany

Abstract. Differential privacy (DP) has arisen as the gold standard in protecting an individual's privacy in datasets by adding calibrated noise to each data sample. While the application to categorical data is straightforward, its usability in the context of images has been limited. Contrary to categorical data the meaning of an image is inherent in the spatial correlation of neighboring pixels making the simple application of noise infeasible. Invertible Neural Networks (INN) have shown excellent generative performance while still providing the ability to quantify the exact likelihood. Their principle is based on transforming a complicated distribution into a simple one e.g. an image into a spherical Gaussian. We hypothesize that adding noise to the latent space of an INN can enable differentially private image modification. Manipulation of the latent space leads to a modified image while preserving important details. Further, by conditioning the INN on meta-data provided with the dataset we aim at leaving dimensions important for downstream tasks like classification untouched while altering other parts that potentially contain identifying information. We term our method *content-aware differential privacy* (CADP). We conduct experiments on publicly available benchmarking datasets as well as dedicated medical ones. In addition, we show the generalizability of our method to categorical data. The source code is publicly available at https://github.com/Cardio-AI/CADP.

Keywords: Differential Privacy · Invertible Neural Networks · Normalizing Flows

Supplementary Information The online version contains supplementary material available at https://doi.org/10.1007/978-3-031-18523-6_9.

1   Introduction

The predictive performances of algorithms especially neural networks are heavily dependent on the amount of data they are trained with. In contrast, privacy regulations aiming at hiding individual sensitive information hinder the application of machine learning tools on heterogeneous multi-center data. Since it is not our objective to argue about the benefits of these privacy regulations, we strive to find methods that allow publishing of sensitive data simultaneously to maintaining individual's privacy. While such methods are trivial to implement for categorical data (e.g. a data base with entries for sex, age, gender, etc.) complex data such as images pose a difficult objective. Contrary to categorical data images obtain their meaning by the spatial relationship of individual pixels. Perturbing pixels by adding random noise would not hinder a human or a machine observer from re-identifying the image's content; recognizing people by their face being the most obvious example. Older techniques rely on blurring or pixelation of people's faces, e.g. Google Street View [11].

Training of machine learning models with such samples would tremendously decrease their predictive performance because a great deal of features are lost in the process which the model never sees (see Fig. 1). This is of utmost importance in the medical domain as we must ensure the model learns on valid features for detecting pathologies.

We hypothesize that the tools of machine learning namely neural networks based on Normalizing Flows (NF) known as Invertible Neural Networks (INN) may be used to address the privacy issue when dealing with images and medical ones in particular [2]. Our contribution is three-fold:

- First, we provide mathematically grounded evidence that INNs provide a valuable tool to obtain ϵ-differentially private images that exhibit all features of natural images (e.g. sharpness or authenticity). ϵ quantifies the probability of data leakage, the lower ϵ the more privacy is guaranteed.

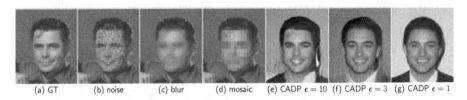

(a) GT   (b) noise   (c) blur   (d) mosaic   (e) CADP $\epsilon = 10$ (f) CADP $\epsilon = 3$ (g) CADP $\epsilon = 1$

Fig. 1. Example of face anonymization with Differential Privacy [17]. Compared to conventional approaches based on noise (a), blur (b), and mosaic (d) our content-aware approach (e)–(g) changes the identity of the image. For $\epsilon = 10$ (e) one can still see strong similarities between reconstruction and ground truth as e.g. the lock of hair on the forehead. For small ϵ the similarity decreases as desired to disable re-identification. However, if the subsequent task was to classify the eye color, this would still be possible with the CADP results from (e)-(g), since we can condition the transformation and therefore leave important aspects unaltered.

- Second, by conditioning our network on meta-data provided in conjunction with the dataset (e.g. pathologies) the INN is able to automatically extract dimensions most likely corresponding to classifying those meta variables. We assume these features merit attention for downstream tasks and, thus, should be modified as little as possible self-evident within the bounds of desired privacy. We term this method *Content-Aware DP* (CADP).
- Third, we show the generalizability of our method not just to images but also to categorical data making it a universal tool for obtaining differentially private data.

We focus on the task of protecting images in particular, or data in general in any context, detached from their intended usage.

2   Related Work

Differentially Private Invertible Neural Networks. In general each learning based algorithm can be trained in a privacy preserving fashion by using differentially private stochastic gradient descent (DP-SGD) [1]. DP-SGD achieves differentially private model training by clipping the per-sample gradient and adding calibrated Gaussian noise proportional to the desired level of privacy. Therefore, DP-SGD tweaks the model parameters instead of the input to obtain privacy by e.g. ensuring no inputs might be reconstructed from the model parameters [23].

One can distinguish between input-, output-, and algorithm-perturbation to achieve DP. When the output of the algorithm or the algorithm itself is perturbed as e.g. in DP-SGD the analysis is performed on the non-private data, where one has to be concerned about the composition property (ϵ degrades over multiple analyses of the dataset). Further, since one cannot release the data the possibilities for analysis are limited. We circumvent above mentioned limitations by performing input-perturbation and use the robustness of DP against post-processing (any further processing of differential private data retains privacy guarantees).

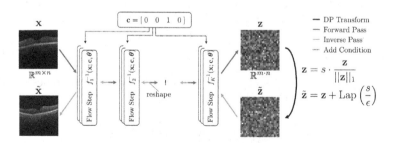

Fig. 2. Content-aware differential privacy (CADP) pipeline. After training the INN to convergence we feed each sample $\mathbf{x}$ with the corresponding condition $\mathbf{c}(\mathbf{y})$ to obtain our latent representation $\mathbf{z}$. After clipping its L_1-norm to the desired sensitivity s, Laplacian distributed noise $\mathrm{Lap}(0, s/\epsilon)$ is added to obtain ϵ-DP. The perturbed $\tilde{\mathbf{z}}$ is fed in reverse to obtain the differentially private image $\tilde{\mathbf{x}}$.

Obviously, INNs can be trained with DP-SGD as well [24]. However, after training one can only use the INN in a generative manner by sampling the latent space $z \sim \mathcal{N}(0; I)$ and obtain data samples that have no relation to in reality occuring data samples and are therefore artificial. Thus, it does not allow for perturbation of the real data samples intended to be published or used for model training. Even worse, using artificial data is also not completely secure against attacks [4] and may even lead to wrong pathologies in generated images [5,15].

Differential Privacy for Images. The most prominent application in the literature about differentially private images deals with faces, as this is the most vivid example. Older approaches rely on pixeling, blurring, obfuscation, or inpainting [10], but this has been proven as ineffective against deep learning based recognizers [18,19]. Another promising path is the generation of fully artificial data with e.g. Generative Adversarial Networks (GAN) with the known drawbacks mentioned above [6,21,24,25]. Ziller et al. claimed to having applied DP to medical images. [27]. However, their approach also only involves training a conventional CNN on medical images with DP-SGD. We take a different path and *alter the content of the input image* in a private manner as we want to preserve as much information as possible and only alter dimensions that are not identification related. To the best of our knowledge DP has never been applied *directly to the content of medical images* before.

3   Methods

3.1   (Conditional) Invertible Neural Networks

INNs deal with the approximation of a complex, unobservable distribution $p(x)$ by a simpler tractable prior $q(z)$, usually a spherical multivariate Gaussian. Let $\mathcal{X} = \{x^{(1)}, ..., x^{(n)}\}$ be n observed i.i.d. samples from $p(x)$. The objective is to approximate $p(x)$ via a model f_θ consisting of a series of K bijective functions $f_\theta = f_1 \odot ... \odot f_K$ parameterized fully by θ transforming $q(z) = \mathcal{N}(0; I)$ into $p(x)$ and vice versa $(f_\theta(x) = z \longleftrightarrow f_\theta^{-1}(z) = x)$.

Such a model can efficiently be used in a generative manner to sample $x \sim p$ by first sampling $z \sim \mathcal{N}(0; I)$ and subsequently transforming the sample as $x = f_\theta(z)$.

Since f_θ exhibits invertibility, exact likelihood evaluation becomes tractable by utilizing the change of variables formula [7,8].

$$\log p(x) = \log q\left(f_\theta^{-1}(z)\right) + \log \left| \det \left(\frac{\partial f_\theta^{-1}(z)}{\partial x} \right) \right| \tag{1}$$

An isotropic Gaussian is usually chosen as prior. Since its covariance matrix is diagonal, components are independent. With INNs sharp image details can be obtained, while simultaneously allowing to modify independent components of the image in latent space [14].

We build on the foundations laid by Ardizzone et al., who incorporated conditions by e.g. concatenation of class labels to the input [3]. This enables the INN to implicitly learn the meta-data dependent distribution in latent space. In the reverse pass we provide the label we would like to obtain, e.g. a pathology, and the INN generates an altered version of the original image that still exhibits the desired pathology $(f_\theta(\mathbf{x}, \mathbf{c}) = \mathbf{z} \longleftrightarrow f_\theta^{-1}(\mathbf{z}, \mathbf{c}) = \mathbf{x})$.

3.2   Content-Aware Differential Privacy

Being termed the gold standard in obscuring data sample sensitive information, DP provides a mathematically grounded, quantifiable measure of leaked information while simultaneously being applicable in a simple manner [26]. From a high-level perspective it guarantees that changing one value in the database ($\mathcal{X}$ and $\mathcal{X}'$) will have only a small effect on the model prediction [9].

$$Pr\left[\mathcal{M}(\mathcal{X}) \in \mathcal{S}\right] \leq \exp(\epsilon) Pr\left[\mathcal{M}(\mathcal{X}') \in \mathcal{S}\right], \tag{2}$$

where $\mathcal{M}$ denotes a randomized mechanism and $\mathcal{S}$ all sets of outputs. The closer the two probabilities are, the less information is leaked (small ϵ). DP is usually obtained by perturbing data with calibrated noise proportional to the function's f (L_1-norm) sensitivity on dataset $\mathcal{X}$, which is the maximum change in the function's value by changing one data point. To achieve pure ϵ-DP the Laplace mechanism is commonly used.

$$s = \max_{\mathcal{X}, \mathcal{X}'} \|f(\mathcal{X}) - f(\mathcal{X}')\|_1 , \quad (3) \qquad \mathcal{M}(\mathcal{X}) = f(\mathcal{X}) + \text{Lap}\left(\frac{s}{\epsilon}\right) . \quad (4)$$

After training an INN to convergence i.e. $f_\theta(\mathcal{X}, \mathcal{C}) \sim \mathcal{N}(\mathbf{0}, \mathbf{I})$, each image and label $(\mathbf{x}_i, \mathbf{y}_i) \in \mathcal{X}$ with corresponding condition $\mathbf{c}_i(\mathbf{y}_i)$ is forwarded through the network (see Fig. 2). The resulting latent space $f_\theta(\mathbf{x}_i, \mathbf{c}_i(\mathbf{y}_i)) = \mathbf{z}_i$ is modified in a differentially private manner by sampling from a Laplace distribution with standard deviation determined by the sensitivity s and the desired ϵ. We clip our sensitivity by dividing each $\mathbf{z}_i$ by its L_1-norm (Algorithm 1) [1]. Since $\mathcal{Z}$ is learned to be an isotropic Gaussian each component is independent and can, thus, be modified individually. INNs can trivially be expanded to be trained on categorical data as well, making our method a general technique for applying DP on data.

Theorem 1 (ϵ-Content-Aware-DP Mechanism). *For an image* $\mathbf{x} \in \mathcal{X}$ *there exists a mechanism* $\mathcal{M}_{\text{CA}}$ *that maps* $\mathbf{x}$ *to its differentially private counterpart* $\tilde{\mathbf{x}} \in \mathcal{X}$. *We say* $\mathcal{M}_{\text{CA}}$ *satisfies* ϵ-DP, *if and only if for all* $\mathbf{x}, \mathbf{x}' \in \mathcal{X}$

$$\mathcal{M}_{\text{CA}} = f_\theta^{-1}\left[f_\theta(\mathbf{x}) + (l_1, ..., l_k)\right] = f_\theta^{-1}\left[\mathbf{z} + (l_1, ..., l_k)\right] = f_\theta^{-1}\left[\tilde{\mathbf{z}}\right] , \tag{5}$$

where f_θ *denotes a function that maps* $\mathbf{x}$ *to a latent vector* $\mathbf{z} \in \mathcal{Z}$ *and by reverse pass* f_θ^{-1} *maps* $\mathbf{z}$ *to* $\mathbf{x}$. $\tilde{\mathbf{z}} = \mathbf{z} + (l_1, ..., l_k)$ *denotes the* ϵ-DP *perturbed version of* $\mathbf{z}$ *with* l_i *i.i.d. random variables drawn from* $\text{Lap}(s/\epsilon)$.

Proof. Let $\mathbf{x} \in \mathcal{R}^{|\mathcal{X}|}$ and $\mathbf{x}' \in \mathcal{R}^{|\mathcal{X}|}$ be such that $||\mathbf{x} - \mathbf{x}'||_1 \leq 1$, and $g(\mathbf{x}) = f_\theta^{-1}(f_\theta(\mathbf{x}))$ be some function $g : \mathcal{R}^{|\mathcal{X}|} \to \mathcal{R}^{|\mathcal{Z}|} \to \mathcal{R}^{|\mathcal{X}|}$. We only consider functions that are volume preserving meaning their Jacobian determinant is equal to one ($|\det(\partial f_\theta(\mathbf{x})/\partial \mathbf{z})| = 1$). Let $p_\mathbf{x}$ denote the probability density function of $\mathcal{M}_{CA}(\mathbf{x}, g, \epsilon)$, and $p_{\mathbf{x}'}$ of $\mathcal{M}_{CA}(\mathbf{x}', g, \epsilon)$. We assume the distance between points is similar in $\mathcal{X}$ and $\mathcal{Z}$ as shown by [14]. We compare the two at some arbitrary point $\mathbf{t} \in \mathcal{R}^{|\mathcal{Z}|}$

$$
\begin{aligned}
\frac{p_\mathbf{x}(\mathbf{t})}{p_{\mathbf{x}'}(\mathbf{t})} &= \prod_{i=1}^{k} \left(\frac{\exp\left(-\frac{\epsilon}{s}|g(\mathbf{x}) - f_\theta^{-1}(\mathbf{t})|\right)}{\exp\left(-\frac{\epsilon}{s}|g(\mathbf{x}') - f_\theta^{-1}(\mathbf{t})|\right)} \right) = \prod_{i=1}^{k} \left(\frac{\exp\left(-\frac{\epsilon}{s}|f_\theta^{-1}(f_\theta(\mathbf{x}) - \mathbf{t})|\right)}{\exp\left(-\frac{\epsilon}{s}|f_\theta^{-1}(f_\theta(\mathbf{x}') - \mathbf{t})|\right)} \right) \\
&= \prod_{i=1}^{k} \left(\exp -\frac{\epsilon}{s}|f_\theta^{-1}(\mathbf{z}_\mathbf{x} - \mathbf{t}) - f_\theta^{-1}(\mathbf{z}_{\mathbf{x}'} - \mathbf{t})| \right) \\
&= \prod_{i=1}^{k} \left(\exp -\frac{\epsilon}{s}|f_\theta^{-1}(\mathbf{z}_\mathbf{x} - \mathbf{z}_{\mathbf{x}'})| \right) \\
&\leq \prod_{i=1}^{k} \exp\left(-\frac{\epsilon|\mathbf{z}_\mathbf{x} - \mathbf{z}_{\mathbf{x}'}|}{s} \right) = \exp\left(\frac{\epsilon||\mathbf{z}_\mathbf{x} - \mathbf{z}_{\mathbf{x}'}||_1}{s} \right) \\
&\leq \exp(\epsilon),
\end{aligned}
\tag{6}
$$

where the first inequality follows from the triangle inequality, and the last follows from the definition of sensitivity and $||\mathbf{x} - \mathbf{x}'||_1 \leq 1$. $\frac{p_\mathbf{x}(\mathbf{t})}{p_{\mathbf{x}'}(\mathbf{t})} \geq \exp(-\epsilon)$ follows by symmetry.

4   Experiments

We apply our approach for content-aware differential privacy to several publicly available datasets to showcase its generalizability. In each case we first train the INN on the training partition and subsequently train a classifier on the differentially private data. Note that our goal is not to reach as high as possible predictive performance but to close the gap between original and differentially private training. To exemplify the principle of content-aware DP we use the MNIST dataset, since the effect of transformations in latent space is obvious [16]. Next, we use two dedicated medical datasets, the first being a collection of retinal optical coherence tomography (OCT) scans with four classes (choroidal neovascularization (CNV), diabetic macular edema (DME), drusen, and healthy) [12] and the second being a series of chest x-ray scans with healthy and pneumonic patients [12], which contain more complicated and indistinct transformations.

Since most works in adding privacy to images deal with the prototype example of identifiability of faces, we also apply our approach to the CelebA Faces dataset (see Fig. 1) [17]. After having investigated our method on image data, we expand it to categorical data i.e. diabetes dataset from scikit-learn [20].

For each dataset we train a separete INN with convolutional subnetworks, with depth (number of downsampling operations) dependent on the image resolution. We chose $d = 2$ for MNIST (28×28), $d = 4$ for OCT and chest x-ray

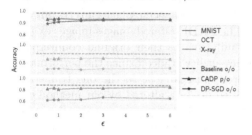

Fig. 3. Differentially private reconstruction of MNIST with different ϵ and $s = \epsilon/2$.

Fig. 4. Accuracy of classifier on different datasets with different ϵ and $s = \min(\epsilon/2, 4)$. Further, we trained the same model with DP-SGD [1]. Training/testing is performed on either original (o) or CADP altered (p) data.

Algorithm 1. CADP

Require: Samples from training set $\mathcal{X} = \{(\mathbf{x}_1, \mathbf{y}_1), ..., (\mathbf{x}_N, \mathbf{y}_N)\}$ with corresponding conditions $\mathcal{C} = \{\mathbf{c}_1(\mathbf{y}_1), ..., \mathbf{c}_N(\mathbf{y}_N)\}$, INN f_θ trained to convergence s.t. $f_\theta(\mathcal{X}) = \mathcal{Z} \sim \mathcal{N}(\mathbf{0}, \mathbf{I})$, sensitivity s, epsilon ϵ

for $(\mathbf{x}_i, \mathbf{y}_i) \in \mathcal{X}$ and $\mathbf{c}_i(\mathbf{y}_i) \in \mathcal{C}$ **do**

    Forward pass
    $\mathbf{z}_i \leftarrow f_\theta(\mathbf{x}_i, \mathbf{c}_i(\mathbf{y}_i))$
    Clip norm of $\mathbf{z}_i$
    $\mathbf{z}_i \leftarrow s \cdot \frac{\mathbf{z}_i}{\|\mathbf{z}_i\|_1}$
    Add calibrated noise
    $\tilde{\mathbf{z}}_i \leftarrow \mathbf{z}_i + \mathrm{Lap}\left(\frac{s}{\epsilon}\right)$
    Reverse Pass
    $\tilde{\mathbf{x}}_i \leftarrow f_\theta^{-1}(\tilde{\mathbf{x}}_i, \mathbf{c}_i(\mathbf{y}_i))$

end for

Output:
    $\tilde{\mathcal{X}} = \{(\tilde{\mathbf{x}}_1, \mathbf{y}_1), ..., (\tilde{\mathbf{x}}_N, \mathbf{y}_N)\}$

(128×128), and $d = 6$ for CelebA $(3 \times 128 \times 128)$. As coupling block we use the volume preserving GIN (general incompressible-flow) [22] for MNIST and diabetes data, and Glow (generative flow) [14] for the other, more complicated datasets. After having trained an INN to convergence we train a classifier with convolutional blocks and two linear layers on the differentially private data. Testing is performed on original data to investigate the amount of true features the model learns. We believe that the performance of the classifier acts as an implicit benchmark to make sure the INN not only reconstructs conditional noise. It is common practice for all works dealing with DP algorithms to be compared to the non-private benchmark. The goal must be to close the still existing gap to incentivize differentially private training by eliminating all its shortcomings. For comparison we also train the same classifier with DP-SGD, the current gold standard [1]. All experiments were performed on a NVIDIA Titan RTX.

5   Results

The results are presented in a two-fold manner. We first show the differentially private adjusted images per class for each dataset with different levels of ϵ. Second, we show the reached accuracy of the classifier on the original, not-CADP altered test data chunk when trained on the original, on the CADP altered dataset, or with DP-SGD.

MNIST. Even for small ϵ our approach generates visually appealing results that are indistinguishable from real digits but exhibit a large difference from the original (see Fig. 3). Attributes being altered are line thickness (e.g. 6), slant (e.g. 1), and even style (e.g. 2). For $\epsilon = 0.2$ a classifier trained on CADP-altered data outperforms the commonly accepted DP-SGD, CADP reaches 92.94% accuracy while DP-SGD only results in 89.24% (c.f. Fig. 4). The gap closes for larger ϵ.

Retinal OCT and Chest X-ray. In retinal OCTs the perturbations are rather subtle and difficult to interpret for a human observer or a non-expert. Identification related attributes like retinal detachments in specific places are (re-)moved impeding de-identification (see Fig. 5). The CADP-altered images images exhibit transformations resulting in large dissimilarites to their original counterpart. However, CADP induces a smaller privacy-utility tradeoff since the performance of the classifier trained on CADP altered data is close to the one trained on original data (Fig. 4). The classifier trained on data altered by our method outperforms the one trained with DP-SGD by 23.63% on average across all ϵ on the OCT test dataset and by 16.52% on the chest X-ray test dataset. We attribute this to the content-awareness of our method, which leaves dimensions corresponding to conditions, i.e. pathologies, unaltered. This is desirable in settings, where one trains a model on private data of another location, e.g. a hospital, and applies it to its own in-house samples.

Categorical Data. INNs can also generate differentially private categorical data as can be seen in Fig. 6 for the diabetes dataset from `scikit-learn` [20]. The data distributions are kept similar but are still altered equipping each data sample with plausible deniability. To obtain the binary feature of sex, we condition the INN on this feature; the others are learned in an unsupervised fashion.

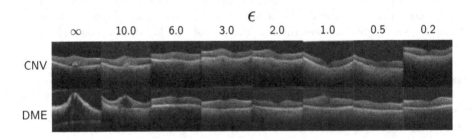

Fig. 5. Content-aware differentially private images from OCT dataset with different ϵ for classes *CNV* and *DME* [12]. The sensitivity is set to $\min(\epsilon/2, 4)$. For high ϵ (e.g. 10) the reconstructed retinal OCT still share similarities as in Fig. 1. For smaller ϵ qualitatively the images look different from their original counterpart. However, the classifier (Fig. 4) still performs well acting as an implicit control of the preserved features.

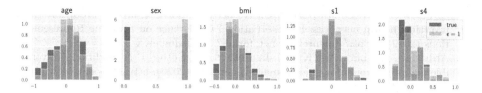

Fig. 6. Content-aware differentially private data from diabetes dataset from `scikit-learn` with $\epsilon = 1$ and sensitivity $s = 1$ [20]. With conditions the INN is able to reconstruct the approximate distributions even if binary distributed.

6 Discussion and Conclusion

We introduced a new method to achieve differentially private images based on invertible neural networks, which we term CADP (content-aware differential privacy). We applied the method to medical images and ensured the identity i.e. pathology of the patient is not changed by conditioning the INN on the class labels. We could show that in three experiments on diverse medical data (images of digits, OCT, and X-ray scans), the subsequent classifiers outperformed conventional approaches by a margin when fed with CADP-generated data. By this we reduce the risk for false diagnosis and increase the safety of patients against wrong diagnoses while providing provable and mathematically grounded privacy guarantees. Hence, CADP pre-processed datasets may be used to increase anonymity of medical image data in the future. However, the level of required anonymity should be decided depending on the individual use case.

Even for small $\epsilon < 1.0$ our method generates visually appealing results that can be used to train a classifier outperforming DP-SGD with the same privacy guarantees. However, clipping of the latent space discards information for reconstruction. In future work, it can be investigated how much information is lost to assure privacy. Further, an in-depth exploration of the latent space can be conducted.

Acknowledgements. This research was supported by grants from the Klaus Tschira Foundation within the Informatics for Life framework, by the DZHK (German Centre for Cardiovascular Research), and by the BMBF (German Ministry of Education and Research). The authors gratefully acknowledge the data storage service SDS@hd supported by the Ministry of Science, Research and the Arts Baden-Württemberg (MWK) and the German Research Foundation (DFG) through grant INST 35/1314-1 FUGG and INST 35/1503-1 FUGG.

References

1. Abadi, M., et al.: Deep learning with differential privacy. In: Proceedings of the 2016 ACM SIGSAC Conference on Computer and Communications Security (2016). https://doi.org/10.1145/2976749.2978318

2. Ardizzone, L., Kruse, J., Rother, C., Köthe, U.: Analyzing inverse problems with invertible neural networks. In: International Conference on Learning Representations (2019). https://openreview.net/forum?id=rJed6j0cKX
3. Ardizzone, L., Lüth, C., Kruse, J., Rother, C., Köthe, U.: Conditional invertible neural networks for guided image generation (2020). https://openreview.net/forum?id=SyxC9TEtPH
4. Bellovin, S., Dutta, P., Reitlinger, N.: Privacy and synthetic datasets. Stan. Technol. Law Rev. (2018)
5. Bhadra, S., Kelkar, V.A., Brooks, F.J., Anastasio, M.A.: On hallucinations in tomographic image reconstruction. IEEE Trans. Med. Imaging **40**, 3249–3260 (2021)
6. Bissoto, A., Perez, F., Valle, E., Avila, S.: Skin lesion synthesis with generative adversarial networks. In: OR 2.0 Context-Aware Operating Theaters, Computer Assisted Robotic Endoscopy, Clinical Image-Based Procedures, and Skin Image Analysis, pp. 294–302 (2018)
7. Dinh, L., Krueger, D., Bengio, Y.: Nice: non-linear independent components estimation. In: International Conference on Learning Representations (2015)
8. Dinh, L., Sohl-Dickstein, J., Bengio, S.: Density estimation using real NVP. In: International Conference on Learning Representations (2017). https://openreview.net/forum?id=HkpbnH9lx
9. Dwork, C., Roth, A.: Medical imaging deep learning with differential privacy. Sci. Rep. **11**, 1–8 (2021). https://doi.org/10.1038/s41598-021-93030-0
10. Fan, L.: Image pixelization with differential privacy. In: DBSec (2018)
11. Frome, A., et al.: Large-scale privacy protection in google street view. In: International Conference on Computer Vision, pp. 2373–2380 (2009). https://doi.org/10.1109/ICCV.2009.5459413
12. Kermany, D., Zhang, K., Goldbaum, M.: Large dataset of labeled optical coherence tomography (OCT) and chest X-ray images. Cell (2018). https://doi.org/10.17632/rscbjbr9sj.3
13. Kingma, D.P., Ba, J.: Adam: a method for stochastic optimization. In: International Conference of Learning Representations (2015)
14. Kingma, D.P., Dhariwal, P.: Glow: generative flow with invertible 1×1 convolutions. In: Advances in Neural Information Processing Systems, vol. 31 (2018)
15. Laves, M.H., Tölle, M., Ortmaier, T.: Uncertainty estimation in medical image denoising with Bayesian deep image prior. In: Uncertainty for Safe Utilization of Machine Learning in Medical Imaging, and Graphs in Biomedical Image Analysis, pp. 81–96 (2020)
16. LeCun, Y., Cortes, C., Burges, C.: MNIST handwritten digit database. ATT Labs, vol. 2 (2010). https://yann.lecun.com/exdb/mnist
17. Liu, Z., Luo, P., Wang, X., Tang, X.: Deep learning face attributes in the wild. In: International Conference on Computer Vision (ICCV), December 2015
18. McPherson, R., Shokri, R., Shmatikov, V.: Defeating image obfuscation with deep learning (2016)
19. Oh, S.J., Benenson, R., Fritz, M., Schiele, B.: Faceless person recognition: privacy implications in social media. In: Leibe, B., Matas, J., Sebe, N., Welling, M. (eds.) ECCV 2016. LNCS, vol. 9907, pp. 19–35. Springer, Cham (2016). https://doi.org/10.1007/978-3-319-46487-9_2
20. Pedregosa, F., et al.: Scikit-learn: machine learning in Python. J. Mach. Learn. Res. **12**, 2825–2830 (2011)
21. Schütte, A.D., et al.: Overcoming barriers to data sharing with medical image generation: a comprehensive evaluation. NPJ Digit. Med. **4**, 1–14 (2021). https://doi.org/10.1038/s41746-021-00507-3

22. Sorrenson, P., Rother, C., Köthe, U.: Disentanglement by nonlinear ICA with general incompressible-flow networks (GIN). In: International Conference on Learning Representations (2020). https://openreview.net/forum?id=rygeHgSFDH
23. Usynin, D., et al.: Adversarial interference and its mitigations in privacy-preserving collaborative machine learning. Nat. Mach. Intell. **3**(9), 749–758 (2021). https://doi.org/10.1038/s42256-021-00390-3
24. Waites, C., Cummings, R.: Differentially private normalizing flows for privacy-preserving density estimation. In: AAAI/ACM Conference on AI, Ethics, and Society (2021)
25. Yoon, J., Jordon, J., van der Schaar, M.: PATE-GAN: generating synthetic data with differential privacy guarantees. In: International Conference on Learning Representations (2019). https://openreview.net/forum?id=S1zk9iRqF7
26. Ziller, A., Usynin, D., Braren, R., Makowski, M., Rueckert, D., Kaissis, G.: The algorithmic foundations of differential privacy. Found. Trends Theor. Comput. Sci. **9**, 211–407 (2014). https://doi.org/10.1561/0400000042
27. Ziller, A., Usynin, D., Braren, R., Makowski, M., Rueckert, D., Kaissis, G.: Medical imaging deep learning with differential privacy. Sci. Rep. **11**(1), 1–8 (2021). https://doi.org/10.1038/s41598-021-93030-0

DeMed: A Novel and Efficient Decentralized Learning Framework for Medical Images Classification on Blockchain

Garima Aggarwal[1], Chun-Yin Huang[1], Di Fan[2], Xiaoxiao Li[1],
and Zehua Wang[1(✉)]

[1] University of British Columbia, Vancouver, Canada
{xiaoxiao.li,zwang}@ece.ubc.ca
[2] University of South California, Los Angeles, CA, USA

Abstract. Training predictive models with decentralized medical data can boost the healthcare research and is important for healthcare applications. Although the federated learning (FL) was proposed to build the predictive models, how to improve the security and robustness of a learning system to resist the accidental or malicious modification of data records are still the open questions. In this paper, we describe DeMed, a privacy-preserving decentralized medical image analysis framework empowered by blockchain technology. While blockchain is limited in serial computing, the decentralized data interaction in blockchain is very desired to preserve the data privacy when training models. To adapt blockchain in medical image analysis, our framework consists of the self-supervised learning part running on users' local devices and the smart contract part running on blockchain. The prior is to obtain the provable linearly separable low-dimensional representations of local medical images and the latter is to obtain the classifier by synthetically absorbing users' self-supervised learning results. The proposed DeMed is validated on two independent medical image classification tasks on pathological data and chest X-ray. Our work provides an open platform and arena for FL, where everyone can deploy a smart contract to attract contributors for medical image classification in a secure and decentralized manner while preserving the privacy in medical images.

Keywords: Blockchain · Federated learning · Self-supervised learning

1 Introduction

Machine learning (ML) models have shown their advantage in many different tasks in healthcare filed. The medical image analysis is one of the most important applications. To effectively train a high-quality deep learning model, the

---

G. Aggarwal and C.-Y. Huang—These authors contributed equally to this work.

S. Albarqouni et al. (Eds.): DeCaF 2022/FAIR 2022, LNCS 13573, pp. 100–109, 2022.
https://doi.org/10.1007/978-3-031-18523-6_10

aggregation of a significant amount of patient information is required. Multi-institutional healthcare predictive model can accelerate research and facilitate quality improvement on patient-care by leveraging different data sources and learning a model from data originated from the other institutions. However, improper data disclosure could place sensitive personal health information at risk. In addition, regulations such as GDPR [22] and HIPPA [8] strictly require protecting user information and granting transparent authorizations for the use of healthcare data.

Although federated learning [19] (FL) can be a solution to training ML models in a multi-party setting without data sharing, the users in FL still must share other forms of sensitive information (*e.g.*, model gradients or weights) to a *centralized service*. Such sharing is problematic when the central third party is not trustworthy, as prior work has demonstrated that adversaries can attack the model or data by the poisoning attack [26] and inversion attack [28] through observation of the target's shared model updates in the central server.

The blockchain [20] has emerged as a more appropriate system to facilitate private, verifiable, crowd-sourced decentralized computation, which is based on peer-to-peer networking and coordination while maintaining confidentiality without the need for a central coordinator, thereby going beyond FL. In a blockchain system, the data records are not saved in a centralized data server but maintained by network peers with consecutive data blocks. Further, the blockchain system provides an open platform and arena for FL, which enables sharing ML models among all parties without an intermediary. With blockchain and smart contact (SC), it is not the privilege of the big institutes to propose and train the learning models, but everyone can deploy a SC to attract contributors for medical image classification in a decentralized manner. However, there are inevitable obstacles to launching deep learning (DL)-based FL on the blockchain. First, latency and capacity are two fundamental elements that limit the throughput on blockchain. For example, on the Ethereum blockchain, the cost necessary to perform a transaction on the network is known as 'gas cost'. Transmission of DL models with hundreds of thousands of parameters hampers their practical utility. Second, without a central controller, if something goes wrong in a model training, *i.e.*, receiving weights from malicious users, we don't have a clear idea of how to identify the problem and correct it.

To overcome the aforementioned limitations, we propose `DeMed`, which is a framework for decentralized medical image analysis. It can reduce the input dimension of medical data to the point where the features are provably separable using a simple linear classifier. To this end, we first leverage the state-of-the-art reconstruction-based self-supervised learning (SSL) method, MAE [14], for low-dimensional representation learning. We then propose a *lightweight yet reliable* metric to select high quality users. Furthermore, we write a SC [9] using Solidity [6] for model parameter transmission. We tested the system on microscopic and X-Ray image classification tasks [21,23], and achieve comparable performance with Swarm Learning [24] and Centralized Learning, while protecting the model from users that may degrade the model. The comparison between the learning strategies are given in Fig. 1(a).

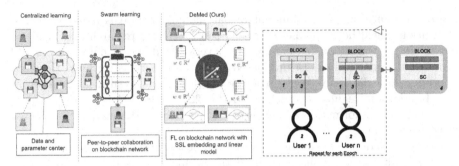

(a) Comparison between learning strategies.   (b) Blockchain module in DeMed

Fig. 1. (a) Comparison with different learning strategy. For centralized learning, a center collects data and be in charge of training the model. For swarm learning, users under SC keep their own data and train the model in peer-to-peer communications. For DeMed, users keep their data, train their own local model, and upload the weights to blockchain. The strategy is similar to federated learning, but the weights are aggregated and protected inside SC. (b) Four steps in the blockchain module of DeMed: i) every global epoch, users download same weights from the SC (blue). ii) Each user trains these weights locally with their respective data and iii) uploads them to the SC (grey). iv) Weights are aggregated after the epoch and original weights are updated to the new aggregated weights, to be used in the next epoch. (Color figure online)

2   Preliminary

2.1   Blockchain

A blockchain system [1] is a decentralized data processing and maintaining system built on top of the peer-to-peer computer networks. Each peer in blockchain saves the data in the bundles (*i.e.*, blocks) which are chained up in chronological order. All the data records in the chain of blocks, so called *blockchain*, are maintained by each peer individually. Having one peer with its local data copy tampered does not affect the global data records, which makes the blockchain system be resistance to tampering. Another attractive feature in blockchain is no single point of failure, when comparing with the traditional database system. Every peer in the peer-to-peer network can provide the data access service to the public. Besides, the evolution history of the data records are fully traceable. Indeed, the data records in the chain of blocks are no more than the state transition events which are called *transactions* in blockchain [2,3].

There are several works utilizing blockchain for FL. For example, [15] uses SVM over blockchain based federated learning which enables different operators to train intelligent driving models without sharing data. [18] investigates blockchain assisted FL that punishes malicious users by the reward system, and ensures robustness in FL training. [10] leverages Private Blockchain and Public Blockchain to attain accountability, privacy, and robustness, and propose an off-chain trojan detection for malicious users. Most of the related works focuses on privacy and robustness concerns in FL. However, to the best of our knowledge, we are the first one that utilizes SSL to facilitate blockchain based training on large Deep Learning models.

2.2   Self-supervised Learning (SSL)

SSL solves auxiliary prediction tasks (known as pretext tasks) without requiring labeled data to learn useful semantic representations. These pretext tasks are created solely using the input features, such as predicting a missing image patch, recovering the color channels of an image from context, predicting missing words in text, or forcing the similarity the different views of images, *etc.* [11,13,14, 27]. They improve the effectiveness of learning representations for downstream prediction tasks. Studies have shown that simple machine learning model, such as linear classifier, can achieve superiors performance by taking the embedded feature learned by SSL. Empirical and theoretical results have shown the features learned by proper SSL strategy are linearly separable using simple classifiers [16].

3   Method

3.1   Overview of the Framework

We aim to train a medical image classifier on a blockchain via SC[1]. Using the DeMed pipeline, the input dimensions of the medical data are reduced to the point where the features are separable by a linear classifier, thus also reducing the number of parameters that need to be stored in the SC. This makes our system viable even without integration of decentralized storage infrastructure. We collect publicly available *in-domain* data to pre-train MAE and distribute the MAE encoder as feature extractor to all users.[2] The users can use the extractor to obtain the features of their own data and only the weights of the linear classifier will be trained and uploaded to the SC where the aggregation is done automatically. In this paper, we implement two different aggregation methods. The blockchain module of DeMed pipeline is shown in Fig. 1(b). Note DeMed is different from two existing learning framework for mult-user data learning: Centralized Learning and Swarm Learning (shown in Fig. 1(a)). Centralized Learning aggregates all weights from the users which requires a server center, while Swarm Learning requires all users to train at the same time at the blockchain side and directly write the whole deep model to SC.

We consider there is a hospital that wants to train a medical image classifier but doesn't have enough data. The hospital initializes a DeMed system for the task and is in charge of collecting *in-domain* unlabeled data, training a SSL representation extractor, and distributing the extractor to the users. The users will

---

[1] https://github.com/ubc-tea/DeMed-DeCaF22/blob/main/contracts/decentraldl.sol.

[2] An alternative way is to pre-train MAE using ImageNet and finetune on the collected data afterwards, if the number of the collected data is low.

contribute their data by uploading the weights of locally trained linear classifier. DeMed is a learning framework that launches FL on blockchain. We aim to do an in depth privacy analysis in future work to investigate the privacy preserving attribute of DeMed.

3.2 Launch Efficient Deep Learning Training on Blockchain

Self-supervised Learning Embedding Space. Motivated by [16], a well-trained SSL backbone can project the data onto a linearly separable space under proper assumptions. We utilize a state-of-the-art reconstruction-based SSL framework, Masked AutoEncoder (MAE) [14], as our feature extractor. MAE utilizes state-of-the-art image classification framework, Vision Transformer (ViT) [12], as the encoder for semantic feature extraction, and uses a lighter version of ViT as decoder. It divides an input image into patches, randomly blocks a certain percentage of image patches, and feeds them into the autoencoder architecture. By blocking out a large amount of image patches, the model is forced to learn a more complete representation. With the aim of positional embedding and transformer architecture, MAE is able to generalize the relationship between each image patch and obtain the semantic information among the whole image, which achieves the state-of-the-art performance in self-supervised image representation training. The pre-trained MAE encoder is then distributed to the users in SC.

Training Federated Linear Model on Blockchain. We deploy the SC in Ethereum [25] blockchain to facilitate privacy-preserving FL. Ethereum can be seen as a transaction-based state machine, and a transaction is a cryptographically signed instruction constructed by an actor. Ethereum blockchain provides a mechanism to facilitate transactions between two consenting parties, which is called the SC. [9] SC is a piece of code, residing on a blockchain based platform, that executes an agreement or a logic. The code itself is replicated on multiple nodes of the blockchain, hence demarking the permanence, security and immutability of agreed upon logic. When the code is executed, a new block is added to the blockchain. The code is executed only on acceptance of all the parameters for the called functions.

In our pipeline, the communication exists between a hospital and the users of the system through the Ethereum and smart contracts. The transactions in our pipeline include storing weights in the SC, downloading the weights from the SC, and aggregating these weights. The only trained weights are from the classifier, which we use a linear layer. To begin with, the hospital will initialize the weights in the blockchain Sect. 3.2. For every epoch, the users download the weights from the blockchain, update the weights on their data, and upload the updated weights to the blockchain. Weights are gathered from all the users in the SC for aggregation.

3.3 Secure Training on Blockchain with User Selection

One essential step in DeMed is model aggregation. Considering the communication cost in writing model weights to SC, we select a portion of users in each global round. In this section, we describe a naïve weights aggregation method and a more advanced aggregation strategies that is robust to malicious users. The logic to choose the users based on any of the following two aggregation methods lies within the hospital. In case of user selection, the users add their norms and cosines to the SC, which help the hospital make a decision on user selection for the secure aggregation. To reduce the gas consumption for blockchain transactions, we could adopt Layer-2 solutions [4] such as the Optimistic Rollup [5] or Zero Knowledge Proof Rollup [7] technologies. They bundle up transactions and submit a summary of the changes required to represent all the transactions in a batch rather than sending each transaction individually.

Naïve Weights Aggregation. To ensure the model sees all the users' data, we divide the users into small sets (batches) where each set has B users. During training, we iteratively feed in B users' data until all users' data are "seen" by the model. For example, the users from i-th set will download the global weights after the weights of users from $(i-1)$-th set are aggregated.

User Selection Weights Aggregation. Although naïve weights aggregation makes use of all users' weights to contribute to the global model, it may lead to unstable convergence and is prone to be attacked by malicious users. Malicious users are those who tries to drag down model training by uploading poisoned weights. Therefore, we propose User Selection (US) weights aggregation that selects users that contribute better weights would allow more efficient training and avoids malicious users. To address this problem, we use the weight drifts (denoted by d) and cosine similarity (denoted by cos) for user selection, which are defined as follows:

$$d = ||W_0 - w_k||_2, \tag{1}$$

and

$$cos = \frac{V \cdot W_k}{max(||V||_2 \cdot ||W_k||_2, \epsilon)}, \tag{2}$$

with $V = W - W_0, W_k = w_k - W_0, \epsilon = e^{-8}$, where V is the direction of the gradient, W is the naïve aggregation of the epoch, w_k and W_k are the local model weights and gradient direction of the k-th user after training for that epoch, and W_0 is initial weights used to train for the model for the particular epoch. Note that this is similar to [17] but we calculate the V based on all the gradients of the *current* run. Furthermore, instead of using a single criteria, we leverage both weight drifts and cosine similarity in user selection, which is detailed in Sect. 4.1. Weight drift and cosine similarity aim to pick users who have weights closest to the other weights in distance and direction, respectively.

4   Experiment

4.1   Experiment Setup and Datasets

Setup. We evaluate DeMed on 2 medical datasets: PCam [21], a microscopic dataset for identifying metastatic tissue in histopathologic scans of lymph node sections and COVIDx [23], a chest X-Ray dataset for COVIDx classification. In our experiments, we divide a dataset into 3 disjoint sets:

- **Public Train Set**: randomly sampled large amount of data from the datasets. This resembles the public available *in-domain* data and is used to pre-trained the SSL representation extractor.
- **Validation Set**: Randomly sampled data points for testing. This simulates the testing set that is kept in the smart contract to examine the weights uploaded by the users.
- **User Train Sets**: Randomly sampled 100 data points for 16 users. This resembles the data that each user has.

For training MAE, the experiments are run on NVIDIA DeForce RTX 3090 Graphic card with PyTorch. We follow the training strategy in [14]. However, due to the hardware limitation, we fix the batch size to 256 and adjust the training epoch accordingly. For DeMed learning, we use the extracted representations to train a linear layer that maps the embedding dimensions into predictions. Here, the embedding dimension of MAE is 1024 and number of classes is 2, so a fully connected (1024×1) layer and BCELoss is applied. Note that although we only simulate 16 users in **User Train Sets**, the system is scalable to more users. We test the performances of scenarios that there are only 2, 4, 8 users are allowed to join per transaction, and found that the accuracies are similar. In the following experiments, we will only show the results for 8 users per transaction (please refer to Table 2).

Due to the lightweight of DeMed, we could launch the blockchain module on CPU only. We used Ganache as a local blockchain for our experiment. The SC for the weights of linear layer was written in Solidity programming language. For training local linear classifier, the experiments run on 8-Core Intel Core i9 processor. Each user will download the global weights, train for 3 epochs locally, and then upload the new weights to the SC. Learning rate is set to $5e^{-3}$, and Adam optimizer is selected.

The Naïve aggregation of weights does not filter out malicious users from the system. Hence, we used model weights drift d (Eq. (1)) and cosine similarity cos (Eq. (2)) to filter out users from our system that would lead to a decline in the accuracy. We first request calculating the d for all users, and band weight submission for those whose d are too large/small (we remove 10 users from this step). Second, we request calculating the cos for the rest 10 users, and pick the 2, 4, 8 number of users with the largest cosine similarity. Finally, we aggregate the weights of the selected users as the final weights for the respective epoch.

4.2 Comparison Between Aggregation Methods

We evaluate training results of the two aggregation methods. We first show that Naïve aggregation and US aggregation result in similar performance. Then we show adding one malicious user will degrade Naïve aggregation's performance while US aggregation is not influenced by the malicious user.

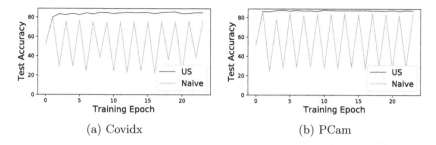

(a) Covidx   (b) PCam

Fig. 2. Comparison of testing accuracy over training epochs for two weights aggregation methods: naïve vs user selection (US). One user is malicious. The zigzag curve for naïve aggregation and worse testing results indicate that it is prone to be attacked by malicious users. We show the results for selecting 8 users per transaction.

Table 1. Testing accuracy for DeMed (2, 4, 8 users) using naïve weights aggregation and user selection (US) weights aggregation.

# users/round	2		4		8	
Aggregation method	Naive	US	Naive	US	Naive	US
CovidX	84.1	84.1	84.6	84.1	84.4	85.2
PCam	86.2	86.5	87.4	87.3	87.2	87.3

Testing Performance. We train the classification model for two datasets on DeMed (2, 4, 8 users cases) using Naïve Weights Aggregation and User Selection(US) Weights Aggregation as shown in Table 1. One can observe that using 8 users per aggregation gives the best results. The user selection method has slightly better accuracy as the best contributing users are selected for weight aggregation, while for Naïve method every user contributes their weights evenly.

Training with Malicious Users. We simulate a malicious user attack by manipulating a user's weight into $W_{poisoned} = -10 \times W_{original}$. The accuracy curve is shown in Fig. 2. One can observe that the curve for naïve aggregation is zigzag. This is because for Naïve user aggregation, the malicious user also contributes it's weights, thus leading to declined accuracy whenever the model *sees* the malicious data. On the other hand, in case of user selection, the malicious user is screened out and accuracy does not decline.

4.3   Comparison Between Learning Strategies

We train classification models for the 2 datasets on DeMed (2, 4, 8 users cases), Swarm Learning, and Centralized Learning, and the testing accuracy are shown in Table 2. One can observe that using 8 users in DeMed results in the best classification performance. Also, we would like to emphasize that DeMed can achieve comparable results while having better flexibility than Swarm Learning and being more privacy preserving than Centralized Learning.

Table 2. Testing accuracy for `DeMed`, swarm learning, and centralized learning.

Method	Centralized learning	Swarm learning	DeMed		
User selection	–	–	2	4	8
CovidX	84.8	84.8	84.1	84.1	85.2
PCam	87.8	87.9	86.5	87.3	87.4

5   Conclusion

We propose `DeMed`, an efficient decentralized learning framework that utilizes pre-trained SSL feature extractor to realize blockchain-based training on SC. By training classifier on the extracted features, we leverage a linear model on SC in a FL fashion. We also design user selection mechanism similar to [17] but with slight difference in finding the most representative users in each aggregation to detect malicious users. Overall, `DeMed` shows comparable model performance to Centralized Learning and Swarm Learning, while preserving security and flexibility. We believe that `DeMed` can facilitate privacy-preserving decentralized learning for medical image analysis.

Acknowledgement. This work is supported in part by the Natural Sciences and Engineering Research Council (NSERC) of Canada (RGPIN-2021-02970, DGECR-2021-00187, DGECR-2022-00430), NVIDIA Hardware Award, and Public Safety Canada (NS-5001-22170).

References

1. Blockchain. https://www.investopedia.com/terms/b/blockchain.asp. Accessed 30 July 2022
2. Blockchain transactions. https://onezero.medium.com/how-does-the-blockchain-work-98c8cd01d2ae. Accessed 30 July 2022
3. Etehreum transactions. https://ethereum.org/en/developers/docs/transactions/. Accessed 30 July 2022
4. Optimistic rollups. https://ethereum.org/en/developers/docs/scaling/. Accessed 30 July 2022
5. Optimistic rollups. https://ethereum.org/en/developers/docs/scaling/optimistic-rollups/. Accessed 30 July 2022
6. Solidity. https://docs.soliditylang.org/en/v0.8.15/. Accessed 30 July 2022
7. Zero-knowledge rollups. https://ethereum.org/en/developers/docs/scaling/zk-rollups/. Accessed 30 July 2022
8. Act, A.: Health insurance portability and accountability act of 1996. Public Law **104**, 191 (1996)
9. Buterin, V.: Ethereum white paper: a next generation smart contract & decentralized application platform (2013). https://github.com/ethereum/wiki/wiki/White-Paper
10. Desai, H.B., Ozdayi, M.S., Kantarcioglu, M.: Blockfla: accountable federated learning via hybrid blockchain architecture. In: Proceedings of the Eleventh ACM Conference on Data and Application Security and Privacy, pp. 101–112 (2021)

11. Devlin, J., Chang, M.W., Lee, K., Toutanova, K.: Bert: pre-training of deep bidirectional transformers for language understanding. arXiv preprint arXiv:1810.04805 (2018)
12. Dosovitskiy, A., et al.: An image is worth 16x16 words: transformers for image recognition at scale. arXiv preprint arXiv:2010.11929 (2020)
13. Grill, J.B., et al.: Bootstrap your own latent-a new approach to self-supervised learning. Adv. Neural. Inf. Process. Syst. **33**, 21271–21284 (2020)
14. He, K., Chen, X., Xie, S., Li, Y., Dollár, P., Girshick, R.: Masked autoencoders are scalable vision learners. arXiv preprint arXiv:2111.06377 (2021)
15. Hua, G., Zhu, L., Wu, J., Shen, C., Zhou, L., Lin, Q.: Blockchain-based federated learning for intelligent control in heavy haul railway. IEEE Access **8**, 176830–176839 (2020)
16. Lee, J.D., Lei, Q., Saunshi, N., Zhuo, J.: Predicting what you already know helps: provable self-supervised learning. In: Advances in Neural Information Processing Systems, vol. 34 (2021)
17. Li, T., Sahu, A.K., Zaheer, M., Sanjabi, M., Talwalkar, A., Smith, V.: Federated optimization in heterogeneous networks. Proc. Mach. Learn. Syst. **2**, 429–450 (2020)
18. Ma, C., et al.: When federated learning meets blockchain: a new distributed learning paradigm. arXiv preprint arXiv:2009.09338 (2020)
19. McMahan, B., Moore, E., Ramage, D., Hampson, S., Arcas, B.A.: Communication-efficient learning of deep networks from decentralized data. In: Artificial Intelligence and Statistics, pp. 1273–1282. PMLR (2017)
20. Nakamoto, S.: Bitcoin: a peer-to-peer electronic cash system. Decent. Bus. Rev. 21260 (2008)
21. Veeling, B.S., Linmans, J., Winkens, J., Cohen, T., Welling, M.: Rotation equivariant CNNs for digital pathology. In: Frangi, A.F., Schnabel, J.A., Davatzikos, C., Alberola-López, C., Fichtinger, G. (eds.) MICCAI 2018. LNCS, vol. 11071, pp. 210–218. Springer, Cham (2018). https://doi.org/10.1007/978-3-030-00934-2_24
22. Voigt, P., Von dem Bussche, A.: The EU general data protection regulation (GDPR). Intersoft consulting (2018)
23. Wang, L., Lin, Z.Q., Wong, A.: COVID-Net: a tailored deep convolutional neural network design for detection of COVID-19 cases from chest X-ray images. Sci. Rep. **10**(1), 19549 (2020). https://doi.org/10.1038/s41598-020-76550-z
24. Warnat-Herresthal, S., et al.: Swarm learning for decentralized and confidential clinical machine learning. Nature **594**(7862), 265–270 (2021)
25. Wood, G.: Ethereum: a secure decentralised generalised transaction ledger. Ethereum Project Yellow Paper **151**, 1–32 (2014)
26. Xie, C., Koyejo, S., Gupta, I.: Zeno: distributed stochastic gradient descent with suspicion-based fault-tolerance. In: International Conference on Machine Learning, pp. 6893–6901. PMLR (2019)
27. Zhang, R., Isola, P., Efros, A.A.: Colorful image colorization. In: Leibe, B., Matas, J., Sebe, N., Welling, M. (eds.) ECCV 2016. LNCS, vol. 9907, pp. 649–666. Springer, Cham (2016). https://doi.org/10.1007/978-3-319-46487-9_40
28. Zhu, L., Han, S.: Deep leakage from gradients. In: Yang, Q., Fan, L., Yu, H. (eds.) Federated Learning. LNCS (LNAI), vol. 12500, pp. 17–31. Springer, Cham (2020). https://doi.org/10.1007/978-3-030-63076-8_2

Cluster Based Secure Multi-party Computation in Federated Learning for Histopathology Images

Seyedeh Maryam Hosseini[1]([✉]), Milad Sikaroudi[1], Morteza Babaei[1,2], and Hamid R. Tizhoosh[1,2,3]

[1] Kimia Lab, University of Waterloo, Waterloo, ON N2L 3G1, Canada
{sm24hoss,milad.sikaroudi,morteza.babaie}@uwaterloo.ca
[2] Vector Institute, MaRS Centre, Toronto, Canada
[3] Department of Artificial Intelligence and Informatics, Mayo Clinic, Rochester, MN, USA
tizhoosh.hamid@mayo.edu

Abstract. Federated learning (FL) is a decentralized method enabling hospitals to collaboratively learn a model without sharing private patient data for training. In FL, participant hospitals periodically exchange training results rather than training samples with a central server. However, having access to model parameters or gradients can expose private training data samples. To address this challenge, we adopt secure multiparty computation (SMC) to establish a privacy-preserving federated learning framework. In our proposed method, the hospitals are divided into clusters. After local training, each hospital splits its model weights among other hospitals in the same cluster such that no single hospital can retrieve other hospitals' weights on its own. Then, all hospitals sum up the received weights, sending the results to the central server. Finally, the central server aggregates the results, retrieving the average of models' weights and updating the model without having access to individual hospitals' weights. We conduct experiments on a publicly available repository, The Cancer Genome Atlas (TCGA). We compare the performance of the proposed framework with differential privacy and federated averaging as the baseline. The results reveal that compared to differential privacy, our framework can achieve higher accuracy with no privacy leakage risk at a cost of higher communication overhead.

Keywords: Federated learning · Decentralized learning · Secure multiparty computation · Privacy preservation · Histopathology imaging

1 Introduction

Machine learning methods rely on a large number of data collected in a centralized location for training purposes. However, most data owners such as medical centers are not willing to share their private data with others because of privacy regulations [13]. To address the data privacy concern, decentralized methods such

S. Albarqouni et al. (Eds.): DeCaF 2022/FAIR 2022, LNCS 13573, pp. 110–118, 2022.
https://doi.org/10.1007/978-3-031-18523-6_11

as Federated learning (FL) are emerging. FL enables learning a model while all participants keep data private, sharing training results with the central server. However, authors in [17] have shown that sharing the model's parameters or gradients is not safe. They demonstrate that having access to the model's weight or gradients can expose training samples. Therefore, privacy-preserving methods in FL have recently been introduced to protect training samples from leakage. There are three different strategies for privacy-preserving FL in the literature to securely share the training results [8,15].

- **Differential Privacy (DF)** [2] protects privacy by adding noise to the training results before sharing with the central server. Although perturbing the training results improves the privacy of the training samples, it adversely impacts accuracy.
- **Secure Multiparty Computation (SMC)** [11] is a privacy-preserving method, enabling hospitals to jointly compute a function on their model's weight without revealing the actual weights values. Although SMC does not perturb the training results, it has communication overhead since hospitals communicate with each other to compute the average weights.
- **Homomorphic Encryption (HE)** [4] relies on encoding/decoding gradients and uses encrypted data for training. It allows computation on encrypted gradients and decryption of the results is equivalent to performing the same operations on gradients without any encryption. This method is efficient in terms of communication cost, however, it is computationally expensive.

The effectiveness of DP in decentralized learning has been investigated in the healthcare domain [3,9]. Authors in [9] preserve accuracy by adding Gaussian noise to the trained model weights, providing extensive experiments on MRI images. In [3], the authors conduct the feasibility study of DP in federated learning. Also, the impact of the design factors of DP in decentralized learning has been investigated on histopathology images.

SMC has played a successful role in cloud computing and the Internet of Things (IOT) [16]. Recently, SMC has been adopted as a privacy-preserving method in federated learning. For example, authors in [10] applied chained SMC in FL to protect model weights from disclosure. In their framework, first, the central server sends one of the participants a random number. Then participants sequentially communicate with each other to compute the average of the local models. This framework imposes extreme latency and cannot be scaled since all the participant has to communicate sequentially. However, in our proposed method, communications happen in parallel within clusters. In this paper, we address the privacy challenges of federated learning by introducing a novel framework based on SMC. Unlike DP, SMC does not compromise the model accuracy since it does not perturb training results. In our proposed method, we divide the hospitals into small clusters. Hospitals within each cluster collaborate to learn the summation of the local weights without having access to individual hospitals' trained weights. We perform experiments on the histopathology lung cancer dataset, comparing the performance of the proposed method with DP and baseline.

2   Method

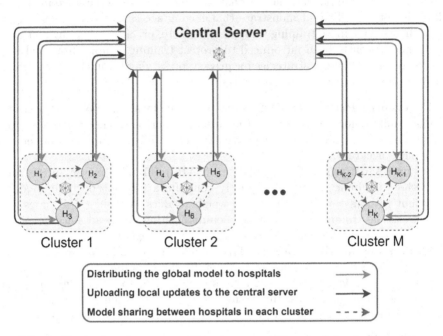

Fig. 1. Cluster-based secure multi-party computation for federated learning.

In this section, we introduce our proposed SMC-based FL method in detail. Figure 1 represents our proposed framework for cluster-based SMC. Before training, hospitals need to be divided into multiple groups. Clustering can be performed in different ways depending on three factors: the geographical distance between hospitals, hardware resources in each hospital, and network communication types deployed in each hospital. For instance, if hospitals are geographically far from each other, hospitals closer to each other can form a cluster. Another real-world scenario is that hospitals may indeed have different hardware resources to train the model causing latency and leading to asynchronous schedules. In these situations, one way to cluster hospitals is to group them into clusters of different sizes to improve total communication overhead between hospitals and the central server. Finally, network communication type is another important factor that impacts clustering in real-world scenarios. Different hospitals may have deployed different communication protocols and APIs to send/receive updates to/from other hospitals. We can group hospitals with the same communication protocols in the same cluster.

In this work, we assume that all hospitals are placed geographically at the same distance from each other, have the same hardware resource and communication prototype. As such, we randomly select hospitals and form clusters of the same size. More specifically, given K hospitals, which will be equally divided into M clusters with size $N = K/M$. Each hospital belongs to one cluster which is denoted by $c = \{1, \ldots, M\}$. Hospital k in cluster c is represented by H_k^c. The set n_c with length N represents indexes of all hospitals in cluster c.

Model training in our proposed approach is performed in three steps.

Step1: Local Training. All hospitals train the model with their local data, updating the model. We denote model parameters trained by the kth hospital with w_k.

Algorithm 1. Proposed method. There are K hospitals, M clusters, T is the number of epochs, E is the number of local epochs, η is learning rate, n_c index of all hospitals in cluster c.

Input: M, C, T, w^0, η, n_c
Output: w^{T-1}

1: **for** $t = 0, \ldots, T - 1$ **do**
2:     Server sends w^t to all hospitals
        % *Step1: Local Training*
3:     **for** $k = 1, 2, \ldots, K$ **do**
4:         $w_k^{t+1} \leftarrow$ **LocalTraining**(k, w^t, η) % update weights
5:     **end for**
        % *SMC*
        $R_k^c \leftarrow 0$
6:     **for** $c = 1, 2, \ldots, M$ **do**
7:         **for** $k \in n_c$ **do**
8:             **for** $i \in n_c$ **do**
9:                 $R_k^c\mathrel{+}= \beta_{i,k}^c w_i^t$
10:            **end for**
11:            Hospital k feedbacks R_k^c to the central server.
12:        **end for**
13:    **end for**
        % *Step3: Aggregation*
14:    Server updates w^{t+1} as
$$w^{t+1} \leftarrow \frac{1}{K} \sum_{k=1}^{K} R_k^c$$
15: **end for**
16: **return** w^{T-1}

LocalTraining(i, w_t, η) :

1: $\mathcal{B} \leftarrow$ (split dataset of ith hospital into batches of size B)
2: **for** local epoch $j = 1, 2, \ldots, E$ **do**
3:     **for** batch $b \in \mathcal{B}$ **do**
4:         $w \leftarrow w_t - \eta \nabla F_k(w_t; b)$ % *$F_k(.)$ is the loss function for hospital k*
5:     **end for**
6: **end for**
7: return w

Step2: SMC. Hospital H_k^c generates N random numbers $\{\beta_{k,j}^c | 0 < \beta_{k,j}^c < 1, j \in n_c\}$ that sum up to one.

$$\sum_{j \in n_c} \beta_{k,j}^c = 1 \tag{1}$$

Then, each hospital k in cluster c, H_k^c, sends portions of its own locally trained model parameters to each of $N - 1$ neighbours in cluster c. Mathematically, H_k^c sends $\beta_{k,j}^c w_k$ to hospital j for all $j \in n_c$. In the end, the kth hospital will have some portion of its own, and some portion of its $N - 1$ neighbor's model parameters as follows:

$$\mathcal{H}_k^c : R_k^c = \sum_{i \in n_c} \beta_{i,k}^c w_i \tag{2}$$

Step3: Aggregation. Finally, each hospital sends R_k^c to the central server, and the central server takes the average of R_k^c of all the hospitals in all clusters as follows:

$$w = \frac{1}{K} \sum_{c=1}^{M} \sum_{k \in n_c} R_k^c = \frac{1}{K} \sum_{c=1}^{M} \sum_{k \in n_c} \sum_{i \in n_c} \beta_{i,k}^c w_i \tag{3}$$

If we exchange the position of the two summations in Eq. 3, we will get

$$w = \frac{1}{K} \sum_{c=1}^{M} \sum_{i \in n_c} \underbrace{\sum_{k \in n_c} \beta_{i,k}^c}_{1} w_i$$

$$= \frac{1}{K} \sum_{c=1}^{M} \sum_{i \in n_c} w_i = \frac{1}{K} \sum_{i=1}^{K} w_i$$

As shown above, the central server can receive the exact average weights without having access to the weights of each individual hospital. These steps have been summarized in Algorithm 1.

Table 1. The summary of the dataset [3].

Client	# Slides	# Patches
C1: Int. Gen. Cons.	267	66,483
C2: Indivumed	211	52,539
C3: Asterand	207	51,543
C4: Johns Hopkins	199	49,551
C5: Christiana H.	223	55,527
C6: Roswell Park	110	27,390

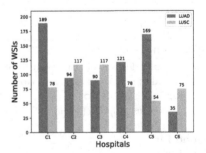

Fig. 2. Label distribution in dataset.

3   Experiments and Results

3.1   Datasets

We evaluate our proposed privacy-preserving FL on The Cancer Genome Atlas (TCGA) [1,14] dataset, the largest publicly available archive of the histopathology whole slide images (WSIs). This annotated dataset has more than $30,000$ H&E stained WSIs that have been collected from various medical centers all over the world. To validate the proposed method, we select TCGA WSIs diagnosed with non-small cell lung cancer (NSCLC) to construct a dataset of multiple institutions. This cancer has two frequent subtypes, namely

- Lung Adenocarcinoma (LUAD)
- Lung Squamous Cell Carcinoma (LUSC).

This study includes hospitals that have WSIs from both LUAD and LUSC subtypes. In TCGA, only six hospitals met this requirement. Therefore, we collected WSIs diagnosed with NSCLC from those six hospitals to create the dataset with six participants. WSIs are extremely large images of size up to $50,000 \times 50,000$ pixels. Therefore, they cannot directly be fed into any neural network. The common approach to deal with these images is to divide them into patches of smaller sizes for further analysis [5]. We divide the selected WSIs into patches of size 1000×1000 pixels. Due to space limitation, we refer readers to [3] for more details on patch extraction and selection of the lung dataset that has been used in our experiments. The statistics of this dataset for each hospital are presented in Table 1 and Fig. 2. The dataset of each hospital has been randomly divided into 80% and 20% groups for training and testing purposes, respectively.

3.2   Experimental Details

Figure 3 illustrates WSI preprocessing as well as the model used to classify lung samples into LUAD and LUSC subtypes. As shown in this figure, for the classification of lung histopathology WSIs, we first employ pretrained DenseNet121 [6] to extract features of length 1024 for each patch. Next, We employ attention-gated multiple instance learning (MIL) to combine feature vectors of patches of each WSI, creating a feature of size 1024 for each WSI classification [7]. The reason why we use MIL is that when we divide a WSI into multiple patches, we are dealing with instances for which only a single WSI level label, medical diagnosis, is provided. Therefore, we require multiple instance learning (MIL) architecture to learn a model that can predict the WSI label given a bag of instances (patches). The attention-based MIL architecture enables the model to combine the features of patches to create one feature vector of length 1024 that will be used for the classification of WSI. This architecture aggregates feature vectors of those patches such that key patches are assigned relatively higher weights. The high-level structure of the MIL classifier has been visualized in Fig. 3. The MIL gated attention classifier is the network that we learn in a decentralized federated learning fashion. Due to space limitations, we refer readers to [7] for more

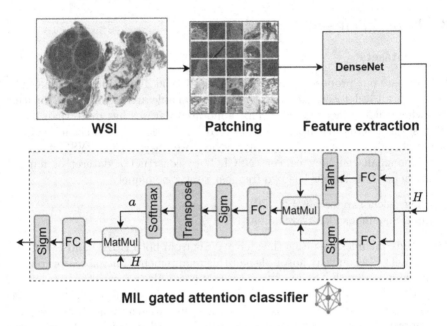

MIL gated attention classifier

Fig. 3. The illustration of the end to end training procedure. First WSIs are divided into patches of size 1000 × 1000. Next the features of patches are extracted using DensNet121. Finally, those features of patches are fed into MIL gated attention classifier.

detail on this MIL network. The histopathology lung dataset includes data from six hospitals. We divide those $K = 6$ hospitals into $M = 2$ clusters of size $N = 3$. We deploy DP according to [9] with additive Gaussian noise standard deviation of 0.03. The standard deviation has been selected to have the highest possible privacy while the classification performance is still acceptable. For all these three methods, we use an Adam optimizer with the following hyper-parameter values, epochs = 300, batch size = 32, number of local epochs = 1, and learning rate = 0.009.

3.3   Results and Discussions

In this section, we present our experimental results on the lung histopathology dataset. We compare our proposed SMC based method with the baseline which is FedAVG [12] without any privacy-preserving consideration. We also compare our method with DP which has been implemented on top of FedAvg. An ideal privacy-preserving method has to have a closed performance to the baseline while preserving privacy of training results. Table 2 shows the performance of each method for each hospital in terms of accuracy and F1 Score. As represented, in each hospital, the proposed method has a closed performance to the baseline and outperforms DP. Additionally, the average performance of our method surpasses DP. Figure 4 and 5 compare methods in terms of the average testing accuracy and average training loss of participant hospitals for 300 rounds of training communication between hospitals and the central server. As can be seen, the proposed method performs close to the baseline, surpassing DP. To eliminate the impact of random parameters in our experiments, we repeated all the experiments five times and all the results have been provided by taking the average over these five realizations.

Table 2. Experimental results.

Client	Method	ACC	F1-Score
C1	FedAvg	76.38	82.51
	DP	66.12	69.89
	Proposed	75.01	81.08
C2	FedAvg	85.46	87.63
	DP	79.06	81.12
	Proposed	87.20	89.03
C3	FedAvg	81.54	80.96
	DP	74.40	70.27
	Proposed	80.95	80.47
C4	FedAvg	75.01	82.74
	DP	69.37	73.84
	Proposed	75.62	83.12
C5	FedAvg	73.33	82.31
	DP	64.87	68.54
	Proposed	68.88	78.58
C6	FedAvg	68.18	66.74
	DP	68.18	63.34
	Proposed	69.31	66.78
Avg	FedAvg	76.65	80.48
	DP	70.33	71.16
	Proposed	76.16	79.84

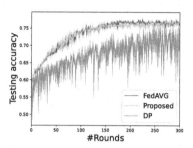

Fig. 4. The average testing accuracy for 300 rounds of training over all hospitals.

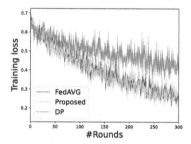

Fig. 5. The average training loss for 300 rounds of training over all hospitals.

4   Conclusions

In this paper, we addressed the privacy-preserving challenge of the federated learning. We have proposed cluster-based SMC to protect individual hospitals' model parameters from disclosure. In the proposed method, neither participant hospitals nor the central server has access to model weights of individual hospitals; however, weights average can be recovered at the central server. Our experimental results suggested that the proposed method outperforms DP in terms of accuracy and F1 Score at the expense of more communication overhead. However, we believe that having slight communication overhead to get higher accuracy is most likely acceptable in the medical domain. Additionally, each hospital needs to perform preprocessing to find suitable additive noise standard deviation in DP method. However, our proposed method does not require any preprocessing since it does not have any hyper-parameter. Therefore, depending on the application, applying cluster-based SMC for privacy-preserving purposes might be preferable compared to other privacy-preserving method such as DP.

References

1. https://www.cancer.gov/tcga
2. Abadi, M., et al.: Deep learning with differential privacy. In: Proceedings of the 2016 ACM SIGSAC Conference on Computer and Communications Security, pp. 308–318 (2016)
3. Adnan, M., Kalra, S., Cresswell, J.C., Taylor, G.W., Tizhoosh, H.R.: Federated learning and differential privacy for medical image analysis. Sci. Rep. **12**(1), 1–10 (2022)
4. Brutzkus, A., Gilad-Bachrach, R., Elisha, O.: Low latency privacy preserving inference. In: International Conference on Machine Learning, pp. 812–821. PMLR (2019)
5. Hou, L., Samaras, D., Kurc, T.M., Gao, Y., Davis, J.E., Saltz, J.H.: Patch-based convolutional neural network for whole slide tissue image classification. In: Proceedings of the IEEE Conference on Computer Vision and Pattern Recognition, pp. 2424–2433 (2016)
6. Huang, G., Liu, Z., Van Der Maaten, L., Weinberger, K.Q.: Densely connected convolutional networks. In: Proceedings of the IEEE Conference on Computer Vision and Pattern Recognition, pp. 4700–4708 (2017)
7. Ilse, M., Tomczak, J., Welling, M.: Attention-based deep multiple instance learning. In: International Conference on Machine Learning, pp. 2127–2136. PMLR (2018)
8. Kaissis, G.A., Makowski, M.R., Rückert, D., Braren, R.F.: Secure, privacy-preserving and federated machine learning in medical imaging. Nat. Mach. Intell. **2**(6), 305–311 (2020)
9. Li, X., Gu, Y., Dvornek, N., Staib, L.H., Ventola, P., Duncan, J.S.: Multi-site fMRI analysis using privacy-preserving federated learning and domain adaptation: Abide results. Med. Image Anal. **65**, 101765 (2020)
10. Li, Y., Zhou, Y., Jolfaei, A., Yu, D., Xu, G., Zheng, X.: Privacy-preserving federated learning framework based on chained secure multiparty computing. IEEE Internet Things J. **8**(8), 6178–6186 (2020)
11. Lindell, Y.: Secure multiparty computation. Commun. ACM **64**(1), 86–96 (2020)
12. McMahan, B., Moore, E., Ramage, D., Hampson, S., Arcas, B.A.: Communication-efficient learning of deep networks from decentralized data. In: Artificial Intelligence and Statistics, pp. 1273–1282. PMLR (2017)
13. Rieke, N., et al.: The future of digital health with federated learning. NPJ Digit. Med. **3**(1), 1–7 (2020)
14. Weinstein, J.N., et al.: The cancer genome atlas pan-cancer analysis project. Nat. Genet. **45**(10), 1113–1120 (2013)
15. Yin, X., Zhu, Y., Hu, J.: A comprehensive survey of privacy-preserving federated learning: a taxonomy, review, and future directions. ACM Comput. Surv. (CSUR) **54**(6), 1–36 (2021)
16. Zhao, C., et al.: Secure multi-party computation: theory, practice and applications. Inf. Sci. **476**, 357–372 (2019)
17. Zhu, L., Liu, Z., Han, S.: Deep leakage from gradients. In: Advances in Neural Information Processing Systems 32 (2019)

Towards More Efficient Data Valuation in Healthcare Federated Learning Using Ensembling

Sourav Kumar[1]([✉])[iD], A. Lakshminarayanan[2][iD], Ken Chang[1][iD], Feri Guretno[2][iD], Ivan Ho Mien[2][iD], Jayashree Kalpathy-Cramer[1,3][iD], Pavitra Krishnaswamy[2][iD], and Praveer Singh[1,3][iD]

[1] Department of Radiology, Athinoula A. Martinos Center for Biomedical Imaging, Massachusetts General Hospital, Boston, MA, USA
`skumar43@mgh.harvard.edu`, `changk4@mskcc.org`
[2] Institute for Infocomm Research, A*STAR, Singapore, Singapore
{`lux,guretnof,ivan_ho,pavitrak`}`@i2r.a-star.edu.sg`
[3] Department of Ophthalmology, University of Colorado School of Medicine, Aurora, CO, USA
{`jayashree.kalpathy-cramer,praveer.singh`}`@cuanschutz.edu`

Abstract. Federated Learning (FL) wherein multiple institutions collaboratively train a machine learning model without sharing data is becoming popular. Participating institutions might not contribute equally - some contribute more data, some better quality data or some more diverse data. To fairly rank the contribution of different institutions, Shapley value (SV) has emerged as the method of choice. Exact SV computation is impossibly expensive, especially when there are hundreds of contributors. Existing SV computation techniques use approximations. However, in healthcare where the number of contributing institutions are likely not of a colossal scale, computing exact SVs is still exorbitantly expensive, but not impossible. For such settings, we propose an efficient SV computation technique called SaFE (Shapley Value for Federated Learning using Ensembling). We empirically show that SaFE computes values that are close to exact SVs, and that it performs better than current SV approximations. This is particularly relevant in medical imaging setting where widespread heterogeneity across institutions is rampant and fast accurate data valuation is required to determine the contribution of each participant in multi-institutional collaborative learning.

Keywords: Federated Learning · Data valuation · Healthcare AI

1 Introduction

Federated Learning (FL) allows machine learning (ML) models to be trained on data from multiple data contributors without the need to bring data to a central location [23]. With the growing adoption of FL in enterprise including healthcare [31], it is important to quantitatively determine the contribution of indi-

---

S. Kumar and A. Lakshminarayanan—Equally contributing first authors.
P. Krishnaswamy and P. Singh—Equal senior authors.

© The Author(s), under exclusive license to Springer Nature Switzerland AG 2022
S. Albarqouni et al. (Eds.): DeCaF 2022/FAIR 2022, LNCS 13573, pp. 119–129, 2022.
https://doi.org/10.1007/978-3-031-18523-6_12

vidual data sources (henceforth referred to as institutions) to the performance of the global model. This data valuation technique must be fair and accurate. Shapley value (SV) [33], a technique from co-operative game theory can be used to evaluate the contribution that each institution's data bring to a global model. In a cooperative game, the contribution of each player is determined by calculating the average of all marginal contributions that the particular player brings to all possible coalitions not involving that player. SV can be used to value the data contributions of different institutions participating in FL. However, calculating SV is computationally very expensive. To determine the contribution of each institution requires training an exponential number of FL models (2^n models [16]), which becomes utterly infeasible due to astronomical computational and communication costs, even with a small number of participants. It is impossible to compute exact SV in a reasonable time when contributing institutions number in hundreds, with current techniques using approximations [7,12].

In healthcare settings, the number of contributing institutions is unlikely to be in the hundreds. For example, recent FL training research for predicting clinical outcomes of COVID-19 patients involved twenty contributing institutions [10]. Given infrastructure and legal constraints, it is reasonable to expect 30 or fewer participating institutions in healthcare FL. Though calculating exact SV with thirty institutions is still exorbitantly expensive (2^{30} FL models to compute), yet such calculations are not infeasible.

Generalizable AI models will immensely benefit from diverse data from varied sources. This is especially relevant in healthcare because there is so much heterogeneity across medical cohorts - variability across geographies, across socioeconomic levels, across different data acquisition devices and techniques. Unfortunately, healthcare data is hard to share, due to legal and ethical reasons. FL can solve this sharing problem, but contributing healthcare institutions will still want to be fairly rewarded for participating in such collaborations, specifically because annotated healthcare data - which requires specialized labelling skills, is precious. In addition, noisy labels are not uncommon in healthcare and SV computations can be useful for identifying poor quality data contributors. SV can also be used to detect malicious institutions as well as identify institutions whose contributions are marginal [37].

We propose SaFE (Shapley value for Federated Learning using Ensembling) to calculate SV when number of contributing institutions is not immensely large (less than 30). SaFE uses models trained on each institution's data as a proxy to the data itself. We still create 2^n models, but we use simpler models (logistic regression models), which we then aggregate using ensembling in a data-centre environment, making SaFE computationally tractable. Using empirical studies, we show that SaFE is fast, computes SV close to exact values, and performs better than existing SV approximations.

2   Related Work

The term Federated Learning was introduced in 2016 by Mcmahan et al. [28]. There are two types of FL settings - cross-device and cross-silo [18]. Mobile device applications with thousands of devices are considered cross-device e.g. Google's mobile keyboard prediction [14] and Apple's "Hey Siri" [1], while enterprise applications where a comparatively smaller number of reliable institutions train a model (e.g. healthcare), is considered cross-silo. Cross-silo FL has been proposed in domains such as financial risk prediction [6], drug discovery [5,9] and cybersecurity [30]. There is increasing interest in FL for a variety of healthcare applications e.g., image segmentation [21], multi-institutional medical collaboration [19,32,34], digital health [38], COVID-19 research [10] and pathology [26]. However, data valuation for FL in healthcare applications is yet to be explored.

There has been considerable work on data valuation using SV in centralized setting, including in the medical domain [13,15–17,36]. J. Kang, Z. Xiaong et al. [20] assume prior knowledge of data quality of different participating institutions and propose mechanisms to maximize participation. SV is also used to compute feature importance for explainable AI [27]. In [36], S. Tang, A. Ghorbani et al. use a technique called Data Shapley to compute the contribution of single datum to a model which is trained on a centralized chest X-Ray dataset. The computed SV is used to identify low quality data, to create better models for pneumonia detection. Since it is impossible to compute exact SV for any dataset with more than a handful of data points, Data Shapley uses Monte Carlo (MC) approximation methods, thus using only a randomly selected subset of data points in the computation. However, there are relatively limited studies on data valuation using approximate SV for FL.

The few studies exploring computation of SV for cross-device FL settings [24,35,37], cannot consider contributions from all devices at the same time. In particular, this limits the applicability of these methods for cross-silo settings, which is relevant to medical use cases where all institutions contribute at the same time. We further note that the approximate SV computation methods may have difficulties in fairly assessing the value of data from different institutions. For example, two institutions with fairly large proportion of samples from a minority class/race/ethnicity might both be of high value compared to other institutions, but the valuation might change based on whether one or both of them have been sampled in the Monte Carlo approximation.

3 Background: SV Computation

Even though it is possible to value data based on attributes such as age, volume and lineage, increasingly SV has become the method of choice for data valuation. Let v denote a utility function (performance score) with respect to which SVs are calculated. v is a mapping $2^n \rightarrow R$, where n is the total number of players (users). The SV ϕ_i for the player i is defined as the average of marginal contribution the player brings to all coalitions(subsets of the players) S which do not involve the player i. So $S = \{s \mid s \in \mathcal{P}(N) \ni i \notin s\}$ or we can denote $(S \subseteq N \setminus \{i\})$ where $N = \{1, 2, 3, \ldots, n\}$

$$\phi_i(v) = \sum_{S \subseteq N \setminus \{i\}} \frac{|S|!(n - |S| - 1)!}{n!} (v(S \cup \{i\}) - v(S)) \tag{1}$$

where $|S|$ denotes the cardinality. Approximation methods use Monte Carlo or Truncated Monte Carlo [13, 36], both of which are based on random sampling of different data permutations. This random sampling is repeated for many different permutations (until a convergence criterion is met), after which the approximate SV is computed by averaging over all calculated marginal contributions. Truncated in the truncated Monte Carlo means that the method stops parsing the current permutation and moves to a new permutation if the contribution of current is below a certain threshold.

4   Shapley Value for Federated Learning Using Ensembling

Step-1: Traditional FL: Train a FL model, using the FedAvg technique or similar model aggregation technique. At the end of FL training, every participating institution has a globally trained FL model.

Step-2: Fine-Tuning: Every participating institution uses the globally trained FL model to fine-tune a locally created model, using its own dataset. In our scheme, to enable faster SV computation in Step-3, we create a logistic regression (LR) model, trained using per-datum feature vectors extracted using a scheme similar to that proposed by S. Tang, A, Ghorbani et al. [36]. Unlike [36], which uses a pretrained CNN CheXNet, we use the FL model created in Step-1. This locally trained LR model is sent back to the global server.

Step-3: SV using Ensembling: On the global server, we compute all 2^n models using ensembling [3] of LR models from Step-2. Unlike current Monte Carlo techniques to compute SV approximations, we compute SV using a simpler model (LR) and ensembling. For ensembling, we combine the Softmax predictions from each LR model to get a combined prediction.

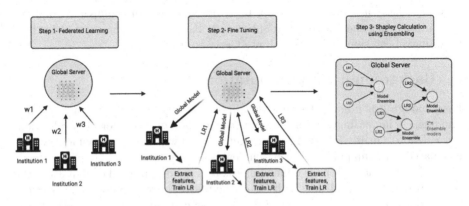

Fig. 1. Shapley For Federated Learning using Ensembling (SaFE)

Algorithm 1. Proposed Methodology to compute Shapley Value

Input: n participants, A global model (G), FeatureExtract- function for feature extraction from trained G, TrainLR- function to train a LR model, GetEnsemble- function that takes a subset and the set of all LR models and returns the ensemble of LR models for that subset, v- Performance score metric
Output: $\phi_i, \ldots, \phi_n$ (Shapley values for all users)

1: Initialize the global model(G) with initial weights
2: Perform Federated Learning and obtain a trained Model G
3: **for** each user i=1..n in parallel **do**
4:     Send global model to each user
5:     $F_i \leftarrow FeatureExtract(G, D_i)$
6:     $L_i \leftarrow TrainLR(F_i)$
7: **end for**
8: $\mathcal{L} \leftarrow \{L_1, \ldots, L_n\}$ local trained logistic regression models are made available to the central server
9: Initialize all $\phi_i \leftarrow 0$
10: **for** each user i=1..n **do**
11:     $\mathcal{S} \leftarrow$ subsets of $\{1 \ldots n\}$ not containing i
12:     **for** s in $\mathcal{S}$ **do**
13:         $\phi_i \leftarrow \phi_i + \frac{1}{n}\binom{n-1}{|s|}^{-1}$(v(GetEnsemble($\mathcal{L}$,s $\cup\{i\}$)-v(GetEnsemble($\mathcal{L}$, s)))
14:     **end for**
15: **end for**
16: **return** $\phi_i, \ldots, \phi_n$

Time Cost Analysis. Training exponential number of models for even simple datasets e.g. MNIST, CIFAR takes several hours. In our experimental set-up (Linux desktop with Intel Xeon E5-2637v4 CPU, 3.5 Ghz clock, 32 GB RAM with 2 Nvidia GTX 1080 GPUs), training one FL model for MNIST (five institutions) using a simple CNN on a single GPU takes approximately 15 min. For a more complex dataset (ROP) and a more complex CNN, one FL model takes approximately 30 min. Training a 3D CNN for brain imaging using 2 GPUs takes longer, around 45 min. Computing exact SV for MNIST and ROP took approximately 3 and 6 h respectively, including computing 2^5 FL models. Note that FL training was simulated on a single machine, so data exchange between institutions and the global server was inter-process, not over the Internet, which could an order of magnitude slower and costlier.

These time costs appear reasonable, but as the number of institutions increase, the time cost increases exponentially. For example, with 20 institutions, assuming FL training costs similar to MNIST (15 min per FL training), computing 2^{20} models will take an incredible 30 years. If we make the utterly unreasonable assumption that each institution can train 1000 models in parallel (using 1000 GPU VMs), we can reduce this time cost to 3 years. However, if there are 30 institutions, even with 1000 GPU VMs, the time-cost is 30 years!

Using SaFE, we compute one FL model and 20 LR models (one for each of the 20 institutions) and 2^{20} ensembled models at the central server. Ensembling models is inexpensive. In our experimental setup creating one ensembled model takes approximately 15 ms. With MNIST and ROP datasets, SaFE takes approximately 20 min and 35 min respectively. Ensembling does not require GPU and can be parallelized. With 20 institutions, we still compute 2^{20} models, but the time to compute SV using SaFE is 4.5 h. For 30 institutions, if we leverage 1000 parallel cloud CPU VMs, we can still compute SV in a very reasonable 4.5 h.

More SaFE Advantages

1. The ensembled model created using LR models of all participating institutions performs as well as the global FL model (see result sections).

2. Ensembling LR models is much faster compared to training FL models and does not require GPU.

3. Ensembling is done on the global server, so communication costs of training 2^n FL trained models is not incurred.

4. SV computation (Steps 2 and 3 in Fig. 1) is done separate and independent of Step-1. Since Step-3 is done centrally, this allows parallelization of the SV computation.

5. Step 2 and 3 do not leak private information any more than the FL training (Step-1). Only locally trained LR model is sent to the global parameter server, no institutional data is shared with the central server.

5   Experimental Evaluation

We use four different datasets - 2 well known computer vision toy datasets, namely CIFAR10 [22] and MNIST [11]; and 2 real world medical datasets:

Retinopathy Of Prematurity (ROP): This contains 5600 fundoscopic images from 7 different institutions classified by disease severity, namely No, Plus, and Pre-Plus [25].

Brain-MRI: Two different datasets were used to create an MRI dataset for classification. The pathological brain images are from the Brain Tumour Segmentation (BraTS) 2019 dataset [29] which contains 335 patients. The IXI Dataset [4] was used for healthy brain scans and contains 550 images. T1 contrast enhanced (T1ce) images were used from both datasets to create this dataset.

With all the 4 datasets, we perform experiments under both IID and non-IID settings. For MNIST, CIFAR10 and ROP, we split the dataset assuming 5 institutions. For brain-MRI dataset, we split assuming 4 institutions (to reduce computational costs for our experiments). We also assume that the testset is located at global server, against which the performance of different models are tested. For each of the 4 datasets, we first extract this global testset (20% datapoints from each dataset), before creating the institutional splits. For MNIST and CIFAR the global testset is the datasets' original test split.

For **IID**, we use the same number of samples with nearly identical label distribution. Next, for **non-IID (MNIST and CIFAR10)**, we introduce non-iidness in label distribution, by keeping the number of data samples in each institution fixed but creating highly skewed label distribution splits. Institution 1 has surplus of classes 0, 1 (95% for 0, 1 and rest 5% for other classes); institution 2 has surplus of classes 2, 3 and so forth. Lastly, for **non-IID (ROP and Brain MRI)**, since both datasets have just three classes, we maintain uneven label distribution by identifying the majority label within the two datasets and dividing that majority label amongst the different institutions in a linearly increasing fashion. The opposite is done with the minority labels. They are distributed among the splits in a linearly decreasing fashion. This ensures an increasing percentage of majority labels and decreasing one for minority labels across splits.

Note that we chose these data splits to demonstrate the effectiveness of our SaFE method to compute SV, not to demonstrate the effectiveness of the ML learning algorithm.

Experimental Setup. To compute exact SV in FL training, we need 2^n models. In out MNIST and CIFAR-10 experiments, we train 2^5 FL models, while for Brain-MRI experiments, we train 2^4 models.

For ROP classification, we use a Resnet18 model with pretrained ImageNet weights. For MNIST and CIFAR10 classification, we use a simpler CNN from [28]. For Brain-MRI, we use a 3D Resnet18 mixed convolution network [8] with pretrained weights. The learning rate for Brain-MRI classification is 2.5e−7. For CIFAR10, MNIST and ROP experiments, learning rate is 1e−4. The batch size was 64 for CIFAR10, MNIST, ROP whereas for Brain-MRI experiments, a batch size of 8 was used. We used epoch size of 20 for MNIST, ROP and Brain-MRI dataset and for CIFAR10 it was 50. For logistic regression models, the solver used was saga with elasticnet regularization with l1 ratio of 0.5.

We used a Linux desktop with Intel Xeon E5-2637v4 CPU, clocked at 3.5 GHZ, with 32 GB RAM and two Nvidia GTX 1080 GPUs. A single GPU was used for CIFAR10, MNIST and ROP experiments and both GPUs were used for Brain-MRI classification. Code-base is available on request.

6 Results

LR Ensembling vs Global FL: We compare the performance of the globally ensembled model created using locally fine-tuned LR models (from every contributing institution) and compare it to the performance of the FL model (Step-1 of SaFe). As shown in Table 1 the ensembled model accuracy is very similar to the performance of traditional FL model. For ROP experiments, the AUROCs are 0.96 and 0.95 for IID and non-IID splits respectively for both FL and LR-ensembled models. We observe the same with Brain-MRI as well, with both FL and LR-ensembled models having AUROCs of 0.94.

SV Comparison Results: To compare our proposed SaFE method for computing SV against exact SV computation, we use the cosine similarity measure, commonly used to compare similarity between two vectors [2]. SV computed using SaFE are very similar to exact SV as shown in Table 2. Quite expectedly, the SV for each institution in an IID setting is almost the same. For Brain MRI

Table 1. Ensemble LR performance vs Traditional FL performance

Dataset	LR Ensemble Model acc	Global FL Model acc
MNIST	98.28	98.41
CIFAR10	82	83
ROP	90	94
Brain MRI	93	94
(a) IID		
Dataset	LR Ensemble Model acc	Global FL Model acc
MNIST	96.8	96.78
CIFAR10	73	76
ROP	95	96
Brain MRI	89	91
(b) Non-IID		

and ROP datasets, we observe almost similar SV too. With non-IID splits, the similarity scores are not as close as IID splits, but still very high.

TMC vs SaFE: To compute Truncated Monte Carlo (TMC) SV, we perform random sampling of different permutations of the LR models. We used the implementation by [13] but adapted it to work in a FL setting. SV is calculated by parsing through these permutations and calculating the marginal contribution of every new institution once its added to the existing list of institutions already scanned. This marginal contribution is the difference in performance of the ensemble model due to the added institution while parsing a permutation. This process is repeated for many different permutations and the final SV is the average over all calculated marginal contributions. This technique doesn't consider all possible model ensembles, since it stops sampling permutations after a threshold. As seen in Fig. 2, in comparison to TMC, SaFE is much closer to exact SV.

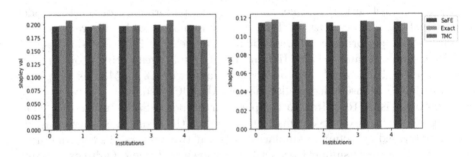

Fig. 2. Shapley for MNIST-IID (left) and CIFAR-IID (right).

Table 2. Calculated Shapley values for different datasets using our SaFe method

Dataset	Expt. Setting	Shapley type	1	2	3	4	5	Similarity
			Institutions					
MNIST	IID	Exact Shapley	0.197	0.197	0.196	0.196	0.196	0.999
		Our Shapley	0.196	0.197	0.196	0.197	0.196	
	NON IID	Exact Shapley	0.195	0.194	0.192	0.191	0.195	0.999
		Our Shapley	0.186	0.197	0.199	0.190	0.193	
CIFAR	IID	Exact Shapley	0.115	0.113	0.111	0.115	0.113	0.999
		Our Shapley	0.116	0.115	0.116	0.114	0.111	
	NON IID	Exact Shapley	0.101	0.070	0.086	0.115	0.100	0.973
		Our Shapley	0.106	0.104	0.097	0.080	0.101	
ROP	IID	Exact Shapley	0.183	0.175	0.181	0.200	0.200	0.997
		Our Shapley	0.182	0.182	0.180	0.180	0.176	
	NON IID	Exact Shapley	0.209	0.202	0.187	0.192	0.176	0.99
		Our Shapley	0.187	0.192	0.186	0.192	0.193	
Brain MRI	IID	Exact Shapley	0.230	0.209	0.230	0.226		0.998
		Our Shapley	0.218	0.216	0.209	0.230		
	NON IID	Exact Shapley	0.235	0.222	0.230	0.225		0.99
		Our Shapley	0.187	0.210	0.176	0.176		

7 Conclusion

When healthcare institutions participate in collaborative FL training, the contributions that their data make to the global model might not be equal. Some institutions might contribute more data, some better quality data or some more diverse data. To fairly rank the data valuation of datasets, Shapley value (SV) has emerged as the method of choice. But SV computation is impossibly expensive, when there are immensely large number of participating institutions. Even in healthcare FL, where we have a sizeable number of participants, calculating SV can be exorbitant. Existing SV techniques use approximations, which can result in unfair SV attributions. In this paper, we propose an efficient SV technique called SaFE (Shapley value for Federated Learning using Ensembling), that relies on "model" approximation (ensembling being an instance of it) instead of "SV computation" approximation. We show empirically that SaFe computes SV faster, its SV are close to exact SV, and that SaFe performs better than current approximation techniques. Future work would deepen the theoretical foundation of SaFE to obtain guarantees for different model approximation scenarios.

Acknowledgments. This study was supported by National Science Foundation (NSF) grant NSF1622542 and National Institutes of Health (NIH) grants U01CA154601, U24CA180927, and U24CA180918 to J. Kalpathy-Cramer; as well as by funding and infrastructure for deep learning and medical imaging R&D from the Institute for Infocomm Research, Science and Engineering Research Council, the Agency for Science, Technology and Research (A*STAR), Singapore. This research was carried out in part at the Athinoula A. Martinos Center for Biomedical Imaging at the Massachusetts General Hospital, using resources provided by the Center for Functional Neuroimaging Technologies, P41EB015896, a P41 Biotechnology Resource Grant supported by the National Institute of Biomedical Imaging and Bioengineering (NIBIB), National Institutes of Health. Data Collection as well as Cleaning for the ROP datasets was supported by grants R01 EY19474, R01 EY031331, R21 EY031883, and P30 EY10572 from the National Institutes of Health (Bethesda, MD), and by unrestricted departmental funding and a Career Development Award (JPC) from Research to Prevent Blindness (New York, NY).

References

1. Apple WWDC 2019. https://developer.apple.com/videos/play/wwdc2019/708
2. Cosine Similarity. https://www.sciencedirect.com/topics/computer-science/cosine-similarity
3. Ensemble Models. https://www.sciencedirect.com/topics/computer-science/ensemble-modeling
4. IXI dataset. https://brain-development.org/ixi-dataset/
5. VentureBeat: Federated learning platform for drug discovery. https://venturebeat.com/2020/09/17/major-pharma-companies-including-novartis-and-merck-build-federated-learning-platform-for-drug-discovery/9
6. WeBank: WeBank and Swiss Re sign cooperation MOU (2019). https://www.fedai.org/news/webank-and-swiss-re-signed-cooperation-mou/
7. Castro, J., Gomez, D., Tejada, J.: Polynomial calculation of the Shapley value based on sampling. Comput. Oper. Res. **36**, 1726–1730 (2009)
8. Chatterjee, S., Nizamani, F.A., Nürnberger, A., Speck, O.: Classification of brain tumours in MR images using deep spatio spatial models. Sci. Rep. **12**(1), 1–11 (2022)
9. Choudhury, O., Park, Y., Salonidis, T., Gkoulalas-Divanis, A.: Predicting adverse drug reactions on distributed health data using federated learning. In: AMIA Symposium 2019, pp. 313–322 (2020)
10. Dayan, I., Roth, H., Zhong, A., Harouni, A.: Federated learning for predicting clinical outcomes in patients with COVID-19. Nat. Med. **27**, 1–9 (2021)
11. Deng, L.: The MNIST database of handwritten digit images for machine learning research. IEEE Sig. Process. Mag. **29**(6), 141–142 (2012)
12. Fatima, S.S., Wooldridge, M., Jennings, N.R.: A linear approximation method for the Shapley value. Artif. Intell. **172**(14), 1673–1699 (2008)
13. Ghorbani, A., Zou, J.: Data Shapley: equitable valuation of data for machine learning. In: Proceedings of the 36th International Conference on Machine Learning, vol. 97, pp. 2242–2251. PMLR, Long Beach, CA, 09–15 June 2019
14. Hard, A., Rao, K., Mathews, R., Beaufays, F.: Federated Learning for Mobile Keyboard Prediction. arXiv abs/1811.03604 (2018)
15. Jia, R., et al.: Towards efficient data valuation based on the Shapley value. In: AISTATS. Naha, Okinawa, Japan (2019)
16. Jia, R., et al.: Efficient task-specific data valuation for nearest neighbor algorithms. Proc. VLDB Endow. **12**(11), 1610–1623 (2019)
17. Jia, R., et al.: Scalability vs. utility: do we have to sacrifice one for the other in data importance quantification? In: 2021 IEEE/CVF Conference on Computer Vision and Pattern Recognition (CVPR), pp. 8235–8243. Nashville, TN, USA (2021)
18. Kairouz, P., McMahan, H.B., Avent, B.: Advances and open problems in federated learning. Found. Trends Mach. Learn. **14**(1–2), 1–210 (2021)

19. Kaissis, G., Ziller, A., Passerat-Palmbach, J., Ryffel, T., Usynin, D.: End-to-end privacy preserving deep learning on multi-institutional medical imaging. Nat. Mach. Intell. **3**(6), 473–484 (2021)
20. Kang, J., Xiong, Z.: Incentive mechanism for reliable federated learning: a joint optimization approach to combining reputation and contract theory. IEEE Internet Things J. **6**(6), 10700–10714 (2019)
21. KhoKhar, F.A., Shah, J.H.: A review on federated learning towards image processing. Comput. Electr. Eng. **99**, 107818 (2022)
22. Krizhevsky, A., Nair, V., Hinton, G.: Cifar-10. http://www.cs.toronto.edu/~kriz/cifar.html
23. Li, Q., Wen, Z.: A survey on federated learning systems: vision, hype and reality for data privacy and protection. IEEE Trans. Knowl. Data Eng. 1 (2021)
24. Liu, Z., Chen, Y., Yu, H., Liu, Y., Cui, L.: GTG-Shapley: efficient and accurate participant contribution evaluation in federated learning. ACM Trans. Intell. Syst. Technol. **13**(4), 1–21 (2022)
25. Lu, C., et al.: Federated learning for multi-center collaboration in ophthalmology: improving classification performance in retinopathy of prematurity. Ophthalmol. Retina (2022)
26. Lu, M.Y., et al.: Federated learning for computational pathology on gigapixel whole slide images. Med. Image Anal. **76**, 102298 (2022)
27. Lundberg, S.M., Lee, S.I.: A unified approach to interpreting model predictions. In: Guyon, I., et al. (eds.) Advances in Neural Information Processing Systems, vol. 30. Curran Associates Inc., Long Beach, CA (2017)
28. McMahan, B., Moore, E., Ramage, D.: Communication-efficient learning of deep networks from decentralized data. In: Proceedings of the 20th International Conference on Artificial Intelligence and Statistics. Proceedings of Machine Learning Research, vol. 54, pp. 1273–1282. PMLR, Ft. Lauderdale, FL, 20–22 April 2017
29. Menze, B.H., Jakab, A.: The multimodal brain tumor image segmentation benchmark (BRATS). IEEE Trans. Med. Imag. **34**(10), 1993–2024 (2015)
30. Nguyen, T.D., Marchal, S., Miettinen, M., Fereidooni, H.: DIOT: a federated self-learning anomaly detection system for IoT. In: 2019 IEEE 39th International Conference on Distributed Computing Systems (ICDCS), pp. 756–767. Dallas, Texas (2019)
31. Rieke, N., Hancox, J., Li, W., Milletarì, F., Roth, H.R., Albarqouni, S.: The future of digital health with federated learning. NPJ Digit. Med. **3**(1), 1–7 (2020)
32. Sadilek, A., Liu, L., Nguyen, D., Kamruzzaman, M., Serghio, S.: Privacy-first health research with federated learning. NPJ Digit. Med. **4**(1), 1–8 (2021)
33. Shapley, L.S.: A Value for N-Person Games. RAND Corporation, Santa Monica, CA (1952)
34. Sheller, M., Edwards, B., Reina, G., Martin, J., Pati, S., Kotrotsou, A.: Federated learning in medicine: facilitating multi-institutional collaborations without sharing patient data. Sci. Rep. **10**(1), 1–12 (2020)
35. Song, T.: Profit allocation for federated learning. In: 2019 IEEE International Conference on Big Data (Big Data), pp. 2577–2586 (2019). https://doi.org/10.1109/BigData47090.2019.9006327
36. Tang, S., et al.: Data valuation for medical imaging using Shapley value and application to a large-scale chest X-ray dataset. Sci. Rep. **11**(1), 8366 (2021)
37. Wang, T., Rausch, J., Zhang, C., Jia, R., Song, D.: A Principled Approach to Data Valuation for Federated Learning. CoRR abs/2009.06192 (2020)
38. Xu, J., Glicksberg, B.S., Su, C., Walker, P., Bian, J., Wang, F.: Federated learning for healthcare informatics. J. Healthc. Inform. Res. **5**(1), 1–19 (2021)

Towards Real-World Federated Learning in Medical Image Analysis Using Kaapana

Klaus Kades[1,2]([✉]) [iD], Jonas Scherer[1,3] [iD], Maximilian Zenk[1] [iD],
Marius Kempf[4] [iD], and Klaus Maier-Hein[1,5] [iD]

[1] Division of Medical Image Computing, German Cancer Research Center (DKFZ),
Heidelberg, Germany
k.kades@dkfz.de
[2] Faculty of Mathematics and Computer Science, Heidelberg University,
Heidelberg, Germany
[3] Medical Faculty, Heidelberg University, Heidelberg, Germany
[4] Karlsruhe Service Research Institute (KSRI), Karlsruhe, Germany
[5] Pattern Analysis and Learning Group, Heidelberg University Hospital,
Heidelberg, Germany

Abstract. The Radiological Cooperative Network (RACOON) is dedicated to strengthening Covid-19 research by establishing a standardized digital infrastructure across all university hospitals in Germany. Using a combination of structured reporting together with advanced image analysis methods, it is possible to train new models for a standardized and automated biomarker extraction that can be easily rolled out across the consortium. A major challenge consists in providing generic and robust tools that work well on relevant data from all hospitals, not just on those where the model was originally trained. Potential solutions are federated approaches that incorporate data from all sites for model generation. In this work, we therefore extend the Kaapana framework used in RACOON to enable real-world federated learning in clinical environments. In addition, we create a benchmark of the nnU-Net when applied in multi-site settings by conducting intra- and cross-site experiments on a multi-site prostate segmentation dataset.

Keywords: Federated learning · Platforms · nnU-Net · Segmentation

1 Introduction

The outbreak of the Covid-19 virus has shown that hospital-overarching application of machine learning algorithms is a key concept in fighting a pandemic [27]. A standardized application of machine learning algorithms across clinics requires from an organizational point of view national and international collaborations. For this reason, the Radiological Cooperative Network (RACOON) was

Supplementary Information The online version contains supplementary material available at https://doi.org/10.1007/978-3-031-18523-6_13.

established in Germany in 2021 in order to enable Covid-19 research across all German university clinics. From a technical point of view, a standardized infrastructure is required for the deployment of algorithms inside hospitals and for federated scenarios across hospitals [19,21,28]. From a methodological point of view, algorithms are required which perform well and robust on in-house data as well as on unseen data from other clinics.

Besides the availability of well-curated medical data, the application of federated learning in healthcare faces security and heterogeneity challenges. Additional challenges are the management and administration of training large models as well as the avoidance of data leakage in order to ensure data privacy [12,13,21]. In contrast to NVIDIA Clara Federated or the OpenMined-based Privacy-preserving Medical Image Analysis software framework (PriMIA) [11,22,23], the used Kaapana-based infrastructure within RACOON does not support federated use cases so far. For this reason, one main contribution of this work is an extension of the Kaapana toolkit with a federated functionality, which is tailored to the technical and political requirements within RACOON, to allow the application of federated use cases.

In addition to the technical challenges, current state-of-the-art algorithms often lack good performance on unseen, out-of-distribution data. This holds also for the nnU-Net [6,7,9]. In RACOON, one main objective is to train segmentation algorithms in order to automate and standardize the assessment of Covid-19-related tissue alterations. For this, Covid-19 relevant anatomies and pathologies were segmented in the lung of a site-overarching patient cohort. One way of creating robust and well-performing algorithms is to train the model on more heterogeneous data [1], which in the case of RACOON requires a federated training strategy due to data privacy regulations. Therefore, another main contribution of this work is the adaptation of the nnU-Net to be used for federated learning and to assess its performance on train and test data coming from the same clinical site or from different clinical sites against single-site, centralized and ensemble-trained models on the example of a multi-site prostate segmentation dataset [14,15].

2   Related Work

Federated learning for medical use cases poses challenges in various aspects, ranging from learning methodology over data protection and privacy to the technical infrastructure and algorithm implementation [21,28]. The authors of [13] systematically analyse different federated learning strategies as well as domain-independent open-source software solutions for federated learning which include FATE, TensorFlow Federated, OpenMined, PaddleFl or FedML. In the medical domain, the open-source software framework PriMIA (Privacy-preserving Medical Image Analysis) [11] is presented for the application of privacy-preserving deep learning algorithms on multi-institutional medical imaging data. A widely used non-open-source solution is the healthcare application framework NVIDIA Clara which features federated learning with its NVIDIA Clara Train SDK.

[2,3,22–24] prove its successful application in multiple real-world scenarios. Apart from NVIDIA, efforts for federated learning in the imaging domain are pursued by OpenFL or Substra in conjunction with the Medical Open Network for Artificial Intelligence (MONAI) framework.

A key difference of our solution compared to most existing tools is that it requires only unidirectional communication from the clients to the central instance, which is a prerequisite for the application in RACOON. Furthermore, our solution wraps the federated functionality in an agnostic way around a locally running workflow without the need of any customization in the code itself.

Federated learning and its challenges in a clinical environment are analysed and summarized from a methodological point of view in [20,21]. A focus on differential privacy is set in [12,29]. Centralized versus local and alternative federated learning strategies are assessed in [5,26]. In our work, we follow the model averaging approach introduced by [17]. [2,22–24] compare amongst others local and federated trained models across multiple institutions. Publicly available datasets often used to benchmark federated learning and domain shifts in medical imaging are the BRATS dataset [18,26] and the multi-site prostate segmentation dataset from [8,10,14–16]. Federated learning was applied on Covid-19 data by [2–5]. In this work, we use the multi-site prostate segmentation dataset to benchmark our implementation. The question of domain generalizability and cross-domain performance were tackled amongst others in [6,7,16], where [6] propose an approach of how to improve generalizibility of the nnU-Net and [7] introduce a method to detect when the nnU-Net fails on out-of-distribution data.

3   Methods

To enable federated learning in RACOON, it is needed to, firstly, add a backend and a user interface to Kaapana that manages the federated communication between the clinical sites and the central instance, secondly, add the possibility of locally running workflows to share data with the central instance and, lastly, adjust the nnU-Net to work in the federated setup. Since Kaapana itself is a medical imaging platform, we try to reuse most of its existing technology stack to add the needed features. A detailed description of the technology stack and how a typical local workflow looks like in Kaapana is given in [25].

The demands on the backend and the user interface are mainly driven by the setup of RACOON, which consists of multiple clinical sites that have a one-way communication with a dedicated central instance. Therefore, we added a FastAPI backend to Kapaana that allows a secure unidirectional SSL communication from the local to the central site. The FastAPI uses a custom token based authentication for the communication to the central instance. Any file transfer is forwarded to the MinIO S3 object storage, available on the central Kaapana instance. In addition to the usage of so-called pre-signed URLs the transferred files can be protected via Fernet encryption. The backend itself manages all running workflows (jobs) that run locally as well as on the remote sites in the open-source workflow-management-platform Apache Airflow. Therefore, to execute a job on a local site, the job has to be submitted on the central instance and afterwards actively fetched and accepted by the local site. Following this kind of a job queuing architecture, our implementation allows in the first place to execute a workflow on a remote instance, which during a federated training we do periodically. The backend is operated by a dedicated user interface which allows to register local and central instances. In addition, it allows to manage whether to automatically or manually fetch and execute a job as well as which jobs (workflows) and which tag-based image data are available for a remote execution. Finally, it shows detailed information of submitted jobs and their current state. Screenshots of the interface are available online[1].

In Airflow data processing workflows are represented by Directed Acyclic Graphs (DAGs) consisting of multiple building blocks called operators. A simplified version of the nnU-Net training workflow is illustrated in Fig. 1. Federated training of the nnU-Net requires a dynamic exchange of data between locally running workflows and the central instance. In our implementation we try to allow this data exchange as flexible as possible, i.e. any workflow that runs locally should be usable in a federated setting without any customization to the workflow itself. This is achieved by adding to each operator a configurable pre-hook to download data and a post-hook to upload data to the central instance. In addition, we add the functionality to skip operators and to load local data, e.g. pre-processed data which are needed for training, from a previous workflow. Since a federated training increases the difficulty of a robust, error-free training, we added at different levels in the pipeline multiple error exceptions and retries. In addition, we added the possibility to recover a training at its training step in case it stopped for unexpected reasons. From a security perspective, the central instance has no possibility to maliciously manipulate the locally running workflows, which are deployed upon installation of the local instance.

Adjustments to the nnU-Net are necessary because it creates the segmentation pipeline based on local data characteristics, so-called fingerprints, which are likely to be inconsistent in a federated setup. In detail, a fingerprint of a training dataset is created to dynamically configure the pre-processing pipeline and the model architecture. To work with consistent models in a federated training, we concatenate all locally created fingerprints on the central instance in a preparation round, before the model configuration and pre-processing is started at the local sites.

4   Experiments

To benchmark the proposed extension in a multi-site setting, we implement the federated training of the nnU-Net in Kaapana and run experiments on a setup consisting of six independent Kaapana instances which serve as clients and one Kaapana instance which serves as the central instance. We run experiments on the pre-processed multi-site prostate MRI segmentation dataset[2], which consists of data from six different institutions with varying number of cases and acquisition protocols [14,15]. As in [8,14,16], the peripheral zone (PZ) and central

---

[1] https://kaapana.readthedocs.io/en/release-0.1.3/.
[2] https://liuquande.github.io/SAML/.

gland (CG) segmentations of the RUNMC (Site A) and BMC (Site B) datasets are merged together to have a consistent ground truth across all sites.

In federated settings like RACOON, a common challenge is to learn an accurate model despite the existing data heterogeneity. Therefore, in a first experiment ("seen" setup), we evaluate the performance of models trained and tested on data from the same sites with a training and testing split of 70% and 30%, respectively. The test cases of each site are listed in the appendix, Table 2. However, we note that unlike [10], the train test split is done on case- instead of slice-level and unlike [8], we do not use a validation split. In a second experiment ("unseen" setup), we evaluate the domain generalizability for the use case in which a site does not participate in the federated training. Like [8,14,16], we apply the leave-one-domain-out strategy, i.e., we train on K-1 seen sites and test on the omitted unseen target site. In contrast to [8], we do not use an extra validation split of the unseen site, but test on all cases of the unseen site.

In all experiments, we compare the performance of nnU-Net models trained on all source domains in a centralized (denoted as DeepAll) or federated fashion. Additionally, we train nnU-Nets on every single site independently and create an ensemble of these (using only the source domain models in the leave-one-out experiments). In contrast to existing works ([8,10,14]), we evaluate a $2D$ and a $3D$-full-resolution model architecture, despite the large variance on slice thickness between the different sites. To keep the overall computational costs low, but still train with as many cases as possible, we train all models without a validation set and without cross-validation. However, to make sure local models are neither over- nor underfitting, we ran preliminarily single-site experiments with cross-validation. In all presented experiments, we train each model for 500 epochs with respectively 250 batches per epoch and use the final model for testing. The rest of the hyperparameter are either hard-coded or dynamically determined from the nnUNet. More information about its selection can be found in [9]. During the federated training, we apply federated averaging (FedAvg) [17],

$$x^{(t+1)} = x^{(t)} + \sum_{k=1}^{K} \frac{\Delta_k^{(t)}}{K} \quad , \tag{1}$$

after every epoch, where x denotes the parameters of the model and K the number of clients. We note that we weight clients equally in our experiments, to optimize all local objectives equally. The performances of the models are evaluated for each case based on the Dice score (Dice) and the Average Surface Distance (ASD). The federated extensions and the implementation of the federated training of the nnU-Net are integrated in the open source platform toolkit Kaapana[3].

5   Results

Figure 1 illustrates how we implement the federated training of the nnU-Net in Kaapana with all its steps and the client-central communication in detail.

---

[3] https://github.com/kaapana/kaapana.

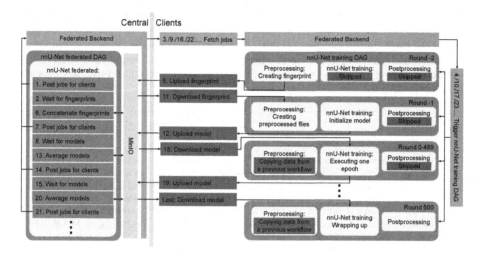

Fig. 1. Overview of the federated learning rounds while training the nnU-Net. The left site corresponds to the central instance, with the federated backend, MinIO and the nnU-Net federated operator. The right site represents a client instance with a simplified view of the nnU-Net training DAG and its operators.The green boxes correspond to Airflow DAGs and operator and all red boxes represent pre- or post-hooks of the operators. (Color figure online)

After authenticating client instances with the central instance, the central instance submits jobs (1./7....), which are fetched by the corresponding clients (3./9...). In a preparation round only the pre-processing of the nnU-Net is executed. Its generated fingerprint of the local datasets are uploaded by a post-hook to MinIO (5.) and concatenated on the central instance (6.). All requests to MinIO are forwarded by the federated backend. In a second round, the fingerprints are downloaded by a pre-hook (11.) and used to configure the nnU-Net. After pre-processing the image data, the nnU-Net training operator initializes the model weights and biases and uploads them to central (12.), where the models are averaged. In the following training rounds, a pre-hook of the pre-processing operator copies the pre-processed data from one run to the next. A pre- and post- hook download and upload the model for the nnU-Net training operator, which executes one epoch of training, respectively. In the final round, the final model is downloaded and some post-processing steps are executed, including the storage of the trained model and the generation of a training report.

For the experiments from Sect. 4, Table 1 reports the Dice (%) and ASD (mm) for the $2D$ and $3D - fullres$ nnU-Net model as well as the results from [8,14,16]. Since the $2D$ nnU-Net models trained on single sites could not determine a prediction on all target domain cases, we only report the ensemble performance for the $3D$ trained models. Furthermore, We note that the reported Dice scores represent the arithmetic mean over all test cases per site. The "Average" column is the unweighted average over the reported per-site mean scores. The average rank

Table 1. Dice (%) and ASD (mm) scores for all experiments in comparison with existing methods, along with the average scores over the sites, the average rank per site and the total number of cases per dataset. We note that for the "seen" experiments, the test set includes 30% of all cases, whereas for the "unseen" experiments, all cases are used for testing. The best nnU-Net scores are marked as bold and the best overall scores are underlined.

Setup	Dataset algorithm	RUNMC # 30	BMC # 30	I2CVB # 19	UCL # 13	BIDMC # 12	HK # 312	Average	Rank
Seen	DCA-Net [8]	91.83 0.72	91.59 0.81	89.93 0.77	91.99 0.64	90.68 0.93	90.57 0.82	90.93 0.78	
2D	Intra-site	87.74 0.79	91.14 0.72	81.12 2.05	88.06 0.82	69.83 2.35	85.11 1.08	83.83 1.30	5.05
	DeepAll	88.55 0.73	91.04 0.73	79.21 2.32	90.14 0.67	80.98 1.58	89.46 0.71	86.57 1.12	3.67
	Federated	88.27 0.77	90.88 0.70	**84.50** 2.00	**90.59 0.61**	78.01 1.62	88.97 0.77	86.87 1.08	3.72
3D	Ensemble	87.48 0.92	86.27 3.46	48.28 20.93	88.02 0.88	58.32 15.54	82.51 8.00	75.15 8.29	6.12
	Intra-site	89.58 0.78	90.46 0.74	83.64 2.14	88.19 1.25	73.95 40.65	84.96 1.01	85.13 7.76	4.07
	DeepAll	**90.00 0.67**	**91.57** 0.64	82.27 2.14	90.02 0.70	87.64 **1.26**	90.49 0.66	88.66 1.01	2.78
	Federated	89.96 0.69	91.50 **0.61**	**84.50** 1.95	90.16 0.63	**87.70** 1.28	**90.99 0.62**	**89.14 0.96**	2.60
Unseen	SAML [14]	89.66 1.38	87.53 1.46	84.43 2.07	88.67 1.56	87.37 1.77	88.34 1.22	87.67 1.58	
	ELCFS [16]	90.19	87.17	85.26	88.23	83.02	90.47	87.39	
	DCA-Net [8]	90.61 1.12	88.31 1.14	84.89 1.76	89.22 1.09	86.78 1.58	89.17 1.02	88.16 1.29	
2D	DeepAll	84.89 1.37	83.10 **1.26**	71.17 4.54	85.88 **1.04**	74.18 4.73	86.24 1.20	80.91 2.36	3.22
	Federated	**85.84 1.11**	81.96 1.33	**76.52 4.52**	84.94 1.53	73.19 **2.56**	86.09 1.03	81.42 **2.01**	3.18
3D	Ensemble	76.53 38.57	84.99 2.25	49.14 37.49	84.34 16.68	72.15 18.96	85.81 5.72	75.49 19.95	3.56
	DeepAll	83.97 4.91	80.37 16.77	58.45 24.77	85.59 8.34	78.98 25.48	**89.24** 1.47	79.43 13.62	2.78
	Federated	85.01 3.65	**85.36** 8.05	67.63 16.34	**86.97** 1.78	**81.95** 21.16	88.51 1.86	**82.57** 8.81	2.25

("Rank") is computed by first taking the arithmetic mean of a case-based ranking of the models per dataset, before averaging it again over the sites. Ranks are calculated independently for the "unseen" and "seen" experiments, but across the different architectures and algorithms. We find that in all experiments the differences in Dice scores between the centralized and the federated trained nnU-Nets are non-significant (Mann-Whitney U test, Benjamini-Hochberg corrected: all $p > .05$). Cross-site performances with standard deviations of the individually trained models are attached in the appendix in Table 3 and Table 4.

To get an intuition about the variability in performance for the different cases, we illustrate in Fig. 2 box plots of the Dice scores on all datasets for the different algorithms and for the $3D$ trained nnU-Net architecture. The plot of the Dice scores for the $2D$ trained nn-UNets along with an illustration of the training loss of the centralized and federated trained nnU-Net models is attached in the appendix in Fig. 3 and 4.

6   Discussion

The two key features added to Kaapana in this work are on the one hand the possibility to trigger a workflow on a remote instance in a well-controlled environment and on the other hand the possibility to transfer the generated file-based output of Airflow operators to the object storage of another instance. With this functionalities, we enable in general the implementation of all kind of network topologies like decentralized or hierarchical and federated learning compute plans

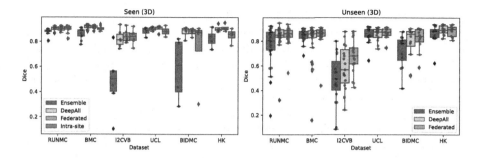

Fig. 2. Distribution of Dice scores of each dataset and algorithm for the "seen" and "unseen" experiments and for the $3D$ nnU-Net architecture.

like sequential or peer-to-peer. The design choice to run a separated workflow for each federated round provides full flexibility when creating a federated learning pipeline. In this work, we were able to setup a federated training of the nnU-Net with federated averaging without the need to modify anything in the local running nnU-Net workflow.

The experimental results with nnU-Net show that our federated learning implementation can reach the same performance as centralized training, suggesting that the potential improvements of nnU-Net through advanced federated learning methods are small. Reasons for the slightly, but not significantly, better results of the federated trained nnU-Net might originate from the fact, that in contrast to the federated approach, the centralized approach does not distinguish to which site a case belongs to and might be biased towards some sites, due to the imbalanced number of cases between different sites. Furthermore, for the $3D$ models, we observe that an ensemble of the models often has difficulties to reach the performance of federated or centralized trained nnU-Nets. In both experiments, we were not able to outperform existing state-of-the-art models. One reason for this might be that no further measures were taken to adjust the nnU-Net for the multi-site setting. In addition, the numbers of the DCA-Net baseline cannot be compared directly to ours because of inconsistent train, validation and test data splits. In the "seen" experiments, we found that additional training data from other sites can for some sites slightly enhance the performance in comparison to intra-site trained models. However, given the, in our application, still very high performance of the intra-site trained models, the question arises whether federated learning is needed for sites with enough training data. In the experiments on nnU-Net's capability to generalize to unseen sites we underpin the result from [6,7] that there is a necessity to validate and to improve the performance of nnU-Net on data from unseen sites.

An important next step is to use the proposed system in a real-world setting, e.g. within the RACOON project, where Kaapana is already being used across clinics. Furthermore, federated learning capabilities of Kaapana can be further augmented, for example by adding a certificate-based authentication or integrating common functionalities of federated learning toolkits like homomorphic encryption, encrypted computation or differential privacy. The main bottleneck of training the nnU-Net federated is the communication cost between each federated round. Therefore, interesting research topics include decreasing the model size of nnU-Net, trying out different hyperparameter settings like increasing the number of local epochs per federated round or investigating different federated aggregation or optimization methods. As mentioned above, another topic of interest is to improve the generalizability of nnU-Net on unseen data, by incorporating methods presented in [6,8,10,16] into nnU-Net. Finally, it will be interesting to add the federated functionality to more, also non-imaging workflows and to try out different federated setups like peer-to-peer federated learning.

Acknowledgements. This research was supported by the German Cancer Consortium (DKTK, Strategic Initiative *Joint Imaging Platform*), the Helmholtz Association within the project *Trustworthy Federated Data Analytics (TFDA)* (funding number ZT-I-OO1 4) and by the German Federal Ministry of Education and Research (BMBF) as part of the University Medicine Network (Project *RACOON*, 01KX2021). Furthermore, we thank Niklas Kühl from the Karlsruhe Service Research Institute (KSRI) and our colleagues at the German Cancer Research Center who were involved in making this work possible, especially Constantin Ulrich, Fabian Isensee, Markus Bujotzek, Maximilian Fischer, Michael Baumgartner, Peter Neher, Piermarco Pascale and Philipp Schader.

References

1. Cahan, E.M., et al.: Putting the data before the algorithm in big data addressing personalized healthcare. npj Dig. Med. **2**(1), 1–6 (2019). https://doi.org/10.1038/s41746-019-0157-2. www.nature.com/articles/s41746-019-0157-2
2. Dayan, I., et al.: Federated learning for predicting clinical outcomes in patients with covid-19. Nat. Med. **27**(10), 1735–1743 (2021). https://doi.org/10.1038/s41591-021-01506-3
3. Dong, Y., et al.: Federated semi-supervised learning for covid region segmentation in chest ct using multi-national data from china, italy, japan. Med. Image Anal. **70**, 101992–101992 (2021)
4. Dou, Q., et al.: Federated deep learning for detecting covid-19 lung abnormalities in ct: a privacy-preserving multinational validation study. npj Dig. Med. 4(1), 60 (2021). https://doi.org/10.1038/s41746-021-00431-6
5. Feki, I., Ammar, S., Kessentini, Y., Muhammad, K.: Federated learning for covid-19 screening from chest x-ray images. Appl. Soft Comput. **106** (2021). https://doi.org/10.1016/j.asoc.2021.107330
6. Full, P.M., Isensee, F., Jäger, P.F., Maier-Hein, K.: Studying robustness of semantic segmentation under domain shift in cardiac MRI. In: Puyol Anton, E., et al. (eds.) STACOM 2020. LNCS, vol. 12592, pp. 238–249. Springer, Cham (2021). https://doi.org/10.1007/978-3-030-68107-4_24
7. Gonzalez, C., Gotkowski, K., Bucher, A., Fischbach, R., Kaltenborn, I., Mukhopadhyay, A.: Detecting when pre-trained nnU-net models fail silently for covid-19 lung

lesion segmentation. In: de Bruijne, M., Cattin, P.C., Cotin, S., Padoy, N., Speidel, S., Zheng, Y., Essert, C. (eds.) MICCAI 2021. LNCS, vol. 12907, pp. 304–314. Springer, Cham (2021). https://doi.org/10.1007/978-3-030-87234-2_29

8. Gu, R., Zhang, J., Huang, R., Lei, W., Wang, G., Zhang, S.: Domain composition and attention for unseen-domain generalizable medical image segmentation. In: de Bruijne, M., et al. (eds.) MICCAI 2021. LNCS, vol. 12903, pp. 241–250. Springer, Cham (2021). https://doi.org/10.1007/978-3-030-87199-4_23

9. Isensee, F., Jaeger, P.F., Kohl, S.A.A., Petersen, J., Maier-Hein, K.H.: nnu-net: a self-configuring method for deep learning-based biomedical image segmentation. Nat. Methods **18**(2), 203–211 (2021). https://doi.org/10.1038/s41592-020-01008-z

10. Jiang, M., Wang, Z., Dou, Q.: Harmofl: harmonizing local and global drifts in federated learning on heterogeneous medical images. In: AAAI Conference on Artificial Intelligence (2022)

11. Kaissis, G., et al.: End-to-end privacy preserving deep learning on multi-institutional medical imaging. Nat. Mach. Intell. **3**(6), 473–484 (2021). https://doi.org/10.1038/s42256-021-00337-8

12. Kaissis, G.A., Makowski, M.R., Rückert, D., Braren, R.F.: Secure, privacy-preserving and federated machine learning in medical imaging. Nat. Mach. Intell. **2**(6), 305–311 (2020). https://doi.org/10.1038/s42256-020-0186-1

13. Li, Q., et al.: A survey on federated learning systems: vision, hype and reality for data privacy and protection. IEEE Trans. Knowl. Data Eng. 1 (2021). https://doi.org/10.1109/TKDE.2021.3124599

14. Liu, Q., Dou, Q., Heng, P.-A.: Shape-aware meta-learning for generalizing prostate MRI segmentation to unseen domains. In: Martel, A.L., et al. (eds.) MICCAI 2020. LNCS, vol. 12262, pp. 475–485. Springer, Cham (2020). https://doi.org/10.1007/978-3-030-59713-9_46

15. Liu, Q., et al.: Ms-net: multi-site network for improving prostate segmentation with heterogeneous MRI data. IEEE Trans. Med. Imaging **39**, 2713–2724 (2020)

16. Liu, Q., et al.: Feddg: federated domain generalization on medical image segmentation via episodic learning in continuous frequency space. In: The IEEE/CVF Conference on Computer Vision and Pattern Recognition (CVPR) (2021)

17. McMahan, H.B., Moore, E., Ramage, D., Arcas, B.A.: Federated learning of deep networks using model averaging. ArXiv abs/1602.05629 (2016)

18. Menze, B.H., et al.: The multimodal brain tumor image segmentation benchmark (brats). IEEE Trans. Med. Imaging **34**(10), 1993–2024 (2015). https://doi.org/10.1109/TMI.2014.2377694

19. Peiffer-Smadja, N., et al.: Machine learning for covid-19 needs global collaboration and data-sharing. Nat. Mach. Intell. **2**(6), 293–294 (2020). https://doi.org/10.1038/s42256-020-0181-6

20. Prayitno, et al.: A systematic review of federated learning in the healthcare area: From the perspective of data properties and applications. Appl. Sci. **11**(23) (2021). https://doi.org/10.3390/app112311191

21. Rieke, N., et al.: The future of digital health with federated learning. npj Dig. Med. **3**(1), 119 (2020). https://doi.org/10.1038/s41746-020-00323-1

22. Roth, H.R., et al.: Federated whole prostate segmentation in MRI with personalized neural architectures. In: de Bruijne, M., Cattin, P.C., Cotin, S., Padoy, N., Speidel, S., Zheng, Y., Essert, C. (eds.) MICCAI 2021. LNCS, vol. 12903, pp. 357–366. Springer, Cham (2021). https://doi.org/10.1007/978-3-030-87199-4_34

23. Roth, H.R., et al.: Federated learning for breast density classification: a real-world implementation. In: Albarqouni, S., et al. (eds.) DART/DCL -2020. LNCS, vol. 12444, pp. 181–191. Springer, Cham (2020). https://doi.org/10.1007/978-3-030-60548-3_18

24. Sarma, K.V., et al.: Federated learning improves site performance in multicenter deep learning without data sharing. J. Am. Med. Inf. Assoc. **28**(6), 1259–1264 (2021). https://doi.org/10.1093/jamia/ocaa341

25. Scherer, J., et al.: Joint imaging platform for federated clinical data analytics. JCO Clin. Cancer Inf. **4**, 1027–1038 (2020). https://doi.org/10.1200/CCI.20.00045

26. Sheller, M.J.E.A.: Federated learning in medicine: facilitating multi-institutional collaborations without sharing patient data. Sci. Rep. **10**(1), 12598 (2020). https://doi.org/10.1038/s41598-020-69250-1

27. Ting, D.S.W., Carin, L., Dzau, V., Wong, T.Y.: Digital technology and covid-19. Nat. Med. **26**(4), 459–461 (2020). https://doi.org/10.1038/s41591-020-0824-5

28. Xu, J., et al.: Federated learning for healthcare informatics. J. Healthc. Inf. Res. **5**(1), 1–19 (2021). https://doi.org/10.1007/s41666-020-00082-4

29. Ziller, A., et al.: Medical imaging deep learning with differential privacy. Sci. Rep. **11**(1), 13524 (2021). https://doi.org/10.1038/s41598-021-93030-0

Towards Sparsified Federated Neuroimaging Models via Weight Pruning

Dimitris Stripelis[1]([✉]), Umang Gupta[1], Nikhil Dhinagar[2], Greg Ver Steeg[1], Paul M. Thompson[2], and José Luis Ambite[1]

[1] Information Sciences Institute, University of Southern California, Los Angeles, CA 90292, USA
{stripeli,umanggup,gregv,ambite}@isi.edu
[2] Imaging Genetics Center, Stevens Neuroimaging and Informatics Institute, University of Southern California, Los Angeles, CA 90292, USA
{dhinagar,thompson}@ini.usc.edu

Abstract. Federated training of large deep neural networks can often be restrictive due to the increasing costs of communicating the updates with increasing model sizes. Various model pruning techniques have been designed in centralized settings to reduce inference times. Combining centralized pruning techniques with federated training seems intuitive for reducing communication costs—by pruning the model parameters right before the communication step. Moreover, such a progressive model pruning approach during training can also reduce training times/costs. To this end, we propose *FedSparsify*, which performs model pruning during federated training. In our experiments in centralized and federated settings on the brain age prediction task (estimating a person's age from their brain MRI), we demonstrate that models can be pruned up to 95% sparsity without affecting performance even in challenging federated learning environments with highly heterogeneous data distributions. One surprising benefit of model pruning is improved model privacy. We demonstrate that models with high sparsity are less susceptible to membership inference attacks, a type of privacy attack.

Keywords: Neuroimaging · Federated learning · Model pruning · Security & Privacy

1 Introduction

Federated Learning [16,18,32] enables distributed training of machine learning and deep learning models across geographically dispersed data silos. In this setting, no data ever leaves its original location, making it appealing for training

---

D. Stripelis and U. Gupta—Equal contribution.

Supplementary Information The online version contains supplementary material available at https://doi.org/10.1007/978-3-031-18523-6_14.

S. Albarqouni et al. (Eds.): DeCaF 2022/FAIR 2022, LNCS 13573, pp. 141–151, 2022.
https://doi.org/10.1007/978-3-031-18523-6_14

models over private data that cannot be shared. For these reasons, Federated Learning has witnessed widespread adoption across multiple disciplines, especially in biomedical settings [3,24,26]. Federated training of neural networks involves exchanging/communicating parameters that are updated during local training on private datasets. This parameter exchange incurs high communication costs, limiting the size of neural networks that can be learned [25]. To circumvent this, model pruning techniques that have been extensively studied in centralized settings [6,9,17] for improving models' training and inference time seem a natural fit towards this direction.

In this work, we propose a federated training approach incorporating model pruning by directly extending previous work on model pruning in centralized settings [6,35]. Similar to these, we use a simple pruning approach of removing weights with the lowest magnitude. However, we consider federated learning environments with heterogeneous data distributions. The learning task is to predict brain age from T1-weighted MRI scans obtained from the UK BioBank dataset [19]. We show that with our progressive model pruning strategy, i.e., increasing the sparsity in the model with each federation round, we can learn a neural network model with less than 5% parameters of the original model while preserving most of the performance.

Even though Federated Learning avoids private data sharing, models trained using federated learning are not always private and may leak sensitive information [8,23,33]. This can often be attributed to overfitting or memorization [8,30]. Pruning parameters excessively can reduce the memorization capacity of neural networks. Inspired by this intuition, we evaluate the empirical privacy of the obtained sparsified models through membership inference attacks. We observe that pruned models at extreme degrees of sparsification (>95%) are less susceptible to membership inference attacks while maintaining learning performance. This suggests a triple win for using pruning during federated training—a) reduced communication costs, b) reduced inference costs due to small sized final models, and c) reduced privacy leakage.

Existing federated model pruning strategies focus on reducing the required communication cost during training in order to achieve specific levels of model performance [1,12]. However, in this work we aim to train highly sparsified models of similar performance to the non-sparsified counterparts while at the same time exploring the privacy gains of federated model sparsification against membership inference attacks. To the best of our knowledge, this is the first work that studies the learning performance and privacy properties of model pruning for deep learning models in the federated neuroimaging domain.

2   Neuroimaging Learning Environments

An extensive number of machine learning and deep learning approaches have been recently proposed [31] with great success [4,34] across multiple biomedical imaging tasks, such as image reconstruction, automated segmentation and predictive analytics. In this work, we evaluate such deep learning approaches for the

BrainAGE prediction task over a set of challenging neuroimaging environments in centralized and federated settings.

Brain Age Prediction Task. Brain age prediction involves creating a machine learning model to predict a person's chronological age from their brain MRI scan, after training the model on large amounts of data from healthy individuals. When this trained model is applied to new scans from patients and healthy controls, the age difference between each individual's true chronological age and that predicted from their MRI scan has been found to be associated with a broad range of neurological and psychiatric disorders, and with mortality [2,22]. This age prediction task is formulated as a regression task also known as the Brain Age Gap Estimation (BrainAGE). Various efficient deep learning architectures have been recently proposed based on RNNs [13,15] and CNNs [7,22] with highly accurate brain age estimations. In our work, we use a 3D-CNN model, similar to [15,27] consisting of seven blocks. The first five blocks are composed of a $3 \times 3 \times 3$ 3D convolutional layer, instance norm, a $2 \times 2 \times 2$ max-pool and ReLU activation functions. The sixth block is a $1 \times 1 \times 1$ 3D convolutional layer followed by an instance norm and ReLU activation. The final block has an average pooling layer, and a $1 \times 1 \times 1$ 3D convolutional layer. We test the performance of the model on the BrainAGE task over the UK BioBank dataset [19]. Out of the 16,356 subjects with neuroimaging in dataset, we selected 10,446 subjects with no neurological pathology and psychiatric diagnosis as defined by the ICD-10 criteria.

Centralized Environment. For centralized training, we follow the same setup as [7,15]. We consider 10,466 healthy subjects from the UKBB dataset and split them into train, test and validation sets of sizes 7,312, 2,172 and 940 respectively.

Federated Learning Environments. In our federated learning environment, we consider a centralized (star-shaped) topology [24] where a single controller orchestrates the execution of the participating learners. The controller aggregates learners' local models based on the number of training examples each model was trained on and learners train the global model on their local dataset using Vanilla SGD [18]. We refer to this federated training procedure as *FedAvg* [18].

Similar to the centralized settings, our learning task is BrainAGE prediction and the learning model is a 3D-CNN [22,27]. We partition the MRI scans of the training and validation datasets from the centralized environment across 8 learners in four federated learning environments [27,29] of heterogeneous data amounts (Uniform, Skewed) and distributions (IID, Non-IID) per learner (see Fig. 1). Uniform and Skewed refer to the cases where learners have an equal and rightly skewed number of training samples, respectively. IID and Non-IID refer to the cases where the age range of the local data distribution of the scans owned by a learner captures the global range or a subset, respectively.

Measuring Privacy via Membership Inference Attacks. To measure how much information the model leaks about the training set, we consider *Membership Inference Attack*. A Membership Inference Attack is often the preferred approach to evaluate practical privacy leakage from machine learning models [10,20].

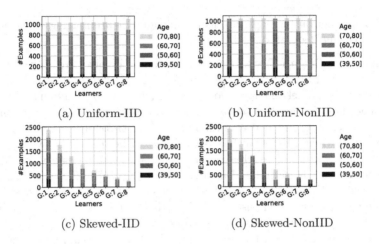

(a) Uniform-IID   (b) Uniform-NonIID

(c) Skewed-IID   (d) Skewed-NonIID

Fig. 1. UKBB federated learning environments.

Unlike differential privacy which considers worst-case privacy leakage, membership inference attacks can be seen as evaluating average case practical privacy leakages. In particular, given a sample (a subject's brain MRI in our case), these attacks infer if the sample was used during training or not. Discovering whether the subject's MRI is in the training set can reveal the personal medical history of the subject, which is undesirable. We use the same attack setups as in [8].

In particular, for evaluating models trained in our centralized environment we use their white-box attack setup. We consider access to some actual training and unseen samples for training the attack model; this is a stronger attack setup. One can also launch attacks without accessing actual training samples by training shadow models [8,21]. We create a balanced test set of training and unseen examples, and report the accuracy of correct predictions as "attack accuracy". Lower attack accuracy is more private, and hence better.

For models trained in our federated environments, we consider one of the learners as malicious and launching attacks against other learners. In our federated environments we consider 8 learners, which translates to 56 (7 × 8) attacks. The learner may train attack models using their private training set and some unseen examples. We report the accuracy of correctly differentiating between other learners' training examples and unseen samples as the "attack accuracy" and report the average accuracy, as in [8]. We also report the number of successful attacks, since due to data heterogeneity not all attacks are successful. We use features derived from the predictions, labels, and gradients of the last two layers of the 3D-CNN to train the attack models.

3   Model Pruning

In this section, we discuss model pruning approach for centralized and federated environments for neuroimaging tasks. We evaluate the efficacy of the weight magnitude-based pruning approach on a 3D-CNN trained on centralized and distributed MRI scans.

Centralized Model Pruning. Neural networks can often have redundant parameters which do not affect the outcome. One of the simplest ways of identifying such parameters is by looking at the magnitude of parameters. Parameters with low absolute values do not influence the output much and thus can be safely pruned [6,35]. We use this simple approach for pruning. [35] showed that gradual parameters pruning during training is more effective than one-shot pruning at the end. Our federated pruning approach exploits this observation. However, in the centralized setting, we prune in one step at the end of 90th epoch, followed by finetuning for 10 epochs.

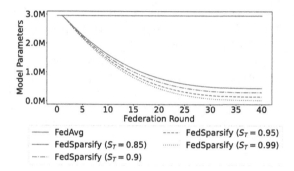

Fig. 2. Federated models number of parameters progression with (FedSparsify) and without (FedAvg) sparsification.

Federated Model Pruning. We develop our sparsified federated training on top of FedAvg. The global model is pruned at the controller after the controller aggregates the local model updates from the participating learners. Once the new (sparsified) global model is computed, the controller sends new global model to the learners along with the associated binary mask representing pruned and unpruned parameters. We use weight magnitude-based pruning approach [35] and remove the weights with lowest absolute values. A parameter once pruned is never resurrected. To enforce this during local training, each learner applies the binary mask at every training step (see also Algorithm 1 in Appendix). As we prune during every federation round, our pruning strategy follows a progressive schedule similar to [28,35]. The percentage of additional parameters pruned in each round follows an exponentially decreasing schedule, and the overall sparsity at round t is governed by this formula:

$$s_t = S_T + (S_0 - S_T)\left(1 - \frac{F\lfloor t/F \rfloor - t_0}{T - t_0}\right)^n \tag{1}$$

Here T is total number of federation rounds, S_0 and S_T are the initial and desired final sparsity, F is frequency of sparsification, and t_0 is the initial sparsification round. The exponent n controls the exponential sparsification rate. We refer to this pruning strategy as *FedSparsify*. In our experimental evaluation, we explore different final sparsities, i.e., $S_T = \{85\%, 90\%, 95\%, 99\%\}$. Throughout our experiments, we set the rate of sparsification n to 3, we prune the global model at every federation round, i.e., $F = 1$, for a total number of 40 federation rounds, $T = 40$, and we start the sparsification schedule at federation round 1, $t_0 = 1$. Figure 2 presents the progression of global model parameters of this sparsification schedule over the course of 40 federation rounds.

4   Results

We train the 3D-CNN model[1] for the brain age prediction task in different learning setups. We perform one-shot pruning in the centralized setup to achieve different sparsity levels. For the federated learning setup, we vary S_T, the final sparsity level in Eq. 1 and prune progressively before communicating updated weights to the learners (see Algorithm 1). In all environments the model is trained using Vanilla SGD with a batch size of 1 and learning rate of $1e^{-5}$. During federated training learners train the global model locally for 4 epochs in between federation rounds. All experiments were run on a dedicated GPU server equipped with 4 Quadro RTX 6000/8000 graphics cards of 50 GB RAM each, 31 Intel(R) Xeon(R) Gold 5217 CPU @ 3.00 GHz, and 251 GB DDR4 RAM.

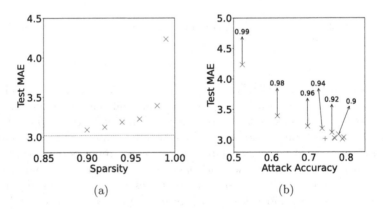

Fig. 3. Centralized BrainAGE model performance at different sparsity levels (left plot) and model vulnerability to membership inference attacks with respect to model performance (right plot).

Model Pruning Does Not Hurt Performance. We first study model performance at different sparsity levels by evaluating the models on a held-out test set. These results are summarized in Fig. 3a for centralized training. Even

---

[1] https://github.com/dstripelis/FedSparsify.

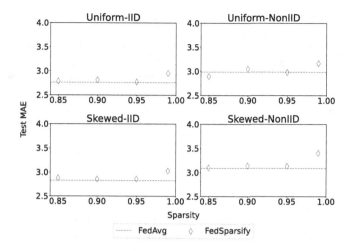

Fig. 4. Federated BrainAGE models learning performance at different degrees of sparsification across all four federated learning environments. Dashed line represents performance of non-sparsified model.

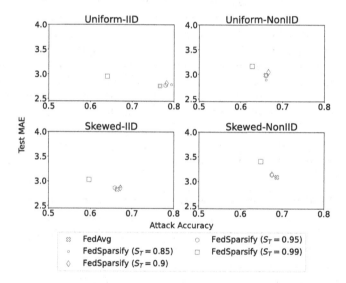

Fig. 5. Federated BrainAGE models vulnerability to membership inference attacks with respect to learning performance across all federated environments.

through the one-step pruning approach, we observe that most of the model performance is preserved when 90% of the parameters are removed. This validates the applicability of weight magnitude-based pruning for deep learning models on neuroimaging tasks. We apply our proposed progressive pruning procedure for federated training at different final sparsity levels across four different environments. The results are summarized in Fig. 4. In all cases, model performance is

Table 1. Federated models comparison in the *Skewed-IID* environment.

Sparsity	Params	Size (MBs)	Comm. (MM)	Test MAE	MIA (Success)	Throughput
0.0	2,950,401	10.85	1888	2.879	0.66 (50)	64.31
0.85	442,561	2.09	714	2.881	0.671 (52)	69.06
0.9	295,041	1.43	645	2.859	0.672 (51)	71.28
0.95	147,521	0.73	576	2.861	0.659 (54)	78.27
0.99	29,505	0.16	521	3.024	0.596 (47)	128.55

not affected at 95% sparsity level and performs the same as the FedAvg model, which is trained without pruning. Even when only 1% of the parameters are preserved, i.e., 99% sparsity, the model performance degrades slightly. Table 1 provides a quantitative comparison of the total number of parameters and memory/disk size of the final model, the cumulative communication cost in terms of the total number of parameters exchanged during training[2], and the model's learning performance. Our pruning schedule can learn a highly sparsified federated learning model with 3 to 3.5 times lower communication cost than its unpruned counterpart (cf. 521 million to 1888 million parameters). Moreover, the reduced number of the final model parameters also leads to reduced model space/memory footprint, with the sparsified models at 95% and 99% sparsification being 67 times smaller than the original model. Following previous work [14] on model efficiency evaluation[3], we benchmark the inference time for sparse and non-sparse models by recording the total number of processing items per second (i.e., Throughput - items/sec) that each model can perform. Specifically, we take the final model learned with (FedSparsify) and without sparsfication (FedAvg) and stress test its inference time by allocating a total execution time of 60 s with a warmup period of 10 s. As we show in Table 1, as sparsification increases model throughput increases too, leading to improved inference efficiency especially at 99% sparsity.

Excessive Model Pruning May Reduce Privacy Vulnerability. Intuitively, pruning can reduce the ability of a neural network to memorize training data and thus reduce privacy vulnerability. To this end, we evaluate pruned models for privacy leakage using membership inference attacks (Fig. 3b and Fig. 5). We find that at extreme sparsity levels (>95% for centralized settings and 99% for federated setting) the attack accuracy reduces suggesting that these models are less vulnerable to privacy leakage compared to non-sparsified models. Compared to the non-sparsified model, the sparsified models are 10% to 20% less vulnerable in case Skewed IID and Uniform IID environments, respectively, and 5% for the Non-IID environments.

---

[2] Communication cost is computed as $\sum_t^T 2N_Z^t L$. T represents the total number of federation rounds, N_Z^t the non-zero model parameters at round t and L the number of participating learners. Factor 2 accounts for the model parameters sent from the controller to the learners and from the learners to the controller within a round.

[3] https://github.com/neuralmagic/deepsparse.

5   Discussion

We investigated model pruning for deep learning models in the neuroimaging domain through the BrainAGE prediction task in both centralized and federated learning environments. We demonstrated that sparsified models are equally performant as their non-sparsified counterparts even at extreme sparsity levels across all investigated environments. We also evaluated the effectiveness of sparsified models in improving model resiliency against membership inference attacks. We discovered that highly sparsified models could reduce vulnerability to this privacy attack. The vulnerability to membership inference attack is related to the mutual information between the training dataset and activations [11] or model parameters [5]. These results could provide a plausible theoretical explanation as to why pruning reduces the information about the training dataset in neural network weights compared to weights obtained by training without pruning. In the future, we plan to analyze the relation between model sparsification and model privacy and provide a theoretical framework to understand the connection between them better. We also plan to improve model privacy by introducing notions of stochasticity while applying model weight pruning.

References

1. Bibikar, S., Vikalo, H., Wang, Z., Chen, X.: Federated dynamic sparse training: computing less, communicating less, yet learning better (2021)
2. Cole, J.H., Leech, R., Sharp, D.J., Alzheimer's Disease Neuroimaging Initiative: Prediction of brain age suggests accelerated atrophy after traumatic brain injury. Ann. Neurol. **77**(4), 571–581 (2015)
3. Dayan, I., et al.: Federated learning for predicting clinical outcomes in patients with Covid-19. Nat. Med. **27**(10), 1735–1743 (2021)
4. Ezzati, A., et al.: Predictive value of ATN biomarker profiles in estimating disease progression in Alzheimer's disease dementia. Alzheimer's & Dementia **17**(11), 1855–1867 (2021)
5. Farokhi, F., Kaafar, M.A.: Modelling and quantifying membership information leakage in machine learning. arXiv preprint arXiv:2001.10648 (2020)
6. Frankle, J., Carbin, M.: The lottery ticket hypothesis: finding sparse, trainable neural networks. In: International Conference on Learning Representations (2018)
7. Gupta, U., Lam, P.K., Ver Steeg, G., Thompson, P.M.: Improved brain age estimation with slice-based set networks. In: 2021 IEEE 18th International Symposium on Biomedical Imaging (ISBI), pp. 840–844. IEEE (2021)
8. Gupta, U., Stripelis, D., Lam, P.K., Thompson, P., Ambite, J.L., Ver Steeg, G.: Membership inference attacks on deep regression models for neuroimaging. In: Medical Imaging with Deep Learning, pp. 228–251. PMLR (2021)
9. Hoefler, T., Alistarh, D., Ben-Nun, T., Dryden, N., Peste, A.: Sparsity in deep learning: pruning and growth for efficient inference and training in neural networks. J. Mach. Learn. Res. **22**(241), 1–124 (2021)
10. Jayaraman, B., Wang, L., Evans, D., Gu, Q.: Revisiting membership inference under realistic assumptions. arXiv preprint arXiv:2005.10881 (2020)
11. Jha, S.K., et al.: An extension of Fano's inequality for characterizing model susceptibility to membership inference attacks. arXiv preprint arXiv:2009.08097 (2020)

12. Jiang, Y., et al.: Model pruning enables efficient federated learning on edge devices. IEEE Trans. Neural Netw. Learn. Syst. (2022)
13. Jónsson, B.A., et al.: Brain age prediction using deep learning uncovers associated sequence variants. Nat. Commun. **10**(1), 1–10 (2019)
14. Kurtz, M., et al.: Inducing and exploiting activation sparsity for fast inference on deep neural networks. In: International Conference on Machine Learning, pp. 5533–5543. PMLR (2020)
15. Lam, P.K., et al.: Accurate brain age prediction using recurrent slice-based networks. In: 16th International Symposium on Medical Information Processing and Analysis, vol. 11583, p. 1158303. International Society for Optics and Photonics (2020)
16. Li, T., Sahu, A.K., Talwalkar, A., Smith, V.: Federated learning: challenges, methods, and future directions. IEEE Signal Process. Mag. **37**(3), 50–60 (2020)
17. Liu, Z., Sun, M., Zhou, T., Huang, G., Darrell, T.: Rethinking the value of network pruning. In: International Conference on Learning Representations (2018)
18. McMahan, B., Moore, E., Ramage, D., Hampson, S., Arcas, B.A.: Communication-efficient learning of deep networks from decentralized data. In: Artificial Intelligence and Statistics, pp. 1273–1282. PMLR (2017)
19. Miller, K.L., et al.: Multimodal population brain imaging in the UK biobank prospective epidemiological study. Nat. Neurosci. **19**(11), 1523–1536 (2016)
20. Nasr, M., Shokri, R., Houmansadr, A.: Comprehensive privacy analysis of deep learning: passive and active white-box inference attacks against centralized and federated learning. In: IEEE Symposium on Security and Privacy (SP) (2019)
21. Nasr, M., Shokri, R., Houmansadr, A.: Machine learning with membership privacy using adversarial regularization. In: Proceedings of the 2018 ACM SIGSAC Conference on Computer and Communications Security, pp. 634–646 (2018)
22. Peng, H., Gong, W., Beckmann, C.F., Vedaldi, A., Smith, S.M.: Accurate brain age prediction with lightweight deep neural networks. Med. Image Anal. **68**, 101871 (2021)
23. Pustozerova, A., Mayer, R.: Information leaks in federated learning. In: Proceedings of the Network and Distributed System Security Symposium, vol. 10 (2020)
24. Rieke, N., et al.: The future of digital health with federated learning. NPJ Digit. Med. **3**(1), 1–7 (2020)
25. Ro, J.H., et al.: Scaling language model size in cross-device federated learning. In: ACL Workshop on Federated Learning for Natural Language Processing (2022)
26. Sheller, M.J., et al.: Federated learning in medicine: facilitating multi-institutional collaborations without sharing patient data. Sci. Rep. **10**(1), 1–12 (2020)
27. Stripelis, D., Ambite, J.L., Lam, P., Thompson, P.: Scaling neuroscience research using federated learning. In: 2021 IEEE 18th International Symposium on Biomedical Imaging (ISBI), pp. 1191–1195. IEEE (2021)
28. Stripelis, D., Gupta, U., Steeg, G.V., Ambite, J.L.: Federated progressive sparsification (purge, merge, tune)+. arXiv preprint arXiv:2204.12430 (2022)
29. Stripelis, D., Thompson, P.M., Ambite, J.L.: Semi-synchronous federated learning for energy-efficient training and accelerated convergence in cross-silo settings. ACM Trans. Intell. Syst. Technol. (TIST) (2022)
30. Truex, S., Liu, L., Gursoy, M.E., Yu, L., Wei, W.: Towards demystifying membership inference attacks. arXiv preprint arXiv:1807.09173 (2018)
31. Wainberg, M., Merico, D., Delong, A., Frey, B.J.: Deep learning in biomedicine. Nat. Biotechnol. **36**(9), 829–838 (2018)
32. Yang, Q., Liu, Y., Cheng, Y., Kang, Y., Chen, T., Yu, H.: Federated learning. Synthesis Lectures Artif. Intell. Mach. Learn. **13**(3), 1–207 (2019)

33. Zari, O., Xu, C., Neglia, G.: Efficient passive membership inference attack in federated learning. In: NeurIPS PriML Workshop (2021)
34. Zhu, B., Liu, J.Z., Cauley, S.F., Rosen, B.R., Rosen, M.S.: Image reconstruction by domain-transform manifold learning. Nature **555**(7697), 487–492 (2018)
35. Zhu, M., Gupta, S.: To prune, or not to prune: exploring the efficacy of pruning for model compression. arXiv preprint arXiv:1710.01878 (2017)

Affordable AI and Healthcare

Enhancing Portable OCT Image Quality via GANs for AI-Based Eye Disease Detection

Kaveri A. Thakoor[1(✉)], Ari Carter[1], Ge Song[2], Adam Wax[3], Omar Moussa[4], Royce W. S. Chen[4], Christine Hendon[1], and Paul Sajda[1]

[1] Columbia University, New York, NY 10027, USA
{k.thakoor,ac4647,cpf2115,ps629}@columbia.edu
[2] University of Rochester, Rochester, NY 14627, USA
gsong4@u.rochester.edu
[3] Duke University, Durham, NC 27708, USA
a.wax@duke.edu
[4] Columbia University Medical Center, New York, NY 10032, USA
{om2333,rc2631}@cumc.columbia.edu

Abstract. Optical coherence tomography (OCT) is widely used for detection of ophthalmic diseases, such as glaucoma, age-related macular degeneration (AMD), and diabetic retinopathy. Using a low-coherence-length light source, OCT is able to achieve high axial resolution in biological samples; this depth information is used by ophthalmologists to assess retinal structures and characterize disease states. However, OCT systems are often bulky and expensive, costing tens of thousands of dollars and weighing on the order of 50 pounds or more. Such constraints make it difficult for OCT to be accessible in low-resource settings. In the U.S. alone, only 15.3% of diabetic patients meet the recommendation of obtaining annual eye exams; the situation is even worse for minority/under-served populations. In this study, we focus on data acquired with a low-cost, portable OCT (p-OCT) device, characterized by lower resolution, scanning rate, and imaging depth than a commercial OCT system. We use generative adversarial networks (GANs) to enhance the quality of this p-OCT data and then assess the impact of this enhancement on downstream performance of artificial intelligence (AI) algorithms for AMD detection. Using GANs trained on simulated p-OCT data generated from paired commercial OCT data degraded with the point spread function (PSF) of the p-OCT device, we observe improved AI performance on p-OCT data after single-image super-resolution. We also achieve denoising after image-to-image translation. By exhibiting proof-of-principle AI-based AMD detection even on low-quality p-OCT data, this study stimulates future work toward low-cost, portable imaging+AI systems for eye disease detection.

Supported by National Science Foundation Grant DGE 1644869.

Supplementary Information The online version contains supplementary material available at https://doi.org/10.1007/978-3-031-18523-6_15.

Keywords: Portable optical coherence tomography · Generative adversarial networks · Eye disease

1 Introduction

1.1 Background and Motivation

Much of the Artificial Intelligence (AI) being developed to detect ophthalmic diseases is trained using data and ground-truth that are collected in leading clinics with state-of-the-art equipment and expert ophthalmologists [1,2]. However, perhaps one of the most compelling uses for AI is for under-served areas which must utilize low-cost portable systems and in which high-quality ground truth may not be available given lack of experienced readers [3]. In this paper, we investigate whether we can use generative adversarial networks (GANs) to map the lower quality of data acquired using a portable-OCT (p-OCT) system (about tenfold cheaper than a commercial system) to the higher quality of commercial OCT data on which an AI model was trained to detect AMD. We hypothesize that this mapping will enable the p-OCT data to be "rescaled" to match the resolution and noise characteristics of the high-quality data used to train an AI model, enabling better downstream AI-based AMD classification performance. To test this, we utilize data collected from a p-OCT device developed by Kim *et al.* [4], who have successfully designed, implemented, and characterized a low-cost, portable OCT system tailored for retinal imaging use in clinical/laboratory studies. This p-OCT device was used for imaging human patients and achieved a contrast-to-noise ratio 5.6% less than that achieved by a commercial Heidelberg Spectralis OCT system [5].

Furthermore, since data shortage is a challenge for the development of AI-based tools, future potential applications of p-OCT data/devices include (1) efficient data collection and augmentation for AI training due to the p-OCT's portable form factor, and (2) GAN-based simulation/synthesis of medical data (as shown to be possible in previous work with commercial OCT and fundus images [6,7]) for enhancing data privacy. The above use cases of p-OCT data and GANs are predicated on the assumption of having robust AI algorithms that can achieve high-accuracy eye disease detection even from p-OCT data; we seek to confirm this assumption through our work by using GANs to improve downstream AI performance on p-OCT data. By showing proof-of-principle AI-based AMD detection using low-quality p-OCT data, we aim to equip a broader, diverse population with access to potentially sight-saving imaging+AI technology.

1.2 Past Work

Existing noise removal approaches for natural images have been applied to medical images [8,9] to successfully generate noise-free images even when clean target images are not available for training. In contrast, in this work we specifically seek to map low-quality image statistics of test data to high-quality image statistics to mimic the quality of data on which an existing AI-based AMD detection model has been trained. This requires capturing the resolution difference between low and high-quality data (achieving super-resolution) as well as capturing the spatially-correlated noise differences between low and high-quality data (past approaches [9] often assume spatially uncorrelated/'pixel-wise independent' noise). In order to achieve this, we turn to the class of generative adversarial networks (GANs), particularly conditional GANs, which learn mappings between source and target data. First, we use super-resolution GANs (such as ESRGAN [10]) to enhance the resolution of output images by learning both the scale and noise mapping between low and high-quality data; such GANs enable 'informed hallucination' of missing information to generate super-resolved versions of input low-resolution data. Second, we use image-to-image translation GANs [11] (such as MedGAN [12]) for the denoising of simulated p-OCT images, to attempt to transform their perceptual quality toward that of commercial OCT images.

1.3   Baseline Performance on p-OCT Data and Dataset Details

Through a collaboration with Duke University's Wax Lab, we obtained 221 b-scan images from 59 subjects that were acquired directly with a p-OCT system [5]. We used this data (Institutional Review Board exempt) to test the authors' previously-developed [13,14] deep learning algorithm's (DLA's) robustness to AMD detection using p-OCT input images. (This previous DLA was trained from scratch on 301 commercial OCT b-scan images [14]). We showed the p-OCT images to AMD experts to label for presence of CNV (choroidal neovascularization, characteristic of 'wet AMD') or no AMD; 39 images were excluded due to presence of pathologies other than AMD, and 14 'non-neovascular' ('dry AMD') eyes were excluded in order to directly assess the DLA's binary AMD classification performance with p-OCT data vs. with commercial OCT data. This resulted in 168 p-OCT images (42 classified as neovascular (NV) AMD ('wet AMD') and 126 classified as non-AMD). For training, we utilized a dataset (described in detail in [14]) of 1270 NV AMD vs. non-AMD commercial OCT images (520 NV AMD, 750 non-AMD) captured with a Carl Zeiss Cirrus HD-OCT 5000 device. Thus, the training set is much closer to balanced (40% NV AMD vs. 60% non-AMD) even though the test set is not balanced. Commercial OCT training data and p-OCT test data examples are shown in Fig. 1 (left). Although both image types are impacted by characteristic speckle noise from the OCT instrument, the amount of noise and the distribution of pixel intensities vary significantly between the two images.

To present the baseline performance of the high-performing DLA in a threshold-independent manner (and to control for imbalance in classes, especially relevant for the p-OCT test data), we plotted the AMD detection model's performance via Receiver Operating Characteristic (ROC) curves (Fig. 3, left panel). The Area Under the Curve (AUC) achieved by the model on baseline **commercial OCT** data is **0.8 (95% CI, 0.694–0.906)**, while the baseline AUC on **p-OCT** data prior to any image quality enhancement is **0.518 (95%**

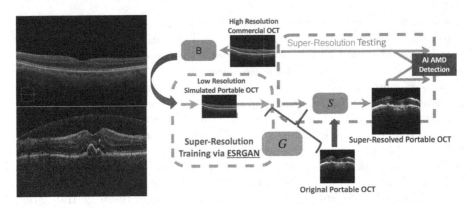

Fig. 1. Left: Original commercial training data (top); histogram-matched p-OCT test data (bottom). **Right:** Image processing pipeline to generate super-resolved images for downstream AI performance evaluation. Commercial OCT data is convolved with the PSF of the p-OCT device, histogram-matched with p-OCT images, and then downsampled by 4x (to form simulated p-OCT data through 'B') prior to being used for paired ESRGAN training. The resulting trained generator ('G') is used to super-resolve ('S') p-OCT test inputs prior to AI-based AMD detection (figure concept from [15]).

CI, 0.396–0.640), barely above chance. To improve the AI model's performance and make it generalizable for p-OCT data, we attempted one GAN-based super-resolution (SR) approach and one GAN-based image-to-image translation approach; these approaches are described in detail in the following sections.

2   Super-Resolving p-OCT Data with ESRGAN

We used the Enhanced Super Resolution Generative Adversarial Network (ESR-GAN) [10], one of the latest state-of-the-art deep learning based super-resolution (SR) techniques, to enhance the resolution of the portable OCT test data prior to downstream classification via a high-performing AMD detection model to evaluate the impact of super-resolution on downstream binary AMD detection.

2.1   ESRGAN Background and Methods

ESRGAN goes beyond the Super-Resolution Generative Adversarial Network (SRGAN) [16] by creating the Enhanced SRGAN. Architectural highlights of ESRGAN that enable its enhanced functionality include the Residual-in-Residual Dense Block (RRDB) [10], which has higher capacity and thus is easier to train than the original SRGAN model, residual scaling [17], and use of a relativistic generator [18]. ESRGAN must be trained with paired low-resolution and high-resolution data (i.e. the same object captured with two imaging instruments). Since we do not have p-OCT and commercial OCT data of the same patients, we simulated paired ESRGAN training data by matching the histogram of the commercial OCT data to that of the p-OCT data, convolving the commercial OCT data with the Point Spread Function (PSF) of the portable OCT, and downsampling the data by a factor of 4 (as dictated by the ESRGAN architecture [10]). This approach resembles past 'Blind Super-resolution' approaches [15] and is appropriate for this situation since we know the point spread function (i.e. degradation kernel) that generated the low-resolution p-OCT data. The pipeline used for generating the paired training data is shown in Fig. 1 (right). Examples of the degraded and ground truth commercial images used for paired training are shown in Fig. 2. We then super-resolved the p-OCT test data using the resulting ESRGAN generator trained (via BasicSR [19]) on the paired, 'simulated p-OCT'/commercial OCT dataset. After histogram-matching the p-OCT test data to the commercial OCT data and denoising via a 5×5 kernel Weiner filter, we inputted the p-OCT data to the trained ESRGAN generator for super-resolution. We then used the super-resolved outputs for downstream AI-based AMD detection.

2.2   ESRGAN Results and Discussion

Training ESRGAN on this paired dataset exhibits qualitatively improved results on validation data, as can be seen by the input and validation output images in Fig. 2. For test data (super-resolved p-OCT data), the improvement is visualized most clearly through the ROC curve in Fig. 3, left panel. AUC achieved by the high-performing AI model on baseline **commercial OCT** data is **0.8 (95% CI, 0.694–0.906)**, while baseline AUC on **portable OCT** data prior to application of super-resolution is **0.518 (95% CI, 0.396–0.640)**. In contrast, after ESRGAN super-resolution (without training on paired commercial OCT and simulated p-OCT data, i.e. just using an 'off-the-shelf' ESRGAN model pretrained on natural images, called **After SR, No Train**), this AUC increases to **0.792 (95% CI, 0.684–0.900)**. After ESRGAN training on paired simulated p-OCT data and commercial OCT data (called **After SR, Train**), AI performance on super-resolved p-OCT data increases to an AUC of **0.897 (95% CI, 0.815–0.979)**. This increase in AUC beyond that achieved on the original commercial OCT data could be due to the super-resolution process in fact increasing the resolution of the p-OCT data beyond that of the original commercial OCT data (the ESRGAN architecture enables a 4× resolution increase compared to input resolution; input resolution is 500×500 pixels, so output resolution is 2000×2000 pixels, while commercial OCT data resolution is only 700×1052 pixels).

It is interesting to note that although the AI performance on super-resolved p-OCT data improves dramatically compared to that on the commercial OCT data and that on the original p-OCT data, this improvement is harder to observe visually/perceptually (see Fig. 4). This is confirmed by computing the BRISQUE scores [20] for sets of these images. The BRISQUE score is a reference-less perceptual image quality metric; lower BRISQUE scores indicate higher perceptual quality. Figure 3 (right panel) shows that, while **commercial OCT** data and

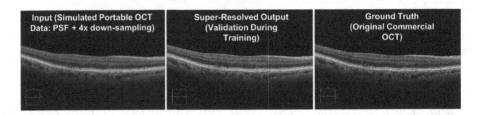

Fig. 2. Left: Simulated portable (degraded commercial) OCT data used for ESRGAN paired training, after histogram matching to p-OCT data, convolving with PSF of the p-OCT device, and 4x bicubic down-sampling; **Center:** SR validation output during training; **Right:** original commercial OCT ground truth.

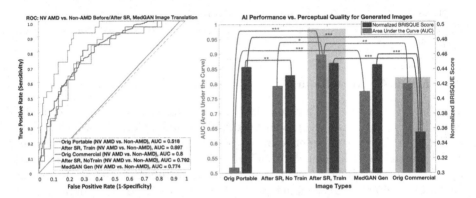

Fig. 3. Left Panel: Receiver Operator Characteristic (ROC) curve comparing performance of AI on **original p-OCT data** (red), on p-OCT data after super-resolution with paired training (**After SR, Train** in yellow), on **commercial OCT data** (violet), and on p-OCT data after super-resolution without training (**After SR, No-Train** in green). Interestingly, super-resolution enhances AI AUC beyond that on the high-quality commercial data, suggesting the value of super-resolution for facilitating AI-based eye disease detection even from p-OCT data. ROC curve in blue shows **MedGAN generated** images (described in Sect. 3) with AUC approaching that of target (commercial OCT) images. **Right Panel:** AUCs and normalized BRISQUE scores for 5 image types. Note inverse relationship between AUC scores and normalized BRISQUE scores for **After SR, Train** (highlighted with light yellow background) and **MedGAN Gen** images; they have significantly higher AUCs (AI performance) compared to **p-OCT images** but significantly poorer (higher) normalized BRISQUE scores (perceptual quality) compared to **commercial OCT** images (highlighted with light green background) [*: $p < 0.05$; **: $p < 0.01$; ***: $p < 0.0001$]. Note overall similarity in normalized BRISQUE scores across all image types. (Color figure online)

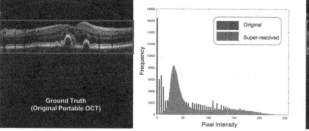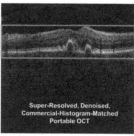

Fig. 4. Left: Original portable OCT image; **Right:** super-resolved, denoised, commercial-OCT-histogram-matched portable OCT image; **Center:** histogram of pixel intensity frequency quantitatively shows super-resolution (increase in presence of varied pixel intensities for red histogram, corresponding to red boxed region in super-resolved (SR) p-OCT image, compared to blue histogram, corresponding to blue boxed region in original p-OCT image). Note shifted peak of SR p-OCT histogram is due to learning histogram of commercial OCT data during paired ESRGAN training. (Color figure online)

super-resolved p-OCT data without training (**After SR, No Train**) have significantly different BRISQUE scores from that of the original **p-OCT** data, the trained, super-resolved (SR) p-OCT data (**After SR, Train**) data has a BRISQUE score that is *not significantly different* from that of the original **p-OCT** data. This aligns with the fact that clinicians who viewed the trained SR p-OCT data also qualitatively described that the trained SR p-OCT data did not provide any additional features beyond what the original p-OCT data provided for their diagnosis. This qualitative finding and the similar BRISQUE scores for the original p-OCT and trained SR p-OCT data, combined with the enhanced AI performance on the SR p-OCT data, are consistent with past work [21], which showed that deep neural networks (DNNs) are less impaired than their human counterparts at deciphering spatially correlated noise. Also, 'noise-trained' DNNs, like the trained ESRGAN here, more closely emulate human vision's robustness to noise than DNNs not trained with noise [21]. This further strengthens the potential value of an SR-enhanced, AI-embedded p-OCT system that could provide high-accuracy automated disease detection, *especially* when a human expert or commercial OCT system are not available, such as in resource-limited environments. The AI's boosted performance on the SR p-OCT data could be attributed to the SR process transforming the original p-OCT data into a space that is more similar to that on which the AMD-detection model has been trained (commercial OCT data). The effective 'transfer learning' during the paired training between simulated p-OCT data and true commercial OCT data also improved AI performance for the trained SR model compared to the non-trained one (when the SR model was only pre-trained on natural images).

3 Enhancing Source Domain Perceptual Image Quality with MedGAN

Given the dramatic improvement in AI performance with super-resolved p-OCT data without accompanying significant improvement in perceptual quality, we also implemented (in Python Tensorflow/Keras) an image-to-image translation [11] GAN to enhance p-OCT perceptual image quality via image denoising.

3.1 MedGAN Background

MedGAN was proposed by Armanious and colleagues [12] as a multi-purpose GAN for the transformation (translation, motion-correction, or denoising) of medical images. Unlike standard GANs, which transform noise into a desired image, MedGAN is conditional, taking as input a source image and transforming it into a desired target image. This type of operation is enabled by MedGAN's particular architecture and the losses that optimize it. Its generator is composed of several U-Net [22] architecture blocks that refine images as they propagate through a sequential encoder-decoder pathway. Modeled after PatchGAN, its discriminator decomposes generated images into 64 patches (each of size 16×16) in order to determine which are most likely to resemble a target image and which are least likely to do so. Together, the generator and discriminator are trained via adversarial loss, which places them in competition, respectively generating realistic images and identifying unrealistic images. While this leads the generator to output broadly sufficient images, they are often blurry. As a result, the generator uses three other loss functions that leverage feature extractors to produce more accurate images. Using the discriminator as a feature extractor, perceptual loss attempts to capture discrepancy between high frequency components of generated and target images, while content and style loss both use layers of VGG-19 [23] to quantify dissimilarities between the generated and target images. These loss formulations are given in the paper's Supplementary Materials. A schematic of our MedGAN denoising use-case and of the components of the MedGAN architecture are shown in Fig. 5, left panel.

3.2 MedGAN Methods

MedGAN Generator. The CasNet generator is built from U-Net modules [22], concatenated sequentially to create a richer output image. The blocks themselves are identically composed of an 8-layer encoding section followed by an 8-layer decoding section. The former employs convolutional layers with kernel sizes of four, stride length of 2, and convolutional filters of size 64, 128, 256, 512, 512, 512, 512, and 512. Given the input image size of $256 \times 256 \times 3$, these parameters eventually yield a $1 \times 1 \times 512$ object, which then feeds into the decoding section, built of 8 deconvolutional blocks with the same stride and kernel parameters as their convolutional counterparts and with filter sizes of 512, 1024, 1024, 1024, 1024, 512, 256, and 128. This section of the block deconvolves the 1×1 object

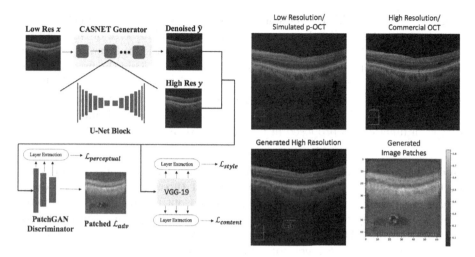

Fig. 5. Left Panel: Our MedGAN use-case is for image denoising; CasNet generator is composed of U-Net blocks; PatchGAN discriminator computes perceptual loss and patched adversarial loss; VGG-19 feature extractor computes style and content losses [12]. **Right Panel:** (Clockwise from top left) An example original low-resolution source image, high resolution target image, a heatmap showing the discriminator's prediction of image patches as real (yellow) or fake (blue), and the final MedGAN-generated image. The MedGAN-generated image is able to achieve a similar level of perceptual quality to the high resolution commercial OCT image, but the persistent artifact at the image's bottom affects this quality. Although these artifacts remained through many iterations of the MedGAN, this particular artifact is low-impact, away from important parts of the image (the retinal layers) and is well contained. (Color figure online)

with 512 channels back to a 256×256 object with 128 channels, allowing for the last deconvolutional layer to feed directly into the next block's first convolutional layer, ensuring modularity of the blocks. To output an image after the last U-Net block, we changed the output filter size of the last filter to 3 (to accommodate our RGB input images), such that a $256 \times 256 \times 3$ image results. Every convolutional and deconvolutional layer is followed by batch normalization and leaky ReLU layers, and the final deconvolutional layer employs a tanh activation function. We modified the original MedGAN architecture by using a sigmoid activation function at the output of the final block (to ensure output images remain in the range $[0, 1]$). Finally, encoding and decoding layers of the same dimension in each block are concatenated to ensure transfer of contextual information throughout the encoding-decoding pathway and to strengthen back-propagation.

MedGAN Discriminator. Unlike classic discriminators that output single values (the probability of the whole generated image being real or fake), MedGAN uses a patch discriminator that returns a 64×64 matrix of values indicating the probability that each 16×16 patch of an input image (either generated or target) is 'real' (each patch equals 1 for a target image, 0 for a generated image.) This approach permits sharper results, especially in conjunction with non-adversarial losses like the perceptual loss. The architecture of this network is relatively straightforward, consisting of two convolutional layers with kernel sizes of 4, strides of 2, and spatial filters with parameters 64 in the first layer and 128 in the second. This ultimately produces a $64 \times 64 \times 128$ object, which can be compressed into a final $64 \times 64 \times 1$ matrix using a convolutional layer with its stride and spatial filter both set to 1, kernel size equal to 4, and a sigmoid activation function, as proposed in the original MedGAN design [12].

MedGAN Training. Training the MedGAN (via Lambda Labs Vector, RTX 3090 GPU) occurs in four iterations. In the first three, the generator produces images upon which losses can be computed and optimized. The discriminator receives no training during these iterations, only being optimized in the fourth and final iteration. This approach emphasizes the training of the generator over the discriminator, as the generator contains a much more complex architecture. This allows the two models to maintain a healthy training equilibrium, rather than creating a situation where the discriminator can dominate the generator.

3.3   MedGAN Results and Discussion

We chose a generator architecture with 6 CasNet blocks (as proposed in the MedGAN paper [12]), as it outperforms 1-block and 3-block architectures based on BRISQUE scores of generated outputs. We found the following loss hyperparameters to be optimal for the portable OCT data based on empirical tuning: Perceptual loss λ_{pi} of 1, Style loss λ_{sj} of 0.0001, and Content loss λ_{cj} of 0.0001. Smaller content and style losses may be preferred, because the VGG-19 feature extractor has been trained on ImageNet [24]; replacing VGG-19 with a network fine-tuned on OCT data may enhance quality of extracted features for p-OCT data, increasing the content/style loss contributions. We trained the model for 100 epochs (48 h) and with up to 1270 input images. Loss definitions and curves for all loss types are shown in the paper's Supplementary Materials. We found that the MedGAN-generated images (when scaled to match target image size) still exhibited significantly higher (poorer) average BRISQUE scores (44.6) than those of target commercial OCT images (35.5); in spite of visible reduction in noise (low perceptual loss) within the generated images, perceptual quality did not quantitatively match that of target images. As a more rigorous test, downstream AI performance using generated images is therefore shown via the blue ROC curve in Fig. 3 (left panel); **MedGAN generated** images exhibit an AUC of **0.774 (95% CI, 0.663–0.885)**, approaching that achieved by the target **commercial OCT** data of **0.8 (95% CI, 0.694–0.906)**. An example generated image and a heatmap indicating probability of 'realness' of patches within generated images according to the discriminator are also shown in Fig. 5, right panel.

We believe that mode collapse contributed to the persistent artifact occurring in the MedGAN output images. In typical GANs, this phenomenon transforms all GAN inputs into a single output image, but mode collapse is not well-defined for conditional GANs like MedGAN. All of MedGAN's generated images appear to have a layer overlaying the original input image, with similar noise patterns and artifact locations in each. Therefore, while the conditional input remains different for all images, the generated artifacts are functionally identical.

4   Conclusions and Future Directions

In the first half of this paper, we used ESRGAN-based super-resolution *to enhance AI-based AMD detection using p-OCT images* and simulated paired training via the p-OCT point spread function. Perceptual quality of super-resolved outputs may be improved by first denoising the p-OCT data via existing high-performing, deep-learning based retinal-OCT denoising techniques [25,26] prior to ESRGAN super-resolution. An alternate future approach could involve using 'GAN-CIRCLE' and the cycle-consistency constraint to achieve super-resolution with unpaired training data and no task specific regularization [27]. In the second half of this paper, we sought to denoise/*improve perceptual quality* of simulated p-OCT data via MedGAN by reducing noise and perceptual loss (between source and target images). This resulted in AI performance close to that of target images, without significant quantitative perceptual quality improvement (lowering of BRISQUE scores). Artifacts in MedGAN-generated images could be eliminated by additional use of regularization and VGG-19 feature extractor fine-tuning on OCT data. Regularization strategies include adding instance noise to the MedGAN training input images and adding gradient penalties to the networks [28]. Another promising future direction is to integrate progressively growing generated images into GAN training [29], which would provide more stable image synthesis. Overall, we observed that GAN-based processing of p-OCT/simulated p-OCT data significantly improved AI-based AMD detection performance, in spite of not significantly changing perceptual quality, as assessed by classical metrics (BRISQUE) and the human eye. Our proof-of-principle findings stimulate future work toward AI-embedded p-OCT devices for eye disease detection, especially in situations when ophthalmic expertise or high quality testing data are not available.

References

1. Briganti, G., Le Moine, O.: Artificial intelligence in medicine: today and tomorrow. Front. Med. **7**, 27 (2020)
2. Moraru, A.D., Costin, D., Moraru, R.L., Branisteanu, D.C.: Artificial intelligence and deep learning in ophthalmology-present and future. Exp. Ther. Med. **20**(4), 3469–3473 (2020)
3. Teikari, P., Najjar, R.P., Schmetterer, L., Milea, D.: Embedded deep learning in ophthalmology: making ophthalmic imaging smarter. Ther. Adv. Ophthalmol. **11**, 2515841419827172 (2019)

4. Kim, S., Crose, M., Eldridge, W.J., Cox, B., Brown, W.J., Wax, A.: Design and implementation of a low-cost, portable OCT system. Biomed. Opt. Express **9**(3), 1232–1243 (2018)
5. Song, G., et al.: First clinical application of low-cost OCT. Transl. Vis. Sci. Technol. **8**(3), 61–61 (2019)
6. Tavakkoli, A., Kamran, S.A., Hossain, K.F., Zuckerbrod, S.L.: A novel deep learning conditional generative adversarial network for producing angiography images from retinal fundus photographs. Sci. Rep. **10**(1), 1–15 (2020)
7. Zheng, C., et al.: Assessment of generative adversarial networks model for synthetic optical coherence tomography images of retinal disorders. Transl. Vis. Sci. Technol. **9**(2), 29–29 (2020)
8. Lehtinen, J., et al.: Noise2Noise: learning image restoration without clean data. arXiv preprint arXiv:1803.04189 (2018)
9. Krull, A., Buchholz, T.O., Jug, F.: Noise2Void-learning denoising from single noisy images. In: Proceedings of the IEEE/CVF Conference on Computer Vision and Pattern Recognition, pp. 2129–2137 (2019)
10. Wang, X., et al.: ESRGAN: enhanced super-resolution generative adversarial networks. In: Leal-Taixé, L., Roth, S. (eds.) ECCV 2018. LNCS, vol. 11133, pp. 63–79. Springer, Cham (2019). https://doi.org/10.1007/978-3-030-11021-5_5
11. Isola, P., Zhu, J.Y., Zhou, T., Efros, A.A.: Image-to-image translation with conditional adversarial networks. In: Proceedings of the IEEE Conference on Computer Vision and Pattern Recognition, pp. 1125–1134 (2017)
12. Armanious, K., et al.: MedGAN: medical image translation using GANs. Comput. Med. Imaging Graph. **79**, 101684 (2020)
13. Thakoor, K., Bordbar, D., Yao, J., Moussa, O., Chen, R., Sajda, P.: Hybrid 3D–2D deep learning for detection of neovascularage-related macular degeneration using optical coherence tomography B-scans and angiography volumes. In: 2021 IEEE 18th International Symposium on Biomedical Imaging (ISBI), pp. 1600–1604 (2021)
14. Thakoor, K.A., et al.: A multimodal deep learning system to distinguish late stages of AMD and to compare expert vs. AI ocular biomarkers. Sci. Rep. **12**(1), 1–11 (2022)
15. Lugmayr, A., Danelljan, M., Timofte, R.: Unsupervised learning for real-world super-resolution. In: 2019 IEEE/CVF International Conference on Computer Vision Workshop (ICCVW), pp. 3408–3416 (2019)
16. Ledig, C., et al.: Photo-realistic single image super-resolution using a generative adversarial network. In: Proceedings of the IEEE Conference on Computer Vision and Pattern Recognition, pp. 4681–4690 (2017)
17. Lim, B., Son, S., Kim, H., Nah, S., Mu Lee, K.: Enhanced deep residual networks for single image super-resolution. In: Proceedings of the IEEE Conference on Computer Vision and Pattern Recognition Workshops, pp. 136–144 (2017)
18. Jolicoeur-Martineau, A.: The relativistic discriminator: a key element missing from standard GAN. arXiv preprint arXiv:1807.00734 (2018)
19. Wang, X., Yu, K., Chan, K.C.K., Dong, C., Loy, C.C.: BasicSR: open source image and video restoration toolbox. github.com/xinntao/BasicSR (2018)
20. Mittal, A., Moorthy, A.K., Bovik, A.C.: No-reference image quality assessment in the spatial domain. IEEE Trans. Image Process. **21**(12), 4695–4708 (2012)
21. Jang, H., McCormack, D., Tong, F.: Noise-trained deep neural networks effectively predict human vision and its neural responses to challenging images. PLoS Biol. **19**(12), e3001418 (2021)

22. Ronneberger, O., Fischer, P., Brox, T.: U-Net: convolutional networks for biomedical image segmentation. In: Navab, N., Hornegger, J., Wells, W.M., Frangi, A.F. (eds.) MICCAI 2015. LNCS, vol. 9351, pp. 234–241. Springer, Cham (2015). https://doi.org/10.1007/978-3-319-24574-4_28

23. Simonyan, K., Zisserman, A.: Very deep convolutional networks for large-scale image recognition. arXiv preprint arXiv:1409.1556 (2014)

24. Deng, J., Dong, W., Socher, R., Li, L.J., Li, K., Fei-Fei, L.: ImageNet: a large-scale hierarchical image database. In: 2009 IEEE Conference on Computer Vision and Pattern Recognition, pp. 248–255 (2009)

25. Halupka, K.J., et al.: Retinal optical coherence tomography image enhancement via deep learning. Biomed. Opt. Express 9(12), 6205–6221 (2018)

26. Qiu, B., et al.: Noise reduction in optical coherence tomography images using a deep neural network with perceptually-sensitive loss function. Biomed. Opt. Express 11(2), 817–830 (2020)

27. You, C., et al.: CT super-resolution GAN constrained by the identical, residual, and cycle learning ensemble (GAN-CIRCLE). IEEE Trans. Med. Imaging 39(1), 188–203 (2019)

28. Mescheder, L., Geiger, A., Nowozin, S.: Which training methods for GANs do actually converge? In: International Conference on Machine Learning, pp. 3481–3490. PMLR (2018)

29. Karras, T., Aila, T., Laine, S., Lehtinen, J.: Progressive growing of GANs for improved quality, stability, and variation. arXiv preprint arXiv:1710.10196 (2017)

Deep Learning-Based Segmentation of Pleural Effusion from Ultrasound Using Coordinate Convolutions

Germain Morilhat[1,2]($\boxtimes$), Naomi Kifle[1,3], Sandra FinesilverSmith[4],
Bram Ruijsink[1,5], Vittoria Vergani[6], Habtamu Tegegne Desita[7],
Zerubabel Tegegne Desita[8], Esther Puyol-Antón[1], Aaron Carass[3],
and Andrew P. King[1]

[1] School of Biomedical Engineering and Imaging Sciences, King's College London,
London, U.K.
[2] IMT Atlantique, Nantes, France
germain.morilhat@gmail.com
[3] Image Analysis and Communications Laboratory, Johns Hopkins University,
Baltimore, U.S.A.
[4] Big Data Institute, Oxford University, Oxford, U.K.
[5] Department of Cardiology, University Medical Center Utrecht,
Utrecht, The Netherlands
[6] King's College Hospital, London, U.K.
[7] Department of Information Technology, University of Gondar, Gondar, Ethiopia
[8] Department of Radiology, University of Gondar, Gondar, Ethiopia

Abstract. Ultrasound imaging plays a crucial role in assessing disease and making diagnoses for a range of conditions, especially so in low-to-middle-income (LMIC) countries. One such application is the assessment of pleural effusion, which can be associated with multiple morbidities including tuberculosis (TB). Currently, assessment of pleural effusion is performed manually by the sonographer during the ultrasound examination, leading to significant intra-/inter-observer variability. In this work, we investigate the use of deep learning (DL) to automate the process of pleural effusion segmentation from ultrasound images. On two ultrasound datasets of suspected TB patients acquired in a LMIC setting, we achieve median Dice Similarity Coefficients (DSCs) of 0.82 and 0.74 respectively using the nnU-net DL model. We also investigate the use of coordinate convolutions in the DL model and find that this results in a statistically significant improvement in the median DSC on the first dataset to 0.85, with no significant change on the second dataset. This work showcases, for the first time, the potential of DL in automating the process of effusion assessment from ultrasound imaging and paves the way for future work on artificial intelligence-assisted acquisition and interpretation of ultrasound images. This could enable accurate and robust assessment of pleural effusion in LMIC settings where there is often a lack of experienced radiologists to perform such assessments.

S. Albarqouni et al. (Eds.): DeCaF 2022/FAIR 2022, LNCS 13573, pp. 168–177, 2022.
https://doi.org/10.1007/978-3-031-18523-6_16

Keywords: Deep learning · CNN · Pleural effusion · Coordinate convolution · Ultrasound

1 Introduction

In 2020 there were an estimated 10 million cases of tuberculosis (TB) worldwide, and the global case fatality ratio was 15% [12]. However, the prognosis for TB is generally good if treatment can be initiated early enough. The gold standard for diagnosis of TB is detection of mycobacterium tuberculosis through a culture test. However, such tests can be expensive and time-consuming, limiting their utility in low-to-middle-income (LMIC) countries [7]. In many LMIC countries radiological indicators play an important role in assessing clinical symptoms associated with TB, with a view to initiating treatment. One such symptom is pleural effusion, which refers to a build-up of excess fluid between the layers of the pleura outside the lungs. It can be caused by TB and several other conditions, including congestive heart failure, kidney failure, cancer, pneumonia, and pulmonary embolism. Pleural effusion can be identified using a chest X-ray but the sensitivity of this method is only good when the effusion volume is large, which makes it unsuitable for initiating early treatment.

Ultrasound imaging allows earlier identification of pleural effusion and grading of its severity, allowing better treatment allocation [9]. However, ultrasound image acquisition and interpretation for pleural effusion assessment require expertise, and in many LMIC countries there is a shortage of skilled sonographers who can perform this task. Even for experienced sonographers, ultrasound-based assessment of pleural effusion is a challenging task, made difficult by the fact that the lungs can change appearance in ultrasound images in the presence of some pathologies, and the appearance of the effusion itself can change as it progresses from exudate to empyema. Furthermore, shadowing caused by the ribs in ultrasound imaging can make it difficult to reliably measure the extent of the effusion. As well as identifying the presence of effusion it is also useful to know its severity. Typically, effusion severity is estimated by manually measuring the "depth" of the effusion in ultrasound (i.e. the perpendicular distance between the pleural boundary and the lung). However, this measurement will vary depending on the probe orientation and how superior/inferior the measurement is taken, and so there is significant inter-/intra-observer variability.

In other applications, deep learning techniques have been used to automate medical image analysis tasks with a view to reducing intra-/inter-observer variability. For example, in ultrasound, deep learning has been applied to cardiac functional quantification [6,10], assessing kidney function [3] and estimating fetal biometrics [15]. Across a range of recent medical image segmentation challenges, the nnU-Net framework [2] has proved to exhibit state-of-the-art performance.

In this paper we investigate the potential of deep learning to automate the task of pleural effusion segmentation from ultrasound imaging. To the best of our knowledge this is the first attempt to automate this challenging task. We employ the state-of-the-art nnU-Net framework and also investigate whether coordinate convolutions can improve performance by explicitly encoding spatial information to improve the model's learning. Coordinate convolutions were first proposed in [5] and have since been shown to improve performance or optimisation properties in medical image segmentation tasks [1]. In our application, due to the standard protocols used for acquiring effusion images, there is good reason to suspect that spatial information may improve segmentation performance and we investigate this hypothesis in this paper. Some previous works have demonstrated this potential in ultrasound image analysis tasks [8,11,13] and here we investigate its potential for the task of pleural effusion segmentation in suspected TB patients.

The primary goal of this work is to demonstrate the feasibility of deep learning methods to tackle the pleural effusion segmentation task. Our first contribution is using the state-of-the-art nnU-Net deep learning model to address this task. Our second contribution is to investigate the use of spatial context information by extending the nnU-net model to use coordinate convolutions.

2   Materials

All ultrasound images were acquired using a SONOACE X7 ultrasound machine by an experienced radiologist at Gondar University Hospital in Ethiopia. Patients underwent clinical examination after reporting with symptoms consistent with a possible diagnosis of TB. All gave informed consent to the use of their images for research purposes and the study was approved by the university's hospital administration. All images were stored in DICOM format and pseudonymised (including blanking of patient details in the image) before being transferred to a password-protected remote file server for subsequent analysis.

A total of 143 images were acquired from 59 patients. The images were obtained at the left and right PLAPS (PosteroLateral Alveolar and/or Pleural Syndrome) and subcostal views [4] with linear array and curved array (abdominal) ultrasound probes. The data were split according to the use of these probes into two datasets of 51 and 92 images, respectively for linear array and curved array. We denote these datasets as Dataset A (linear array) and Dataset B (curved array). All images were annotated at the time of acquisition to measure the extent of the effusion. These annotations consisted of small crosses at the top and bottom of the deepest area of effusion. See Fig. 1 (left column) for example images.

Before being used for training and evaluating the models, each image was automatically cropped using a rectangular/cone mask to remove non-imaging content. Next, we applied an inpainting text algorithm using *keras-ocr* followed by template matching and edge detection algorithms from *opencv* to remove the annotations that were added to the images to measure the effusion. Examples of the outputs of this preprocessing are shown in Fig. 1 (centre column).

All images in both datasets were manually segmented using the ITK-SNAP software [14] (www.itksnap.org) by a trained observer. Examples of ground truth segmentations are shown in Fig. 1 (right column). These segmentations acted as

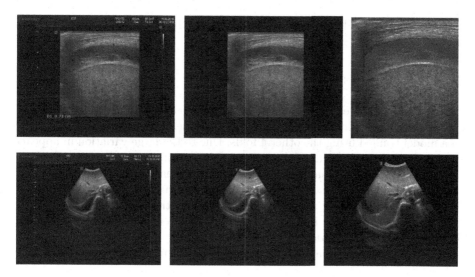

Fig. 1. Sample ultrasound images. Left-to-right: original image, image after cropping and inpainting to remove annotations, further cropping, with ground truth segmentation overlaid in red. Top row: Dataset A. Bottom row: Dataset B. (Color figure online)

ground truths for training and evaluating the proposed models. Additionally, a second trained observer performed independent segmentations of subsets of 10 random images each from the two datasets. These were used to compute an estimate of inter-observer variability in the manual segmentation process.

3   Methods

For our baseline model we employed the nnU-Net deep learning framework [2]. We used the 2-D implementation and the model was trained for 100 epochs to limit computational demands. Training was performed with a batch size of 4 using stochastic gradient descent with Nesterov momentum ($\mu = 0.99$) and an initial learning rate of 0.01. The loss function was the sum of cross entropy and Dice loss. The default nnU-Net data augmentation setting was used which included rotations, scaling, Gaussian noise, Gaussian blur, brightness, contrast, simulation of low resolution, gamma correction and mirroring. The model used for inference was the final model after all training epochs. We chose to use this model rather than the best model over the training epochs so that our results could be treated as test rather than validation results (see Sect. 4).

We also investigated whether using coordinate convolutions [5] could improve the performance of the nnU-Net baseline. Coordinate convolutions work by adding extra channels to the input layer which contain the coordinates of the pixels. In our case, as our images are 2-D this involved adding two extra channels, one containing the x-coordinates and one containing the y-coordinates, with the coordinates being specified in pixels and the origin being at the top left of the image.

4   Experiments

Evaluation for both experiments was performed using a 5-fold cross validation, i.e. the data were split into 5 folds and each was held out in turn and evaluated on a model trained using the other 4 folds. Due to the large variation in appearance between images acquired from the same patients, we performed the cross validation split at the image level rather than the patient level. Because nnU-net performs hyperparameter optimisation using heuristic rules and not using the validation data, and we used the model from the last epoch rather than using the validation data for model selection, these cross validation results can be considered as independent test results.

All models were evaluated using the Dice Similarity Coefficient (DSC),

$$\mathrm{DSC} = \frac{2|X \cap Y|}{|X| + |Y|} \tag{1}$$

where X and Y are the predicted and ground truth segmentations respectively. We report the median and lower/upper quartiles of DSC across the validation/test results of all images.

Additionally, we computed measures of the error and bias in estimation of effusion area, since these are likely to be clinically important measurements in effusion assessment. Specifically, we calculated:

$$\text{Abs. area error \%} = (abs(|X| - |Y|)/|Y|) \times 100\% \tag{2}$$
$$\text{Area bias \%} = ((|X| - |Y|)/|Y|) \times 100\% \tag{3}$$

where $|X|$ and $|Y|$ represent counts of the numbers of foreground pixels in the predicted and ground truth segmentations respectively. We report the median and lower/upper quartiles of these measures.

Finally, we also compute the DSC between the manual segmentations of the two observers on the subsets of 10 images for each dataset. The median DSCs are reported as estimates of inter-observer variability in manual segmentation.

5   Results

Qualitative prediction results of the two proposed models (baseline nnU-Net and nnU-Net with coordinate convolutions) on the two datasets are shown in Fig. 2. Tables 1 and 2 summarise the quantitative performances in terms of DSC and area statistics. Histograms of the DSC values are shown in Fig. 3. The median DSCs between the manual segmentations on the subsets of 10 images (i.e. the estimates of inter-observer variability) are also shown in Table 1.

It can be seen that, despite having fewer images, the baseline model for Dataset A obtained a higher median DSC than the model for Dataset B. For

Dataset A the coordinate convolution model improved the DSC and reduced the area error and bias. In two-tailed Wilcoxon signed rank tests (0.05 significance) the difference between the baseline DSC and that of the coordinate convolution model was found to be statistically significant for Dataset A ($p = 0.0133$) but there was no statistically significant difference for Dataset B ($p = 0.8$). Interestingly, for both Dataset A and Dataset B, both the baseline and coordinate convolution models performed better than the estimate of inter-observer variability. However, we note that the inter-observer variability is quite high (i.e. median DSCs of 0.78 and 0.71), likely reflecting the difficulty and partly subjective nature of the effusion segmentation task. Therefore, it seems likely that the deep learning models are learning to segment effusion in the style of the main observer, which may not always be consistent with the second observer. In addition, the histograms shown in Fig. 3 suggest that there are a significant number of failure cases in the outputs of both models (although fewer for the coordinate convolution model for Dataset A), again reflecting the difficulty of the task.

Table 1. Summary of deep learning model segmentation performances. All figures are the median (lower, upper quartiles) of Dice Similarity Coefficients (DSC) across the entire dataset, computed using a 5-fold cross validation. For the inter-observer variability estimate, we quote only the median DSC.

Dataset	DSCs		
	Baseline	Coord. conv.	Inter-observer var.
A	0.82 (0.7, 0.89)	0.85 (0.73, 0.92)	0.78
B	0.74 (057, 0.88)	0.73 (0.55, 0.88)	0.71

Table 2. Summary of deep learning model performamces in terms of area statistics. All figures are the median (lower, upper quartiles) across the entire dataset, computed using a 5-fold cross validation.

Dataset	Baseline		Coord. conv.	
	Abs. area error %	Area bias %	Abs. area error %	Area bias %
A	20.0 (8.0, 63.4)	1.9 (−17.6, 43.6)	11.2 (4.7, 33.1)	3.5 (−7.8, 19.7)
B	19.9 (5.4, 60.0)	1.5 (−16.1, 37.4)	24.6 (7.9, 52.3)	0.85 (−16.1, 33.4)

6   Discussion and Conclusions

To the best of our knowledge, we have presented the first study into the use of deep learning for automation of pleural effusion assessment from ultrasound images. Our results have demonstrated the potential of deep learning for this challenging task. The performance of the baseline model was superior to that of our reported inter-observer study, although we acknowledge that a number

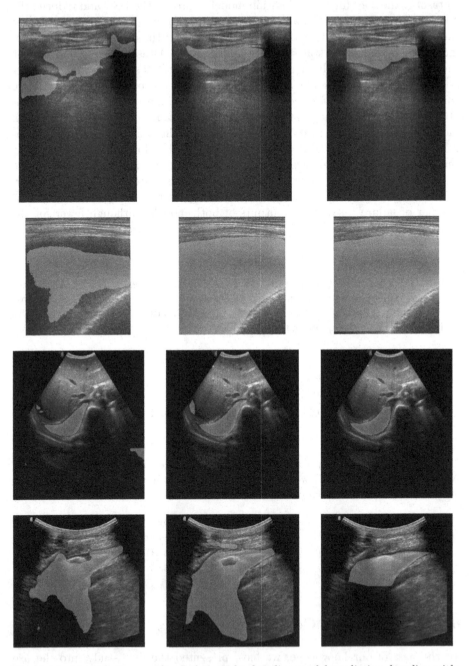

Fig. 2. Model prediction results. Left-to-right: baseline model prediction, baseline with coordinate convolutions prediction, ground truth segmentation. Rows 1–2: Dataset A. Rows 3–4: Dataset B.

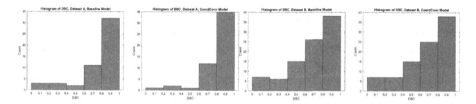

Fig. 3. Histograms of DSC values, from left to right: baseline model (Dataset A), coordinate convolution model (Dataset A), baseline model (Dataset B), coordinate convolution model (Dataset B). Refer to Table 1 for summary statistics.

of failure cases remain (see e.g. the bottom row of Fig. 2). The coordinate convolution model improved performance for one of the two datasets (Dataset A, which was acquired using the linear array probe), but not for the other one. One possible explanation for this difference is that for the linear array probe one of the coordinates represents the distance from the probe (i.e. the y-coordinate). This may have made it easier for the model to exploit this potentially important piece of information. In future work we will examine more closely the impact of presenting spatial information to the model in different ways, e.g. using distance from the probe for the curved array probe dataset. Nevertheless, this work represents an important proof-of-concept, paving the way for future work into artificial intelligence-assisted effusion assessment from ultrasound images. Our eventual aim in this work is to reduce the need for skilled operators (who can be scarce in some LMIC settings) using machine learning techniques.

We have demonstrated the potential of our approach on a dataset of suspected TB patients. However, pleural effusion can be caused by a number of other factors and so we believe that our work will have wider potential applicability, both in LMIC settings and beyond. In fact, not all patients in our dataset were confirmed as TB cases. In addition to pleural effusion, pericardial effusion can also be assessed using ultrasound and we will investigate this possibility in future work. In addition, different aspects of the effusion (which hold clues to the underlying disease process) could potentially be recognised using deep learning models, further reducing the need for skilled operators.

One limitation of our work is the lack of control cases in our database. All of the subjects in the database had effusion identified clinically (although its severity was variable). Expansion of the dataset to include cases with no pleural effusion would enable a more robust model to be trained. Furthermore, it would be beneficial for our ground truths to be reviewed by a panel of trained observers to reach a consensus on where the effusion lies, to reduce uncertainty and variability in assessments between observers.

Our work has focused on the interpretation of ultrasound images, with a view to reducing intra-/inter-observer variability and (eventually) reducing the required skill level to widen access to ultrasound-based pleural effusion assessment in LMIC settings. However, in reality, acquiring good quality images of pleural effusion requires a certain level of skill. Therefore, the impact of our current work would be to speed up the workflows of skilled operators and to reduce intra-/inter-observer variability. However, the standardised BLUE-protocol for lung ultrasound [4] acquisition might require less skill compared to image interpretation. Nevertheless, in the future, we will address the issue of image acquisition, and investigate the potential of machine learning techniques to simplify this process and enable less experienced operators to acquire good quality images. We envisage that this would involve some basic training and a simplified acquisition protocol combined with machine learning-based quality control and real-time integration of our automated effusion assessment model.

Acknowledgements. This work was part-funded by a King's College London Overseas Development Assistance Research Partnership Seed Fund award.

References

1. El Jurdi, R., Dargent, T., Petitjean, C., Honeine, P., Abdallah, F.: Investigating CoordConv for fully and weakly supervised medical image segmentation. In: Proceedings of the IPTA, pp. 1–5 (2020)
2. Isensee, F., Jaeger, P.F., Kohl, S.A.A., Petersen, J., Maier-Hein, K.H.: nnU-Net: a self-configuring method for deep learning-based biomedical image segmentation. Nat. Methods **18**, 203–211 (2021)
3. Kuo, C.C., et al.: Automation of the kidney function prediction and classification through ultrasound-based kidney imaging using deep learning. NPJ Digit. Med. **2**(29) (2019)
4. Lichtenstein, D.A., Mezière, G.A.: The BLUE-points: three standardized points used in the BLUE-protocol for ultrasound assessment of the lung in acute respiratory failure. Crit. Ultrasound J. **3**, 109–110 (2011)
5. Liu, R., et al.: An intriguing failing of convolutional neural networks and the CoordConv solution. In: Proceedings of the NeurIPS, pp. 9605–9616 (2018)
6. Ouyang, D., et al.: Video-based AI for beat-to-beat assessment of cardiac function. Nature **580**(7802), 252–256 (2020)
7. Parsons, L.M., et al.: Laboratory diagnosis of tuberculosis in resource-poor countries: challenges and opportunities. Clin. Microbiol. Rev. **24**(2), 314–350 (2011)
8. Saleh, A., Laradji, I.H., Lammie, C., Vazquez, D., Flavell, C.A., Azghadi, M.R.: A deep learning localization method for measuring abdominal muscle dimensions in ultrasound images. IEEE J. Biomed. Health Inform. **25**(10), 3865–3873 (2021)
9. Soni, N.J., et al.: Ultrasound in the diagnosis and management of pleural effusions. J. Hosp. Med. **10**(12), 811–816 (2015)
10. Tromp, J., et al.: Automated interpretation of systolic and diastolic function on the echocardiogram: a multicohort study. Lancet Digit. Health **7500**(21), 1–9 (2021)
11. Wang, F., et al.: Study on automatic detection and classification of breast nodule using deep convolutional neural network system. J. Thorac. Dis. **12**(9) (2020)
12. World Health Organization: Global tuberculosis report (2021). https://apps.who.int/iris/rest/bitstreams/1379788/retrieve. Accessed 28 July 2022
13. Youn, J., Ommen, M.L., Stuart, M.B., Thomsen, E.V., Larsen, N.B., Jensen, J.A.: Detection and localization of ultrasound scatterers using convolutional neural networks. IEEE Trans. Med. Imaging **39**(12), 3855–3867 (2020)

14. Yushkevich, P.A., et al.: User-guided 3D active contour segmentation of anatomical structures: significantly improved efficiency and reliability. Neuroimage **31**(3), 1116–1128 (2006)
15. ·Zhang, J., Petitjean, C., Lopez, P., Ainouz, S.: Direct estimation of fetal head circumference from ultrasound images based on regression CNN. In: Proceedings of the MIDL, pp. 914–922 (2020)

Verifiable and Energy Efficient Medical Image Analysis with Quantised Self-attentive Deep Neural Networks

Rakshith Sathish[✉], Swanand Khare, and Debdoot Sheet

Indian Institute of Technology Kharagpur, Kharagpur, West Bengal, India
rakshith.sathish@kgpian.iitkgp.ac.in

Abstract. Convolutional Neural Networks have played a significant role in various medical imaging tasks like classification and segmentation. They provide state-of-the-art performance compared to classical image processing algorithms. However, the major downside of these methods is the high computational complexity, reliance on high-performance hardware like GPUs and the inherent black-box nature of the model. In this paper, we propose quantised stand-alone self-attention based models as an alternative to traditional CNNs. In the proposed class of networks, convolutional layers are replaced with stand-alone self-attention layers, and the network parameters are quantised after training. We experimentally validate the performance of our method on classification and segmentation tasks. We observe 50–80% reduction in model size, 60–80% lesser number of parameters, 40–85% fewer FLOPs and 65–80% more energy efficiency during inference on CPUs. The code will be available at https://github.com/Rakshith2597/Quantised-Self-Attentive-Deep-Neural-Network.

Keywords: Self-attention · Quantisation · Medical image analysis

1 Introduction

Deep neural networks have played a significant role in medical image analysis. Since the advent of UNet [18] to UNetr [5], the performance of neural networks on various tasks like classification, segmentation, and restoration has improved considerably. Deeper and broader convolutional neural networks generally show an improvement in performance at the cost of an increase in the number of learnable parameters, model size and total floating-point operations performed during a single forward pass of the data through the network. Moreover, these models require specialised high-performance hardware even during inference. This reliance on larger models and high-performance hardware hinders the last-mile delivery of AI solutions to improve the existing healthcare system, especially in resource constrained developing and under-developed countries.

© The Author(s), under exclusive license to Springer Nature Switzerland AG 2022
S. Albarqouni et al. (Eds.): DeCaF 2022/FAIR 2022, LNCS 13573, pp. 178–189, 2022.
https://doi.org/10.1007/978-3-031-18523-6_17

Challenges: The performance and trustability of deep neural network-based methods are of utmost importance, especially in the medical domain. The performance of these methods decreases as we try to reduce the number of learnable parameters in the model. As an example, in the case of image classification, deeper networks have been shown to be superior to shallow networks with fewer parameters [6,8]. Despite the good performance measured in terms of quantitative evaluation metrics, deep neural network (DNN) are known to make the right decision for the wrong reasons [4]. This limits the trustability of DNN-based frameworks in practical application. Additionally, the black box nature of the convolutional neural networks makes them unreliable for clinical applications. Developing a method that relies on fewer parameters and is clinically verifiable is a challenging task. Also, an efficient model is expected to replicate the performance during inference at a reasonable execution speed even in the absence of GPUs.

Attention-based networks were proposed to augment DNNs with explainability in the case of natural images. However, due to the inherent differences in the nature of images, we cannot assume an equivalent performance in the medical images. As an example, in detecting objects in natural images, the objects of interest often have a well-defined shape and structure, which are absent in the case of medical images. In the case of medical image classification, the biomarkers are usually unstructured pathologies with variable appearance. In this work, we try to verify the effectiveness of replacing convolutions with attention in neural networks for medical images.

Related Works: Transformers [21], based solely on attention mechanisms has revolutionised the way models are designed for natural language tasks. Motivated by their success, [17,26,27] and [25] explored the possibility of using self-attention to solve various vision tasks. Among these, the stand-alone self-attention proposed by [17] established that self-attention could potentially replace convolutional layers altogether. Even though it is efficient compared to other DNNs, such models can be further improved by quantising the weights and activations of the networks [15]. The quantisation of deep neural networks has shown significant progress in recent years [1,24]. The ability to quantise the neural network trained in high precision without substantial loss in performance during inference simplifies the process.

Our Approach: Inspired by the success of [17] in natural image classification tasks, we propose the design of a new class of networks for medical image classification and segmentation, in which we replace the convolution layers with self-attention layers. Furthermore, we optimise the networks for inference by quantising the parameters thereby decreasing energy consumption. To the best of our knowledge, a quantised fully self-attentive network for classification and segmentation of medical images and comparison with its convolutional counterparts has not been attempted so far. Schematic overview of the proposed method is illustrated in Fig. 1.

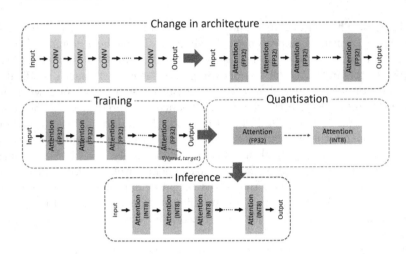

Fig. 1. Overview of the proposed method. Convolutional layers in deep neural network architectures are replaced with self-attention layers and networks with parameters at FP32 precision are trained till convergence. To optimise the model for storage and faster inference, the network parameters are quantised without loss in performance.

2   Method

2.1   Stand-Alone Self-attention

Attention was introduced by [3] for a neural machine translation model. Attention modules can learn to focus on essential regions within a context, making it an important component of neural networks. Self-attention [21] is defined as attention applied to a single context instead of across multiple contexts; that is, *Key*, *Query* and *Values* are derived from the same context. [17] introduced the stand-alone self-attention layer, which can replace convolutions to construct a fully attentional model. Motivated by the initial success of [17] in natural images, we explore the feasibility of using such modules in the proposed class of networks for medical image analysis.

To compute attention for each pixel $\mathbf{x}_{i,j} \in \mathbb{R}^{C_{in} \times 1 \times 1}$ in an image or an activation map, local regions with spatial extent $h \times w$ around $\mathbf{x}_{i,j}$ are used to derive the *keys* and *values*. Learned linear transformations are performed on $\mathbf{x}_{i,j}$ and its local regions to obtain *query* ($\mathbf{Q}$), *keys* ($\mathbf{K}$) and *values* ($\mathbf{V}$) as

$$\mathbf{Q} = \mathbf{W}_{\mathbf{Q}}\mathbf{x}_{i,j} \tag{1}$$

$$\mathbf{K} = \mathbf{W}_{\mathbf{K}}\mathbf{x}_{h,w} \tag{2}$$

$$\mathbf{V} = \mathbf{W}_{\mathbf{V}}\mathbf{x}_{h,w} \tag{3}$$

where $\mathbf{W}_{\mathbf{Q}} \in \mathbb{R}^{C_{out} \times C_{in}}$, $\mathbf{W}_{\mathbf{K}} \in \mathbb{R}^{C_{out} \times C_{in}}$ and $\mathbf{W}_{\mathbf{V}} \in \mathbb{R}^{C_{out} \times C_{in}}$ are learnable transformation matrices and $\mathbf{x}_{h,w} \in \mathbb{R}^{C_{in} \times h \times w}$ is the local region centered at $\mathbf{x}_{i,j}$.

Self-attention on its own does not encode any positional information, which makes it permutation equivariant. Relative positional embedding [19] as used in [17] are incorporated into the attention module. The keys $\mathbf{K} \in \mathbb{R}^{C_{out} \times h \times w}$ are split into $\mathbf{K}_1, \mathbf{K}_2 \in \mathbb{R}^{C_{out}/2 \times h \times w}$ each and column offset $\mathbf{E}_{col}$ and row offset $\mathbf{E}_{row}$ of the positional embedding are added to these separately. After this, we concatenate $\mathbf{K}_1, \mathbf{K}_2$ to obtain a new key ($\mathbf{K}' \in \mathbb{R}^{C_{out} \times h \times w}$) which contains the relative spatial information of pixels in the local region of size $h \times w$. Thus, the relative spatial attention for a pixel x_{ij} is mathematically defined as in Eq. 4 and is graphically illustrated in Fig. 2.

$$\mathbf{y_{i,j}} = \sum_{\{u,v\} \in N_{h,w}(i,j)} softmax_{u,v}(\mathbf{Q}_{i,j}^{\top}\mathbf{K}_{u,v})\mathbf{V}_{u,v} \qquad (4)$$

where $N_{h,w}(i,j)$ is the neighbourhood of size $h \times w$ centered at (i,j).

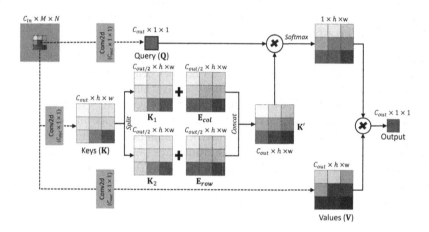

Fig. 2. Self-attention mechanism with local context. Operations are performed on a per-pixel basis to compute attention as shown in the figure. Linear transformations for obtaining query, keys and values are implemented using 2D convolution (*Conv2d*) operation. The learnt relative positional embedding are added to the keys to incorporate the inter-pixel relationships within the local context.

We use these attention blocks instead of 2D convolutional blocks in our networks. During training, all the weights and activations are represented and stored with a precision of FP32. The parameters are quantised to INT8 precision for inference.

2.2   Quantisation of Network Parameters

We perform quantisation using the FBGEMM (FaceBook GEneral Matrix Multiplication) [10] backend of PyTorch for x86 CPUs, which is based on the quantisation scheme proposed by [9]. In order to be able to perform all the arithmetic operations using integer arithmetic operations on quantised values, we require the quantisation scheme to be an affine mapping of integers q to real numbers r as

$$r = S(q - Z) \tag{5}$$

where S and Z are quantisation parameters. We have employed a post-training 8-bit quantisation of all the weights and operations for our proposed model.

2.3 Network Architecture

Classification: The architecture of the proposed classification network is illustrated in Fig. 3(a) with the details of the constituent modules in Fig. 3(c). The network consists of a series of alternating attention blocks and attention down blocks followed by fully-connected linear layers. The feature maps are downsampled using the max-pooling operation. The size of the output linear layer is equal to the number of target classes. The network is trained to perform multi-label classification using a binary cross-entropy loss.

Segmentation: The proposed segmentation network has a fully attention-based encoder-decoder architecture as shown in Fig. 3(b). The encoder unit consists of stand-alone self-attention blocks with ReLU activation and max-pooling operations with the number of feature maps increasing progressively with each attention block. The decoder consists of attention blocks and max-unpooling operations. The size of activation maps of the decoder matches with the corresponding layer in the encoder. The unpooling operations are performed using the indices transferred from the pooling layers in the encoder. To prevent the loss of subtle information, we employ activation concatenation in the decoder, similar to UNet [18]. The network is trained using soft dice loss [12].

3 Experiments

3.1 Datasets

Classification: To evaluate the performance of the fully self-attentive network (SaDNN-cls) on classification tasks, we have used the NIH Chest X-ray dataset of 14 Common Thorax Disease [22]. The dataset comprises $112,120$ frontal-view X-ray images of $30,805$ patients with fourteen disease labels. These disease classes can co-occur in an image; therefore, the classification problem is formulated as multi-label classification. The train, validation and test split provided in the dataset was used for the experiments.

Segmentation: A subset of the medical segmentation decathlon dataset [2] is used to evaluate the performance of the proposed fully-attentive network (SaDNN-seg) for liver segmentation. Out of the 131 ground truth paired 3D CT volumes-Ground truth pairs available in the dataset, 80% were randomly chosen for training, and the remaining 20% were used for testing.

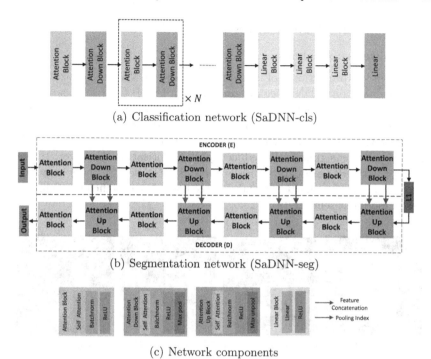

(a) Classification network (SaDNN-cls)

(b) Segmentation network (SaDNN-seg)

(c) Network components

Fig. 3. Architecture of the proposed Self-attentive Deep Neural Networks (SaDNN). Detailed architecture of the networks for classification and segmentation are shown in (a) and (b) respectively. Components of the various blocks in these networks are detailed in (c).

3.2 Implementation Details

Training: The proposed models were trained using an Adam Optimiser [11] with a learning rate of 1×10^{-4}. The models for classification task were trained for 15 epochs and the models for segmentation were trained for 25 epochs.

Baselines: Performance of the proposed quantised self-attention network for the classification task is compared with ResNet-18, ResNet-50 and their 8–bit quantised versions q-ResNet-18, and q-ResNet-50. To assess the performance of the segmentation network, we chose a modified UNet [18] (UNet-small) and SUMNet [13] architecture trained on the same dataset split and their quantised versions q-UNet-small and q-SUMNet as baselines.

System Specifications: All networks were trained on a high-performance server with a NVIDIA $V100$ GPU, $x86_64$ Intel(R) Xeon(R) Silver 4110 CPU @ 2.10 GHz, 96 GB RAM and 1 TB HDD running on Ubuntu 18.01.1 LTS OS. The inference of quantised models was also performed on the same class of CPUs.

4   Results and Discussions

4.1   Qualitative Analysis

visualisation of predictions of the proposed q-SaDNN-seg network and its unquantised version SaDNN-seg are presented in Fig. 4. Over-segmented regions in the predicted segmentation maps are marked in green, under-segmented regions are marked in red and correctly segmented region is shown in white. We observe that the tendency of the original unquantised network SaDNN-seg to over-segment is significantly reduced post quantisation. However, the quantisation of network parameters causes the q-SaDNN-seg to under-segment the target organ. This is reflected in the slightly lower Dice coefficient (DSC) of the proposed model as seen in Table 2.

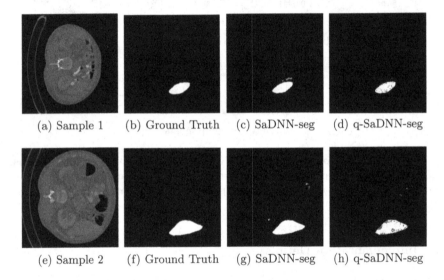

(a) Sample 1   (b) Ground Truth   (c) SaDNN-seg   (d) q-SaDNN-seg

(e) Sample 2   (f) Ground Truth   (g) SaDNN-seg   (h) q-SaDNN-seg

Fig. 4. Comparison of segmentation predictions. Figure shows sample input CT images in (a) and (e) with the corresponding ground truths of liver in (b) and (f) respectively. Segmentation map as predicted by SaDNN-seg, with the over-segmented region marked in green and under-segmented region marked in red are presented in (c) and (g) for the two sample images. Similar visualisation of segmentation by the proposed q-SaDNN-seg are presented in (d) and (h). (Color figure online)

4.2   Quantitative Analysis

The performance of the proposed quantised fully self-attentive network and baselines for multi-label classification task is reported in terms of accuracy in Table 1. It can be observed that the proposed network can achieve performance slightly better than the existing deep residual convolutional neural networks. Table 2 shows the comparison of the proposed segmentation network with the baselines in terms of DSC. The proposed quantised network performs almost as good as the quantised versions of the baseline convolutional neural networks.

Table 1. Evaluation of classification

Model	Accuracy
ResNet-18	0.89
q-ResNet-18	0.88
ResNet-50	0.84
q-ResNet-50	0.83
SaDNN-cls (ours)	**0.90**
q-SaDNN-cls (ours)	0.89

Table 2. Evaluation of segmentation

Model	DSC
UNet-small	0.88
q-UNet-small	0.88
SUMNet	0.89
q-SUMNet	0.89
SaDNN-seg (ours)	**0.88**
q-SaDNN-seg (ours)	0.85

4.3   Computational Analysis

The DNNs used for the experiments exhibited superior classification and segmentation performance in terms of quantitative metrics, but they require a considerable amount of computations and memory access operations to be performed. Deploying a framework which needs excessive computations to be performed results in large energy consumption, which is not feasible in diverse resource-constrained scenarios. Therefore, it is key to have an energy-efficient model without degradation in performance. A rough estimate of energy cost per operation in $45nm$ $0.9V$ IC design can be calculated using Table 3 presented in [7,14,23].

Table 3. Approximate energy cost in 45 nm 0.9 V for different multiplication and addition operations

Operation	Energy (pJ)	
	MUL	ADD
8-bit INT	0.2 pJ	0.03 pJ
16-bit FP	1.1 pJ	0.40 pJ
32-bit FP	3.7 pJ	0.90 pJ

The number of multiplication and addition operations in a standalone self-attention layer [20] can be calculated as

$$Ops_{mul} = Ops_{add} = 2b^2c \qquad (6)$$

where b is the block (local region) size and c is the number of channels.

The total number of parameters, MACs, energy consumed during forward pass and model size of the proposed q-SaDNN-cls and q-SaDNN-seg networks are reported in Table 4 and Table 5 with graphical comparisons in Fig. 5. Models with the least area in the radar charts are more efficient. The proposed q-SaDNN-cls network is 58.59% smaller than quantised ResNet-18 and 80.75% smaller than quantised ResNet-50 in terms of model size. In terms of total MAC units, the propsed networks have 65.93% fewer MACs than ResNet-18, 85.32% fewer than

ResNet-50. Similarly, in terms of the total trainable parameters, the proposed networks have 59.17% lesser parameters than ResNet-18 and 80.62% lesser than ResNet-50.

Table 4. Comparison of classification networks

Model	#Params	MACs	Model size	Energy
ResNet-18	11.17 M	9.10 G	44.79 MB	20.93 J
q-ResNet-18	11.17 M	9.10 G	11.40 MB	1.04 J
ResNet-50	23.53 M	21.11 G	94.45 MB	48.53 J
q-ResNet-50	23.53 M	21.11 G	24.52 MB	2.41 J
SaDNN-cls	**4.56 M**	3.10 G	18.30 MB	7.13 J
q-SaDNN-cls	**4.56 M**	3.10 G	**4.72 MB**	0.35 J

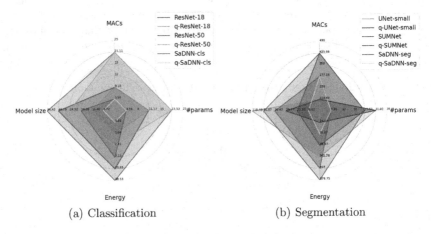

(a) Classification   (b) Segmentation

Fig. 5. Graphical comparison of proposed networks. Figure shows radar chart based comparison of proposed (a) classification network and (b) segmentation network in terms of number of parameters, MACs, model size and energy. The model with the least area within the plot is the best one.

Similar improvement in efficiency of computing can be observed in the case of segmentation as well. The segmentation network q-SaDNN-seg is 73.06% smaller than q-UNet-small and 64.94% smaller than q-SUMNet in terms of model size. In terms of total MAC units, the q-SaDNN-seg has 34.94% fewer than SUMNet. In terms of the trainable parameters, q-SaDNN-seg has 74.37% lesser parameters than UNet-small and 66.21% lesser than SUMNet. It is to be noted that the proposed models are superior in terms energy consumption as well.

Table 5. Comparison of segmentation networks

Model	#Params	MACs	Model size	Energy
UNet-small	31.03 M	218.60 G	118.48 MB	502.78 J
q-UNet-small	31.03 M	218.60 G	29.77 MB	25.13 J
SUMNet	23.53 M	425.98 G	91.07 MB	979.75 J
q-SUMNet	23.53 M	425.98 G	22.88 MB	48.97 J
SaDNN-seg	**7.95 M**	277.15 G	30.47 MB	637 J
q-SaDNN-seg	**7.95 M**	277.15 G	**8.02 MB**	31.87 J

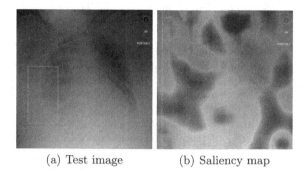

(a) Test image   (b) Saliency map

Fig. 6. Figure shows (a) a sample image from the test set used in our experiments with the clinically relevant region as provided in the dataset marked in green and (b) saliency map of q-SaDNN-cls. Regions shown in red in the saliency map are perceived as most important and those in blue to be least important by the network during prediction. (Color figure online)

4.4   Analysis of Clinical Relevance

Validating the results of the model with respect to clinically relevant information to provide some explanations for the decision made by the model is an important factor that determines trustability. The clinically relevant region provided in the NIH Chest X-ray dataset as marked by a radiologist and the saliency map based explanation generated using RISE [16] for the proposed quantised self-attention deep neural network for classification are shown in Fig. 6. It can be observed that the proposed model focuses on the clinically relevant region while making the decision.

5   Conclusion

We proposed a class of quantised self-attentive neural networks which can be used for medical image classification and segmentation. In these networks, convolutional layers are replaced with attention layers which have fewer learnable parameters. Computation of attention while considering a small local region surrounding a pixel prevents degradation of performance despite the absence of local feature extraction which is typically performed in a CNN. We show that our energy efficient method achieves performance at par with the commonly used CNNs with fewer number of parameters and model size. These attributes make our proposed models affordable and easy to adopt in resource constrained settings.

References

1. Aji, A.F., Heafield, K.: Compressing neural machine translation models with 4-bit precision. In: Workshop on Neural Generation and Translation, pp. 35–42 (2020)
2. Antonelli, M., et al.: The medical segmentation decathlon. arXiv preprint arXiv:2106.05735 (2021)
3. Bahdanau, D., Cho, K., Bengio, Y.: Neural machine translation by jointly learning to align and translate. arXiv preprint arXiv:1409.0473 (2014)
4. Chakravarty, A., Ghosh, N., Sheet, D., Sarkar, T., Sethuraman, R.: Radiologist validated systematic search over deep neural networks for screening musculoskeletal radiographs (2019)
5. Hatamizadeh, A., et al.: UNETR: transformers for 3D medical image segmentation. In: IEEE/CVF Winter Conference on Applications of Computer Vision, pp. 574–584 (2022)
6. He, K., Zhang, X., Ren, S., Sun, J.: Deep residual learning for image recognition. In: Proceedings of the IEEE Conference on Computer Vision and Pattern Recognition, pp. 770–778 (2016)
7. Horowitz, M.: 1.1 computing's energy problem (and what we can do about it). In: IEEE International Solid-State Circuits Conference Digest of Technical Papers, pp. 10–14 (2014)
8. Huang, G., Liu, Z., Van Der Maaten, L., Weinberger, K.Q.: Densely connected convolutional networks. In: Proceedings of the IEEE Conference on Computer Vision and Pattern Recognition, pp. 4700–4708 (2017)
9. Jacob, B., et al.: Quantization and training of neural networks for efficient integer-arithmetic-only inference. In: IEEE Conference on Computer Vision and Pattern Recognition, pp. 2704–2713 (2018)
10. Khudia, D., et al.: FBGEMM: enabling high-performance low-precision deep learning inference. arXiv preprint arXiv:2101.05615 (2021)
11. Kingma, D.P., Ba, J.: Adam: a method for stochastic optimization. arXiv preprint arXiv:1412.6980 (2014)
12. Milletari, F., Navab, N., Ahmadi, S.A.: V-Net: fully convolutional neural networks for volumetric medical image segmentation. In: 2016 Fourth International Conference on 3D Vision (3DV), pp. 565–571 (2016). https://doi.org/10.1109/3DV.2016.79
13. Nandamuri, S., China, D., Mitra, P., Sheet, D.: SUMNet: fully convolutional model for fast segmentation of anatomical structures in ultrasound volumes. In: IEEE International Symposium on Biomedical Imaging, pp. 1729–1732 (2019)
14. Park, S.S., Chung, K.S.: CENNA: cost-effective neural network accelerator. Electronics 9(1), 134 (2020)
15. Paupamah, K., James, S., Klein, R.: Quantisation and pruning for neural network compression and regularisation. In: International SAUPEC/RobMech/PRASA Conference, pp. 1–6. IEEE (2020)

16. Petsiuk, V., Das, A., Saenko, K.: RISE: randomized input sampling for explanation of black-box models. In: British Machine Vision Conference (2018)
17. Ramachandran, P., Parmar, N., Vaswani, A., Bello, I., Levskaya, A., Shlens, J.: Stand-alone self-attention in vision models. arXiv preprint arXiv:1906.05909 (2019)
18. Ronneberger, O., Fischer, P., Brox, T.: U-Net: convolutional networks for biomedical image segmentation. In: Navab, N., Hornegger, J., Wells, W.M., Frangi, A.F. (eds.) MICCAI 2015. LNCS, vol. 9351, pp. 234–241. Springer, Cham (2015). https://doi.org/10.1007/978-3-319-24574-4_28
19. Shaw, P., Uszkoreit, J., Vaswani, A.: Self-attention with relative position representations. arXiv preprint arXiv:1803.02155 (2018)
20. Vaswani, A., Ramachandran, P., Srinivas, A., Parmar, N., Hechtman, B., Shlens, J.: Scaling local self-attention for parameter efficient visual backbones. In: Proceedings of the IEEE/CVF Conference on Computer Vision and Pattern Recognition, pp. 12894–12904 (2021)
21. Vaswani, A., et al.: Attention is all you need. In: Advances in Neural Information Processing Systems, pp. 5998–6008 (2017)
22. Wang, X., Peng, Y., Lu, L., Lu, Z., Bagheri, M., Summers, R.M.: ChestX-ray8: hospital-scale chest X-ray database and benchmarks on weakly-supervised classification and localization of common thorax diseases. In: IEEE Conference on Computer Vision and Pattern Recognition, pp. 2097–2106 (2017)
23. Wu, S., Li, G., Chen, F., Shi, L.: Training and inference with integers in deep neural networks. arXiv preprint arXiv:1802.04680 (2018)
24. Xu, J., Yu, J., Hu, S., Liu, X., Meng, H.M.: Mixed precision low-bit quantization of neural network language models for speech recognition. IEEE/ACM Trans. Audio Speech Lang. Process. **29**, 3679–3693 (2021)
25. Yang, F., Yang, H., Fu, J., Lu, H., Guo, B.: Learning texture transformer network for image super-resolution. In: IEEE/CVF Conference on Computer Vision and Pattern Recognition, pp. 5791–5800 (2020)
26. Ye, L., Rochan, M., Liu, Z., Wang, Y.: Cross-modal self-attention network for referring image segmentation. In: IEEE/CVF Conference on Computer Vision and Pattern Recognition, pp. 10502–10511 (2019)
27. Zhu, X., Su, W., Lu, L., Li, B., Wang, X., Dai, J.: Deformable DETR: deformable transformers for end-to-end object detection. arXiv preprint arXiv:2010.04159 (2020)

LRH-Net: A Multi-level Knowledge Distillation Approach for Low-Resource Heart Network

Ekansh Chauhan[✉], Swathi Guptha, Likith Reddy, and Bapi Raju

International Institute of Information Technology, Hyderabad, India
ekansh.chauhan@research.iiit.ac.in

Abstract. An electrocardiogram (ECG) monitors the electrical activity generated by the heart and is used to detect fatal cardiovascular diseases (CVDs). Conventionally, to capture the precise electrical activity, clinical experts use multiple-lead ECGs (typically 12 leads). Recently, large-scale deep learning models have been used to detect these diseases, however, they require large memory and long inference time. We propose a low-parameter model, Low Resource Heart-Network (LRH-Net), that detects ECG anomalies in a resource-constrained environment. On top, multi-level knowledge distillation (MLKD) is employed to improve model generalization. MLKD distils the dark-knowledge from higher parameter models (teachers) trained on different lead configurations to LRH-Net. The LRH-Net has 106× fewer parameters and 76% faster inference than the teacher model for detecting CVDs. Using MLKD, the performance of LRH-Net on reduced lead data was scaled up to 3.25%, making it suitable for edge devices.

Keywords: Knowledge distillation · Low resource · Cardiovascular diseases · SE-Resnet · Edge computing

1 Introduction

One of the most common causes of death around the globe is cardiovascular diseases (CVDs). According to WHO, in 2021, around 32% of all deaths, i.e., 17.9 million people died from CVDs [27]. These diseases manifest with no severe symptoms and are difficult to diagnose, leading to underestimating the risk or severity. Thus, early diagnosis of these diseases can potentially save millions of lives [24].

Electrocardiography (ECG) is a low-cost and widely used process to monitor abnormal electrical activity in the heart [20]. However, this process can only be used and interpreted by a cardiologist [15]. The advancement of the Internet of Things (IoT) makes real-time capturing of ECG signals feasible using wearable devices. Thereby resulting in massive ECG data, which is used in machine learning techniques to detect CVDs [10,26].

Most of the early literature on CVD used classical feature extraction approaches along with machine learning models [1,2,4,11]. Then, artificial neural networks such as multilayer perceptrons demonstrated great performance

S. Albarqouni et al. (Eds.): DeCaF 2022/FAIR 2022, LNCS 13573, pp. 190–201, 2022.
https://doi.org/10.1007/978-3-031-18523-6_18

and removed the requirement of manually handpicked features to some extent, especially with the advent of deep neural networks [5,13]. However, these networks are typically unconcerned with power consumption, memory consumption and execution time, preferring to be more accurate [7], making them difficult for deploying on low-compute resources. There has always been a trade-off between performance and size – trading off the extent to which size should be decreased and yet retain acceptable performance.

In recent years, most of the work is pivoted on capturing ECG signals using wearable devices using Bluetooth and Internet connectivity of the mobile phones which are later processed on cloud to detect the anomalies. Furthermore, traditional electrocardiography setups use 12 electrodes to monitor heart activity, but using such a setup in a real-time environment would require excessive computation and be inconvenient or tedious process for the end user. Rural areas, on the other hand, have significant contributions to cardio-vascular disease burden, and finding such compute resources is difficult there [16,27]. Therefore, an efficient neural network which takes data from fewer electrodes and requires less memory and inference time is required for an edge computing wearable device.

To the best of our knowledge there is no other solution proposed in the literature for resource constrained environments while considering heterogeneity in datasets (and disease conditions). We propose a low-parameter model called Low Resource Heart-Network (*LRH-Net*) on top of which Multi-Level Knowledge Distillation (MLKD) methods are also proposed to enhance its performance. This novel approach is compared with an existing high-performance large-scale model [28] and a commonly used low-scale model [18] baselines on heterogeneous dataset [21]. The source code for the proposed model and all the experiments that are done are made public to motivate further research in this field[1].

Main contributions of this paper are:

1. A real-time cardiovascular disease detection model which is 106× smaller than a large-scale model and 12× times smaller than the existing low-scale model.
2. A Multi-Level knowledge distillation approach to improve the performance of LRH-Net (student model) and to reduce the number of electrodes and input leads data required for the student model.
3. Performed evaluation on a very diverse, publicly available and combination of multiple datasets to increase its desirability.

2 Methodology

2.1 Pre-processing

The sampling frequency ranges 257 Hz to 1 KHz in the datasets being used. As part of pre-processing, we resampled the data 257 Hz, the minimum in our case. Each ECG is set to be 4096 points long, approximately 16 s. The time series is randomly clipped for longer duration and zero-padded for shorter duration

---

[1] https://github.com/ekansh09/LRH-Net.

signals in order to give a fixed sequence length as an input to the deep learning models. The signal is then normalized using z-score to remove technological biases between datasets i.e., a signal $x_n \in n^{th}$ channel (lead) was transformed using Eq. 1, where $\overline{x_n}$ is the mean and σ_n is the standard deviation across the nth channel.

$$x_n = \frac{x_n - \overline{x_n}}{\sigma_n} \qquad (1)$$

Finally, we also took one-hot encoded phenotypic information such as age (scaled between 0 and 1) and gender, into consideration and represented missing values with additional two mask variables.

2.2   Architecture

The proposed model, LRH-Net, inspired from the ResNet architecture [6] with 3 residual blocks (Res-Blocks) in it and is depicted in Fig. 1. The motivation for using a Resnet based architecture is the power of skip connections that ameliorate the vanishing gradients problem of the back propagation learning scheme and enhance model convergence. Each residual block has two convolution layers, ReLU activation function, batch normalization and one squeeze and excitation (SE) block [9]. The starting filter is always 16 and increased by a factor of two in the case of Res-blocks. SE-Block aids in learning the importance of various features and paying more attention to those that are more important, thereby improving classification performance. We used it to model the spatial relationship among the ECG channels. Additionally, [28] showed that integrating patient's age and gender improves the performance and is easy to feed into an edge device. Considering this, we passed these values through a linear layer followed by concatenation to the features obtained from the average pool layer, that then passes all of them through two more linear layers with ReLU in between in the model to generate the logits.

Knowledge distillation (KD) refers to the idea of model compression where the small model (student model) mimics the larger model (teacher model) using soft labels provided by the teacher model [8]. We used this knowledge distillation method to further improve the performance of LRH-Net. While distilling information from a large network to a smaller network, it is preferable to use a similar kind of architecture for the distillation training [17]. Hence, we used the runner-up network (SE-Resnet) of PhysioNet-2020 challenge proposed in [28] as our Teacher Network (Θ_T).

Recent work on knowledge distillation methods led to an idea of having a multi-teacher approach to reduce the gap between the high parameter model and the low parameter target model by introducing an intermediate size parameter model [17]. Using this as inspiration, we propose a Multi-Level Knowledge Distillation (MLKD) approach to reduce the number of electrodes required to generate fewer lead data and simultaneously enhance the performance of LRH-Net in multiple steps, in a sequential or parallel configuration, to retain the knowledge (representations) from a large-scale model trained on multi-lead ECG data (see Fig. 2). Both sequential and parallel configurations are put to the test in a 2-step

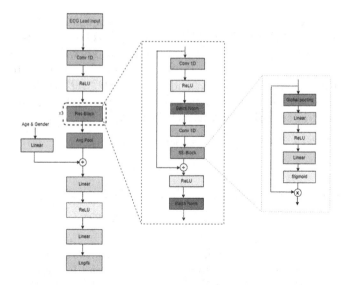

Fig. 1. LRH-Net architecture: proposed low parametric model

procedure. First, by decreasing the number of input channels while maintaining the network's size, and secondly, by reducing the network's size while keeping the input channels constant.

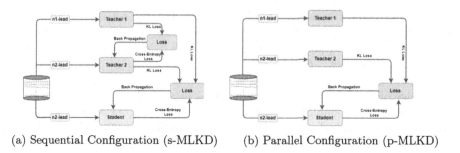

(a) Sequential Configuration (s-MLKD)   (b) Parallel Configuration (p-MLKD)

Fig. 2. Multi-level knowledge distillation (MLKD) methods.

Let n be the number of channels (leads). $\Theta_T^{n_1}$ be the pre-trained teacher network with n_1 input channels and $\Theta_T^{n_2}$ be the teacher network with n_2 ($n_2 < n_1$) input channels. We use Binary cross-entropy (BCE) loss (Eq. 2) as student loss and Kullback-Leibler divergence (KL) loss (Eq. 3) as distillation loss to account the knowledge transfer from the teacher model to the student model.

Sequential MLKD (s-MLKD): At step one ($t = 1$), knowledge is distilled (KD) from $\Theta_T^{n_1}$ to $\Theta_T^{n_2}$. Therefore, from Eqs. 4 and 5, the loss at this step is given by $\mathcal{L}(\Theta_T^{n_2}, \Theta_T^{n_1})$. Now, let the distilled $\Theta_T^{n_2}$ be $\Theta_{T_d}^{n_2}$, where d denotes the distilled model. At second step, we perform KD from $\Theta_T^{n_1}$ and $\Theta_{T_d}^{n_2}$ to LRH-Net with n_2 input channels ($\Theta_L^{n_2}$). We give different weightage to knowledge obtained from each teacher model, denoted as β in Eq. 4. Therefore, the final loss function for a 2-step s-MLKD method is given at 2nd-step as $\mathcal{L}(\Theta_L^{n_2}, \Theta_{T_d}^{n_2}, \Theta_T^{n_1})$. Here, steps are equal to the number of teacher networks, i.e. after each step (except last), we get a trained intermediate teacher network.

$$BCE(p, y) = \tfrac{-1}{N} \sum_i^N \sum_j^M y_{ij} \log p_{ij} + (1 - y_{ij}) \log (1 - p_{ij}) \tag{2}$$

$$KL(p, y) = \sum_{x \in X} y(x) \log \tfrac{y(x)}{p(x)} \tag{3}$$

$$MLKD_{loss}(\Theta_0, \Theta_1, \ldots, \Theta_t) = \sum_{x=1}^t \beta_x KL \left(\tfrac{\log(s(z_0))}{\tau}, \tfrac{s(z_x)}{\tau} \right) \tag{4}$$

$$\mathcal{L}(\Theta_0, \Theta_1, \ldots, \Theta_t; y) = \lambda BCE(\sigma(z_{\Theta_0}), y) + (1 - \lambda) MLKD_{loss}(\Theta_0, \Theta_1, \ldots, \Theta_t) \tag{5}$$

where, p, y are probability and ground truth values. In Eq. 2, N is number of samples in each batch and M is number of classes. In Eq. 3, X is probability space of p, y. Equation 5 represents the loss at every step and in the series notation $(\Theta_0, \Theta_1, \ldots, \Theta_t)$, Θ_0 is student and all other are teacher networks. λ parameter implements the trade-off between BCE-loss and MLKD-loss. z_t represents the logits of Θ_t network. σ is the *Sigmoid* activation function, s is the *SoftMax* activation function and τ is the temperature hyper-parameter used to generate soft-labels. The log-softmax is applied to student's logits in MLKD loss for numerical stability in Pytorch.

Parallel MLKD (p-MLKD): In this scheme, the first step is to train $\Theta_T^{n_2}$ independently and the second step looks almost like the s-MLKD scheme, $\Theta_T^{n_2}$ being different. In p-MLKD, we use two independently pre-trained networks to teach a student network. So, from Eqs. 4 and 5, the final loss function for p-MKLD will be $\mathcal{L}(\Theta_L^{n_2}, \Theta_T^{n_2}, \Theta_T^{n_1})$.

Finally, with s- and p-MLKD schemes, the distilled LRH-Net has the dark knowledge of 12 leads but takes fewer leads as input and outputs logits from the last dense layer. Probability scores are obtained by applying σ (sigmoid) to the output from logits block. Then, a differential evolution genetic technique is used to optimize class thresholds [19]. Our experiments reveal that these thresholds do not vary as the number of leads are varied.

3   Experiments

3.1   Dataset

A total of 43101 standard 12-lead ECG (I, II, III, aVL, aVR, aVF, V1–V6) recordings are used from four publicly available datasets provided by Physionet-2020 challenge [21], i.e., CPSC Database and CPSC-Extra Database, INCART Database, PTB and PTB-XL Database, and the Georgia 12-lead ECG Challenge. It has 24 unique class labels and a signal may have more than one class label assigned to it. The distribution among these 24 classes in the dataset can be visualized from Fig. 3. The signal length varies from 10 s to 30 min.

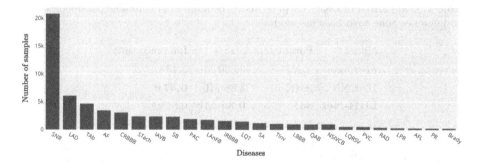

Fig. 3. Dataset distribution

3.2 Implementation Details

The Pytorch framework is used to create the models. LRH-Net is trained for 1 h 40 min using the Adam optimizer with L2 weight decay of 5e−4 for 90 epochs with a batch size of 64. We start with a learning rate of 0.001 and utilise the StepLr scheduler with step size of 20 to change it throughout the training. α and τ are set to 0.3, 7 respectively. Since we used a 2-step approach, the weight list given to the teachers, β, is [0.4, 0.6]. It has 84,516 trainable parameters. All the experiments are carried out using Nvidia Tesla P100 GPUs.

4   Results and Discussion

5-Fold cross-validation is employed to evaluate LRH-Net using the metric provided by the Physionet-2020 challenge called challenge metric score (CM-Score) and the micro-F1-score. Misdiagnoses that result in treatments or outcomes that are similar to the true diagnosis as determined by the cardiologist are given partial credit in the challenge metric. It reflects the clinical reality that some misdiagnoses are more harmful than others and should be scored accordingly [21]. The F1-score is also reported as it more accurately reflects the performance on an imbalanced class data set in one vs all setup.

4.1   Baselines

There are no methods available to reduce ECG leads without compromising on the knowledge of all leads. Also, none of the previously available low-parameter models have trained on diverse multiple-datasets as provided in [21]. Thus, we use four KD techniques mentioned below (see Table 3) and the following two models as our baselines, SE-Resnet (our teacher) and 1D-CNN (see Table 1, 2).

Table 1. Comparison of LRH-Net in terms of the number of trainable parameters, size and inference time with baseline models.

Model	Parameters	Size	Inference time
SE-Resnet	*8.9M*	35.30 Mb	3.43 s
1D-CNN	994K	3.88 Mb	**0.47 s**
LRH-Net	**84K**	**0.35 Mb**	0.84 s

Parameters and Size: Table 1 shows comparison of our proposed model with both the baselines. Empirically, it is noted that the number of parameter are almost directly proportional to the size of the model. In comparison to the baselines, LRH-Net has the fewest parameters which results in a more compact and efficient network. Because LRH-Net's parameters are 106 times smaller than SE-Resnet and 12 times smaller than 1D-CNN, the model size (in mb) is likewise 101 times and 11 times lower respectively.

Inference Time and Complexity: The inference time of a model is directly proportional to the model complexity. The inference time of LRH-Net is significantly smaller than SE-Resnet but slightly more than that of 1D-CNN due to the presence of additional squeeze-and-excitation block within the Res-block and larger kernel size. The kernel size is experimentally chosen and squeeze-and-excitation block is added to help the architecture to draw attention to the fact that the dataset has classes (cardiovascular anomalies) that are not spread out evenly [9].

LRH-Net makes a trade-off between memory consumption and complexity with inference time, which results in superior performance when compared to the baseline (1D-CNN), which has less inference time but poor performance and high memory consumption.

Few studies [14,25] have shown that a 3-lead ECG (I, II, V2) contains the majority of the information found in a 12-lead ECG. Considering this, all the models are tested on standard 12-lead, 3-lead, and 2-lead configurations which are also provided by [22]. The 3-lead configuration is [I, II, V2] and for 2-lead, it is [I, II]. Information from 10, 5, and 4 electrodes (including ground electrode) are required to obtain the data for 12, 3, and 2 leads, respectively.

Table 2 shows the performance comparison between LRH-Net and baselines on various lead configurations. LRH-Net with 83,748 parameters outperforms the existing low-scale baseline model of 1D-CNN with 993,860 parameters by a significant margin for all the lead configurations, i.e., 3.07%, 2.76%, 1.41% increment in CM scores for 12-lead, 3-lead, and 2-lead configurations, respectively. When LRH-Net is compared to SE-Resnet, the model size or parameters are drastically reduced (LRH-Net has fewer parameters), which results in a performance drop of about 10.5% (in CM scores) for all lead configurations.

Table 2. Comparison of LRH-Net in terms of performance with baseline models.

Model	CM-score			F1-score		
	12-lead	3-lead	2-lead	12-lead	3-lead	2-lead
SE-Resnet	*67.43*	*65.37*	*63.34*	*76.65*	*75.42*	*74.86*
1D-CNN	58.66	56.92	55.87	69.50	67.61	67.16
LRH-Net	**60.46**	**58.49**	**56.66**	**72.76**	**71.33**	**70.21**

Knowledge Distillation: The following four knowledge distillation techniques are tested to increase the performance of LRH-Net. Vanilla knowledge distillation [8] is a method of extracting dark knowledge from the logits of deep models. In Fitnets [23], the main idea is to directly match the feature activation of the teacher and the student. In Cross Layer distillation [3], each student layer distills knowledge contained in multiple layers rather than a single fixed intermediate layer from the teacher model. With progressive self-knowledge distillation (PS-KD) [12], on the other hand, a student model itself becomes a teacher model.

Table 3. Evaluation of LRH-Net on various knowledge distillation techniques.

KD technique	Distilled LR-HNet					
	CM-score			F1-score		
	12-lead	3-lead	2-lead	12-lead	3-lead	2-lead
Vanilla KD	**60.67**	**59.49**	**57.27**	**73.41**	73.04	**71.18**
FitNet	60.46	58.88	57.20	72.22	72.61	70.22
PS-KD	57.81	55.80	55.58	68.62	68.05	68.03
Cross-layer	60.17	59.04	57.13	73.34	**73.28**	70.69

Table 3 shows the performance of LRH-Net on multiple lead configurations after being distilled from the pre-trained SE-Resnet on 12-Lead input. When compared to all the recent knowledge distillation techniques, the vanilla KD delivers the best results for our use case. Surprisingly, LRH-Net performance deteriorated when combined with the newest KD-Methods, PS-KD and Cross-Layer and Fitnets. Vanilla KD improved the CM-Score of non-distilled LRH-Net (as compared from LRH-Net results of Table 2) by 0.35%, 1.71%, 1.08% for 12-, 3- and 2-leads, respectively. Cross-Layer KD gives best F1-scores for 3-lead configuration. It can also be noted that the F1-Score is not directly proportional to CM-Score. This latter method is useful when each class is considered independently, i.e., assuming no correlation among the disease classes.

Multi-level Knowledge Distillation: To reduce the knowledge drop while distilling a low-lead, low-parameter model from a high-lead, high-parameter model, we use the multi-level knowledge distillation (MLKD) methods. These methods help the low-scale network in learning dark knowledge from the large-scale network in a step-by-step process. The CM-score and F1-scores of the LRH-Net with 3-lead and 2-lead inputs with sequential and parallel MLKD are reported in Table 4. For both the configurations, the proposed MLKD incorporating Vanilla KD performs better than directly downgrading the leads using simply Vanilla KD (see results in Table 3). The percentage increments in CM-Scores, when LRH-Net using MLKD and non-distilled LRH-Net (see Table 2) are compared are 3.25% and 3.12% for 3- and 2-lead configurations, respectively.

Table 4. Evaluation of LRH-Net on MLKD methods with two teacher networks i.e. (step $(t) = 2$).

Number of leads (n2)	KD-technique	CM-score	F1-score
3-lead	s-MLKD	**60.39**	**73.44**
	p-MLKD	60.36	**72.51**
2-lead	s-MLKD	58.36	71.43
	p-MLKD	**58.43**	**72.66**

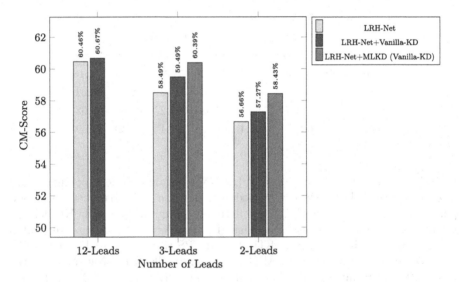

Fig. 4. Bar-plot showing the improvement in LRH-Net's CM-score using Vanilla knowledge distillation (KD) and multi-level knowledge distillation using Vanilla-KD.

Knowledge distillation helps LRH-Net to further reduce its size or parameters with the reduction in number of leads which causes a steady decrease in performance too. This makes it easier to utilise on an edge device because only a small number of electrodes are needed to capture the requisite lead data.

In MLKD, KL losses for the outputs of the student network with both teacher networks result in some amount of conflict in the gradients between these two losses. In the sequential configuration, the second teacher network has been trained to reproduce the outputs of the first teacher network. This will result in less conflict between the two KL loss terms, as the outputs will be closer in the latent-space. In the case of the parallel configuration, both KD loss terms will be in conflict with each other simultaneously to make the outputs of the student network close to each of the teacher networks.

The experimental results shown in the Tables 3 and 4 show that MLKD not only generalizes LRH-Net on fewer leads but also makes it more robust and accurate. LRH-Net after distillation using MLKD with Vanilla KD on 3-Leads is performing almost similar to LRH-Net on 12-Leads (Fig. 4). This could be because the V2 lead (calculated using chest electrode) in a 3-lead configuration has more disease-specific information. However, the low-parameter model is drastically affected in the F1 scores of few hard-to-classify diseases like Sinus Arrhythmia (SA).

5   Conclusion

In this work, we propose the Low Resource Heart-Network (LRH-Net) for detecting cardiovascular diseases. The proposed model is evaluated on a combination of four large heterogenous datasets provided by the PhysioNet-2020 challenge. The proposed low resource model not only enables edge computing on a wearable device but also gives better results as compared to other architectures proposed for wearable devices previously. In addition to compressing the model, our work also focused on using reduced number of leads to reduce the input processing without sacrificing much on the performance using multi-level knowledge distillation (MLKD). As a result, the computational resources, cost, and input channels required for our proposed model are reduced. This approach is carefully designed to increase the ease of use and affordability of an accurate edge device in rural or semi-urban areas. Further research can focus on lowering the performance gap in low-lead configurations by optimizing the number of steps required to distill majority of the critical information by varying the levels of MLKD so that the classification performance on hard-to-classify diseases does not get severely affected.

References

1. Al-Naima, F., Al-Timemy, A.: Neural network based classification of myocardial infarction: a comparative study of Wavelet and Fourier transforms. In: Pattern Recognition, Croatia. IntechOpen, October 2009. https://doi.org/10.5772/7533
2. Alonso-Atienza, F., Morgado, E., Fernández-Martínez, L., García-Alberola, A., Rojo-Álvarez, J.L.: Detection of life-threatening arrhythmias using feature selection and support vector machines. IEEE Trans. Biomed. Eng. **61**(3), 832–840 (2013). https://doi.org/10.1109/TBME.2013.2290800

3. Chen, D., et al.: Cross-layer distillation with semantic calibration. In: Proceedings of the AAAI Conference on Artificial Intelligence, vol. 35, no. 8, pp. 7028–7036 (2021). https://ojs.aaai.org/index.php/AAAI/article/view/16865

4. Coast, D.A., Stern, R.M., Cano, G.G., Briller, S.A.: An approach to cardiac arrhythmia analysis using hidden Markov models. IEEE Trans. Biomed. Eng. **37**(9), 826–836 (1990). https://doi.org/10.1109/10.58593

5. Hannun, A.Y., et al.: Cardiologist-level arrhythmia detection and classification in ambulatory electrocardiograms using a deep neural network. Nat. Med. **25**(1), 65 (2019). https://doi.org/10.1038/s41591-018-0268-3

6. He, K., Zhang, X., Ren, S., Sun, J.: Deep residual learning for image recognition. In: 2016 IEEE Conference on Computer Vision and Pattern Recognition (CVPR), pp. 770–778. IEEE (2016). https://doi.org/10.1109/CVPR.2016.90

7. He, L., Hou, W., Zhen, X., Peng, C.: Recognition of ECG patterns using artificial neural network. In: Sixth International Conference on Intelligent Systems Design and Applications, vol. 2, pp. 477–481. IEEE (2006). https://doi.org/10.1109/ISDA.2006.253883

8. Hinton, G., Vinyals, O., Dean, J.: Distilling the knowledge in a neural network. arXiv, March 2015. https://arxiv.org/abs/1503.02531v1

9. Hu, J., Shen, L., Sun, G.: Squeeze-and-excitation networks. In: 2018 IEEE/CVF Conference on Computer Vision and Pattern Recognition, pp. 7132–7141. IEEE (2018). https://doi.org/10.1109/CVPR.2018.00745

10. Ince, T., Kiranyaz, S., Gabbouj, M.: A generic and robust system for automated patient-specific classification of ECG signals. IEEE Trans. Biomed. Eng. **56**(5), 1415–1426 (2009). https://doi.org/10.1109/TBME.2009.2013934

11. Khorrami, H., Moavenian, M.: A comparative study of DWT, CWT and DCT transformations in ECG arrhythmias classification. Expert Syst. Appl. **37**(8), 5751–5757 (2010). https://doi.org/10.1016/j.eswa.2010.02.033

12. Kim, K., Ji, B., Yoon, D., Hwang, S.: Self-knowledge distillation with progressive refinement of targets. In: Proceedings of the IEEE/CVF International Conference on Computer Vision (ICCV), pp. 6567–6576 (2021)

13. Kiranyaz, S., Ince, T., Gabbouj, M.: Real-time patient-specific ECG classification by 1-D convolutional neural networks. IEEE Trans. Biomed. Eng. **63**(3), 664–675 (2015). https://doi.org/10.1109/TBME.2015.2468589

14. Lee, D., Kwon, H., Lee, H., Seo, C., Park, K.: Optimal lead position in patch-type monitoring sensors for reconstructing 12-lead ECG signals with universal transformation coefficient. Sensors **20**(4), 963 (2020). https://doi.org/10.3390/s20040963

15. Liu, Z., Zhang, X.: ECG-based heart arrhythmia diagnosis through attentional convolutional neural networks. In: 2021 IEEE International Conference on Internet of Things and Intelligence Systems (IoTaIS), pp. 156–162. IEEE, November 2021. https://doi.org/10.1109/IoTaIS53735.2021.9628857

16. Mamaghanian, H., Khaled, N., Atienza, D., Vandergheynst, P.: Compressed sensing for real-time energy-efficient ECG compression on wireless body sensor nodes. IEEE Trans. Biomed. Eng. **58**(9), 2456–2466 (2011). https://doi.org/10.1109/TBME.2011.2156795

17. Mirzadeh, S.I., Farajtabar, M., Li, A., Levine, N., Matsukawa, A., Ghasemzadeh, H.: Improved knowledge distillation via teacher assistant. In: AAAI, vol. 34, no. 04, pp. 5191–5198 (2020). https://doi.org/10.1609/aaai.v34i04.5963

18. Nannavecchia, A., Girardi, F., Fina, P.R., Scalera, M., Dimauro, G.: Personal heart health monitoring based on 1D convolutional neural network. J. Imaging **7**(2), 26 (2021). https://doi.org/10.3390/jimaging7020026

19. Nejedly, P., et al.: Classification of ECG using ensemble of residual CNNs with attention mechanism. In: 2021 Computing in Cardiology (CinC), vol. 48, pp. 1–4. IEEE (2021). https://doi.org/10.23919/CinC53138.2021.9662723

20. Park, J., Cho, H., Balan, R.K., Ko, J.: HeartQuake: accurate low-cost non-invasive ECG monitoring using bed-mounted geophones. Proc. ACM Interact. Mob. Wearable Ubiquitous Technol. 4(3), 1–28 (2020). https://doi.org/10.1145/3411843

21. Reyna, M.A., et al.: Classification of 12-lead ECGs: the PhysioNet/computing in cardiology challenge 2020. In: 2020 Computing in Cardiology, pp. 1–4. IEEE (2020). https://doi.org/10.22489/CinC.2020.236

22. Reyna, M.A., et al.: Will two do? Varying dimensions in electrocardiography: the PhysioNet/computing in cardiology challenge 2021. In: 2021 Computing in Cardiology (CinC), vol. 48, pp. 1–4. IEEE (2021). https://doi.org/10.23919/CinC53138.2021.9662687

23. Romero, A., et al.: FitNets: hints for thin deep nets. In: International Conference on Learning Representations (ICLR) (2015)

24. Romiti, S., Vinciguerra, M., Saade, W., Anso Cortajarena, I., Greco, E.: Artificial intelligence (AI) and cardiovascular diseases: an unexpected alliance. Cardiol. Res. Pract. 2020, 4972346 (2020). https://doi.org/10.1155/2020/4972346

25. Smith, G.H., Van den Heever, D.J., Swart, W.: The reconstruction of a 12-lead electrocardiogram from a reduced lead set using a focus time-delay neural network. Acta Cardiologica Sin. 37(1), 47 (2021). https://doi.org/10.6515/ACS.202101_37(1).20200712A

26. Murdoch, T.B.: The inevitable application of big data to health care. JAMA 309(13) (2013). https://doi.org/10.1001/jama.2013.393

27. World Health Organization: Cardiovascular diseases (CVDs). World Health Organization: WHO, June 2021. https://www.who.int/news-room/fact-sheets/detail/cardiovascular-diseases-(cvds)

28. Zhao, Z., et al.: Adaptive lead weighted ResNet trained with different duration signals for classifying 12-lead ECGs. In: 2020 Computing in Cardiology, pp. 1–4. IEEE (2020). https://doi.org/10.22489/CinC.2020.112

Author Index

Printed in the United States
by Baker & Taylor Publisher Services